HARDWARE HACKING PROJECTS

for Geeks

HARDWARE HACKING PROJECTS

for Geeks

Scott Fullam

O'REILLY®

BEIJING • CAMBRIDGE • FARNHAM • KÖLN • PARIS • SEBASTOPOL • TAIPEI • TOKYO

Hardware Hacking Projects for Geeks

by Scott Fullam

Published by O'Reilly Media, Inc., 1005 Gravenstein Highway North, Sebastopol, CA 95472.

O'Reilly & Associates books may be purchased for educational, business, or sales promotional use. Online editions are also available for most titles (*safari.oreilly.com*). For more information, contact our corporate/institutional sales department: 800-998-9938 or *corporate@oreilly.com*.

Print History:

January 2004:   First Edition.

Editors: Dale Dougherty and Tara McGoldrick

Production Editor: Emily Quill

Cover Designer: Edie Freedman

Interior Designers: David Futato and Melanie Wang

RepKover™ This book uses RepKover™, a durable and flexible lay-flat binding.

0-596-00314-5
[C]

Contents

Part II: Advanced Hacks, Tools, and Techniques

Preface

Introduction

I was inspired in my youth by two early "hackers": Thomas Edison and Ben Franklin. These men were constantly looking at the mechanisms and machines around them and seeking ways to improve their operation. Franklin saw the open fireplace and how it made rooms smoky with little heat to show for all the wood it burned. To fix this, he built an enclosed burning box known today as the Franklin stove. When Franklin grew tired of carrying two sets of glasses around, one for reading and one for distance, he hacked together the first bifocals. Edison was a prolific inventor and hacker. He took devices like the telegraph, stock ticker, and telephone and improved upon them. In his lifetime, Edison had over 1,000 patents to his name.

As a child I was always taking things apart to see how they worked. I used to build my own toys by taking apart ones I already had. Later, when I was a student at MIT, I lived in a dorm that had shared showers with a first-come, first-served usage policy. The only way you could tell if there was someone in the shower was to stand next to the door. Like most college students, I enjoyed sleeping in as long as possible. And as I did not want to stand in a cold bathroom waiting for the shower, I hacked up a sensor to the shower room door with an indicator in my room to tell me when the door was open. When I woke up, I would look for a flashing LED next to my bed indicating that the shower was occupied. This allowed me to wait in my warm bed until the light went off before walking to the shower.

At MIT, my interests included robotics. I built a number of autonomous machines and helped teach a class in robot design. After graduation, this led to a job as a toy designer. Over the course of two years I built close to 100 prototype toys. Many of the prototypes I built were hacked together from existing toys. It was great fun to have a job where I had to think up new things to play with and then build them.

Over the years I have continued to build new and fun toys for personal enjoyment. More than half the fun is getting my hands dirty at a bench. I've also come across a number of other projects that I consider fun and interesting. This book contains an eclectic mix of my own hacks as well as improvements upon other hacks that intrigued me. Although some of the projects may not seem practical at first glance, the knowledge gained by building each project can easily be applied to your own projects. The core equipment from each project can easily be adapted for other uses.

If you have no background in electronics, you may want to first read through Part I, Basic Hacks, Tools, and Techniques. It will help you become familiar with the tools of the trade and some basic soldering techniques, which are core to many of the hacks in the chapters that follow. I also present a list of basic tools required for most projects. If you don't have a hacking bench set up already, you should review the list of basic tools and begin gathering these items.

Goals of This Book

This book is your guide to the world of hardware hacking. The goal of this book is to allow people with no formal electronics- or hardware-engineering skills to hack real hardware. Various pieces of consumer electronic equipment can be modified according to the instructions in this book to do things they were never intended to do. Each chapter includes step-by-step instructions that will allow even a novice hacker to successfully construct that project. At the conclusion of each chapter is a "Bill of Materials" section for the project it covers, including verified suppliers; where appropriate, there are also photographs and diagrams of each step in construction.

Today, almost every appliance we use has some electronics inside of it. After reading this book and trying a few of the hacks, take a look around you and see which of your appliances or electronic gadgets needs "upgrading."

It is my hope that this book will inspire you to become a hacker, and will serve as a jumping-off point for new and clever hacks.

Audience for This Book

This book is intended for several audiences:

- Electronics hobbyists interested in getting their hands dirty and learning by doing.

- Software hackers who want to see what it's like to handle and modify hardware. Many of the projects include interfaces to standalone or networked computers. Once the hardware is built, there is ample opportunity to expand on the simple software projects covered in this book.

I've researched the Web looking for some of the legendary hardware hacks that I've heard about. After collecting the material for these hacks in cooperation with the original developers, I tried to organize the information in a way that will help you do the hack yourself. At the beginning of each chapter, I acknowledge work and materials provided by other developers.

- Budding hackers of all kinds. If you are new to both software and hardware hacking, you can get started quickly with projects that do something interesting immediately.

Organization of This Book

Each project begins with a duration scale representing how much time the project will likely take to complete, a cost scale indicating how much (or how little) it will cost to build each project, and a difficulty scale.

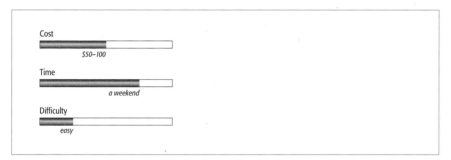

Part I, Basic Hacks, Tools, and Techniques, is an introduction to the tools of the trade for hackers. It covers the common tools and techniques required for hardware hacking, along with some basic electronics theory. This section teaches the basics you'll need for Chapters 1 through 6.

Chapter 1, How to Build a Portable Laptop Power Supply, explains how to build a laptop computer power extender using ordinary D-size batteries, a battery holder, and a connector cable. This project requires a small amount of soldering.

Chapter 2, How to Build an Aquarium Inside a Macintosh, shows how to take a Macintosh Classic computer and turn it into a very nice fish tank. This hack does not involve any circuit boards. You will be cutting out sheets of plastic and gluing them together to form a waterproof tank that sits inside the computer case.

Chapter 3, How to Hack 802.11b Antennas, explains how to build your own directional, long-range antenna for an 802.11b network. You will need to locate an old Primestar dish, and an empty metal can will house the main components.

Chapter 4, How to Build a PC Water-Cooling System, shows how to hack together a water cooler for your PC's CPU to allow it to be overclocked. This hack requires a small amount of simple metalwork, bending a thin sheet of copper and soldering together seams.

About the Photos

Many of the photos used in this book were taken from original sources on the Web. In some cases, the image resolution is low and the clarity of the photograph suffers in print. Nonetheless, we believed it was worth including them in the book. We have made these images available as downloads on the following web site because many of the photos look better on a monitor, and are often available in color.

http://www.oreilly.com/ hardwarehacking

Chapter 5, How to Hack a Furby (and Other Talking Toys), shows how to hack the Furby interactive toy to allow it to speak phrases you program and to react with behavior you specify. Several circuit boards must be populated with electronic components using solder. This chapter also covers how to hack a much simpler talking toy to speak phrases you program.

Chapter 6, How to Hack a Video Periscope for Your Car, shows how to build a video periscope for use in your car. Put this hack together and you can look out over traffic from a small display. You will build a simple circuit board for this hack.

Part II, Advanced Hacks, Tools, and Techniques, covers some of the more advanced tools and techniques you'll need for Chapters 7 through 15.

Chapter 7, How to Build a Digital Video Recorder, explains how to build your own DVR using an old PC, a video capture card, and a few other components.

Chapter 8, How to Hack a Building-Size Display, shows you how to hack a 12-story building into a giant animated display. It also covers how to build a smaller version that can be placed on the side of a house, a dormitory building wall, or any 10- to 20-foot flat surface. This project requires lots of soldering and wiring.

Chapter 9, How to Build a Cubicle Intrusion Detection System, shows you how to build a system for detecting intruders. An inexpensive laser and sensor are used to project a "web" of laser light across any entrance and will sound an alarm when the beam is broken. You'll use an off-the-shelf controller and add a few simple components. This hack requires a small amount of soldering.

Chapter 10, How to Build an Internet Toaster, shows you how to build your own Internet toaster that can be commanded to toast a pattern on the bread based on the weather or any other web-based data.

Chapter 11, How to Build a Home Arcade Machine, explains how to build your own stand-up arcade game cabinet. You will be cutting sheets of plywood, finishing the cabinet, and wiring in a set of arcade-quality controllers. A PC running a piece of software called MAME provides the engine for the games.

Chapter 12, How to Build a Remote Object Tracker, shows how to build a personal "LoJack" system that allows you to track the location of objects by attaching a small box. Some simple connectors must be soldered together for this hack.

Chapter 13, How to Make RC Cars Play Laser Tag, explains how to modify an inexpensive remote-controlled toy car. A system that adds an infrared "laser" and a set of sensors turns the car into a highly interactive toy. Build two of these cars and you can play laser tag. This hack is somewhat involved and requires you to build two small circuit boards.

Chapter 14, How to Build a Wearable Computer, covers wearable computer systems. The chapter reviews major components and explains how you can put together an example system.

Chapter 15, How to Build an Internet Coffeemaker, explains how to build your own web-based coffee machine. An off-the-shelf micro web server with built-in 10BaseT Ethernet will be modified and sensors added to allow you to check the temperature and the amount of coffee in the pot from any web browser. You will solder together a simple circuit board for this project.

Project Downloads

In the interest of keeping down the price of this book, we decided not to include a CD. Instead, we've created a web site to house all the many schematic diagrams, photos, and software listings for each project in this book, ready for you to download. So, don't worry about typing in all that code—you'll find everything here:

> *http://www.oreilly.com/hardwarehacking*

Using Code Examples

This book is here to help you get your job done. In general, you may use the code in this book in your programs and documentation. You do not need to contact us for permission unless you're reproducing a significant portion of the code. For example, writing a program that uses several chunks of code from this book does not require permission. Selling or distributing a CD-ROM of examples from O'Reilly books *does* require permission. Answering a question by citing this book and quoting example code does not require permission. Incorporating a significant amount of example code from this book into your product's documentation *does* require permission.

We appreciate, but do not require, attribution. An attribution usually includes the title, author, publisher, and ISBN. For example: "*Hardware Hacking Projects for Geeks* by Scott Fullam. Copyright 2004 O'Reilly & Associates, Inc., 0-596-00314-5."

If you feel your use of code examples falls outside fair use or the permission given above, feel free to contact O'Reilly at *permissions@oreilly.com*.

How to Contact O'Reilly

Please address comments and questions concerning this book to the publisher:

O'Reilly & Associates, Inc.
1005 Gravenstein Highway North
Sebastopol, CA 95472
(800) 998-9938 (in the United States or Canada)
(707) 829-0515 (international or local)
(707) 829-0104 (fax)

There is a web page for this book, where you can find code files, errata, and additional information. You can access this page at:

http://www.oreilly.com/ hardwarehacking

To comment or ask technical questions about this book, send email to:

bookquestions@oreilly.com

For more information about books, conferences, Resource Centers, and the O'Reilly Network, go to:

http://www.oreilly.com

Acknowledgments

This book began with a phone call from a long-time friend, Jon Orwant. He knew of my penchant for building new toys and hacks and asked me if I would like to put some of those ideas on paper for others to enjoy.

I would like to thank my technical reviewers who read and critiqued my writing. They are: Steve Hazelwood, Eric Faulkner, Bunnie Huang, Matt Biddulph, Raffi Krikorian, Tim Allwine, Nat Torkington, and Shane Warden.

The team at O'Reilly was fantastic at taking my raw work and making it into a real book. My editors were instrumental in making the project a reality.

Last but certainly not least I would like to thank my family and friends for their support, especially my wife Jie. I could not have completed this without her love and patience.

Disclaimer

Much of the information contained in this book is based on personal knowledge and experience. While I believe that the information contained herein is correct, I accept no responsibility for its validity. The hardware designs, software, and descriptive text contained herein are provided for educational purposes only. It is the responsibility of the reader to independently verify all information. Original manufacturer's data should be used at all times when implementing a design.

The author, Scott Fullam, and O'Reilly & Associates, Inc., make no warranty, representation, or guarantee regarding the suitability of any hardware or software described herein for any particular purpose, nor do they assume any liability arising out of the application or use of any product, system, circuit, or software, and specifically disclaim any and all liability, including, without limitation, consequential or incidental damages. The hardware and software described herein are not designed, intended, nor authorized for use in any application intended to support or sustain life or any other application in which the failure of a system could create a situation in which personal injury, death, loss of data or information, or damages to property may occur. Should the reader implement any design described herein for any application, the reader shall indemnify and hold the author, O'Reilly & Associates, Inc., and their respective shareholders, officers, employees, and distributors harmless against all claims, costs, damages and expenses, and reasonable solicitor fees arising out of, directly or indirectly, any claim of personal injury, death, loss of data or information, or damages to property associated with such unintended or unauthorized use.

Basic Hacks, Tools, and Techniques

I

Before you get started on your first hardware hack, it's a good idea to familiarize yourself with some of the tools and practice some basic hacking skills.

The projects in this section require you to use basic hand tools, read schematic diagrams, use a multi-meter, and know how to solder. Read through and practice the techniques presented here to begin your journey as a hardware hacker.

A Tour of My Toolbox

"Voiding the warranty" on any product occurs when you open up a piece of equipment and rummage around to see what new features you can add. More often than not, to hack any given electronic equipment, you will need to construct circuits and/or solder on connectors. All of these activities require some basic tools and knowledge of a few techniques.

Here's what I keep in my toolbox so that whenever I get a hankering to hack, I am ready to go:

Basic soldering equipment. I like to have both a small 12-watt iron for soldering surface mount parts, and a larger 75-watt iron for soldering large connectors. You will also need solder, solder flux, and either a solder sucker or a solder wick. Most of the projects in this book involve soldering, which I'll review later in this chapter.

Basic hand tools. I like to have a set of fine-tipped wire cutters for trimming wires and cutting off the leads of components after they are soldered. A good set of wire strippers also allows you to prepare wires for soldering. A set of needlenose pliers makes it easy to bend component leads to fit in tight spaces. A set of tweezers can help you pick up tiny parts and hold them in place while soldering. I keep a set of jeweler's screwdrivers along with a set of normal drivers to open up enclosures and cases. Fine-blade X-Acto knives are useful for cutting traces on a circuit board. A sheet-metal nibbler will allow you to slowly cut through both plastic and metal cases without having to get out a large power tool. A handheld metal reamer will allow you to cut clean holes through most metal and plastic. The Dremel moto-tool can be a great help in quickly cutting and modifying cases and circuit boards. I strongly recommend a "helping hands" workstand to hold the circuit components you are soldering in place. I also have a magnifying glass to inspect my work. You will likely use one or more of these tools for each project in this book; you can see some of them in Figure I-1. Clockwise from top left are wire strippers, printer's knife, needlenose pliers, wire cutters, and helping hands.

Multi-meter. I have an inexpensive "no-name" brand meter that works well enough. I cover how to use a multi-meter later in this chapter.

Plug boards. These are useful for quickly checking if a circuit idea works before you solder all the parts permanently together. I will cover how to use this in Part II.

Wire. I keep several spools of wire (30-gauge stranded, 24-gauge stranded, solid-core 20-gauge stranded, 16-gauge stranded, and multi-conductor ribbon cable) on hand. It will make your work go faster if you have these readily available.

Hot-melt glue gun. Hot-melt glue is amazing stuff—it's nearly flawless at causing any two solid items to stick together. It is as useful as duct tape and used almost as often by electronics hackers. I have an inexpensive "no-name" brand gun; any brand will do the trick.

These are the basic tools you will want to have on hand for most of the simpler hacks I cover in this book. Part II, Advanced Hacks, Tools, and Techniques will cover the kinds of skills you'll need to tackle the more complicated hacks. Each hack in this book requires only a small subset of the tools described here, but if you're going to call yourself a tinkerer and invent your own hacks, you'll want to be acquainted with all the tools in this toolbox.

The Basics

Hacking hardware usually involves several basic activities: reading schematic drawings that describe circuits, connecting electronic components using solder, and measuring signals in electronic circuits using a multi-meter. Before you jump into the first few projects in this book, you need to know how to perform these activities.

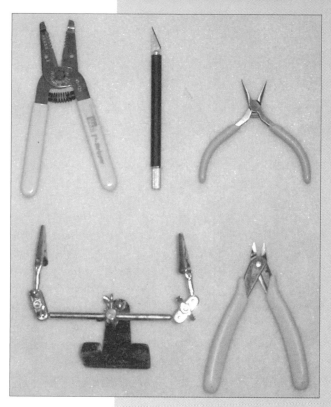

Figure I-1: Hand tools (clockwise from top left are wire strippers, printer's knife, needlenose pliers, wire cutters, and helping hands)

How to read a schematic diagram

The schematic diagram is a standard method for describing how to connect the various parts in an electrical circuit. It shows all of the components used, their values and important part details, and how they connect to the other components. A symbol and a label represent each component.

The circuits in most of the hacking projects in this book will be described using schematic diagrams. Knowing how to read a schematic diagram will also allow you to design and build your own hacking projects.

Schematic diagrams can look complex, but once you know the basic rules of how they are drawn they will be easy to decipher. I will cover the basics of schematic diagram reading in the next few paragraphs, referring back to the example diagram in Figure I-2. Being able to read these diagrams will increase the number of projects you can tackle.

Dots and Lines in Schematic Diagrams

Are you lost yet? Think of the schematic diagram as a roadmap. The electronic components are the buildings and the wires are the roads. When two roads cross without a dot, think of that point as an overpass. When the lines cross with a dot, it is an intersection. Each building has a name, represented by the identification letter/number scheme.

Let's begin by looking at a simple schematic diagram and talking about the meaning of each marking. Figure I-2 shows a typical schematic diagram. Many components of a schematic diagram have a border with letters and numbers along each edge to make it easier to communicate the location of a part. There is usually a title block that describes when the diagram was created and by whom, a brief description, and a revision number. You can see a title block at location 8 in our example. Each electronic part is represented by a symbol of some sort. The symbols vary from simple boxes to more complex drawings. In our example, location 1 shows a voltage regulator. It is represented by a box with an identification called a part reference, shown at 2 as U2, with three lines coming out of it, each with a number next to it. The number shown at 3 is one of the wires, also known as pins, which protrude from the component. The line shown at 4 represents a wire that connects the bottom pin of C2, a capacitor, and point 6, 5, and the bottom pin of C1. The dot at 6 represents a point where three wires are connected. Note that when two lines representing electrical connections cross over each other in a schematic diagram, it does not mean they are connected. At point 10 in the example, two lines representing electrical connections cross, but because there is no dot at the intersection, they are not connected.

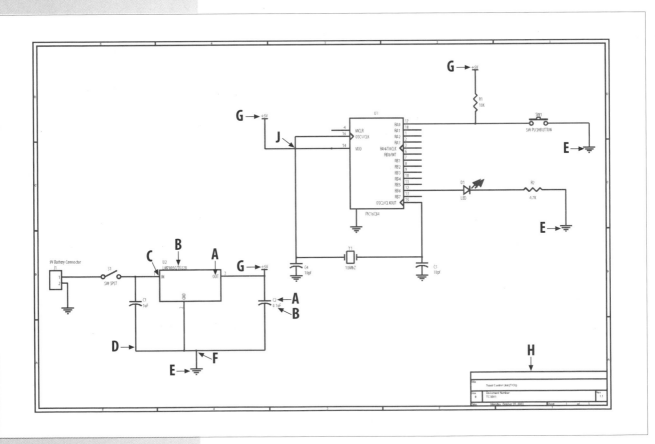

Figure I-2: Example schematic diagram

Sometimes we want to connect many locations in the circuit to the same place. Schematic diagrams often represent this by putting a name next to the line that is connected to this common location. All locations at 7 are connected. This type of naming scheme allows many connections without cluttering the drawing. The power supply to circuits is almost always connected using names on wires. The symbol at 5 is for the ground of the circuit. For now, just connect all of the grounds together.

The symbols you will encounter in a circuit can vary quite a bit; some of the ones you will see in the upcoming chapters are shown in Figure I-3. You should familiarize yourself with them, but you don't need to memorize them now. You can always refer back to this section later.

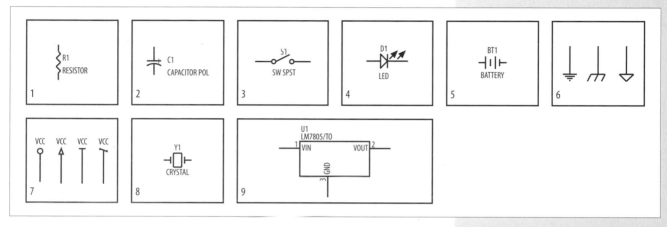

Figure I-3: Basic schematic symbols

The symbols in Figure I-3 can be described as follows:

Item 1 is a resistor. Resistors usually have two pins. You can learn more about how to identify the values of a resistor in Part II. Resistors are often marked with the letter "R" and then an identification number, e.g., "R1."

Item 2 is a capacitor. Capacitors typically have two pins and are sometimes polarized. This means that they have a + side and a – side and must be installed in the proper direction. You can see which side is which by looking on the side of the component package—there will probably be a + or – symbol next to one of the pins. Capacitors are often marked with the letter "C" and then an identification number, e.g., "C1."

Item 3 is a single-throw single-pole switch. This is a technical way to say that the switch opens and closes a single connection. Switches are often marked with the letters "SW" or "S" and then an identification number, e.g., "SW1."

Solder Trivia

In order for electricity to move between circuit elements and allow electronic circuits to operate, connections must be made. You can usually make these connections using an easy-to-apply metal compound. The most common material used is called solder. It is composed of tin and lead with a typical 60/40 mix. This combination melts at a relatively low temperature (360 degrees Fahrenheit) and is therefore easy to melt with hand irons. There are also a large number of alternate formulations, including solder with embedded flux (a material that allows the solder to more easily stick to the metal surfaces being connected) and lead-free solder. See the Solder Flux sidebar for more details.

Item 4 is a light emitting diode (LED). These devices must be installed correctly to work. The pin next to the flat line in the symbol is called the anode and is marked on the component package with a colored stripe. LEDs are often marked with the letters "LED" or "D" and then an identification number, e.g. "D1."

Item 5 is a battery. The + terminal is the side with the wider line; the − is the other side. Batteries are often marked with the letters "BT" or "B" and then an identification number, e.g., "BT1."

The items at 6 are symbols for ground. If a circuit has multiple ground symbols, connect each group separately.

The items at 7 are symbols for circuit power. The label next to each signifies which group it belongs to. Connect only power symbols with the same name.

Item 8 is a crystal. Crystals are used to generate a very accurate timing clock. They can be connected in either direction. Crystals are often marked with the letter "Y" and then an identification number, e.g., "Y1."

Item 9 is a voltage regulator. It takes a "raw" battery and converts it to a stable voltage, which most circuits require. You can identify the location of three pins by checking the data sheet, which is a detailed technical specification from the chip manufacturer. Integrated circuits (which is what a voltage regulator is) are often marked with the letter "U" and then an identification number, e.g., "U1."

The symbols described here are by no means an exhaustive list, and are meant only to get you familiar with some components and whet your appetite for more.

More complicated integrated circuits such as microprocessors are typically represented in schematic diagrams by a box with numbered lines on the sides. The numbered lines represent the signal pins on the IC.

Note that the power and ground connections to integrated circuits (ICs) on a schematic diagram are often omitted in the printed copy. This is because the additional lines on the schematic can make it cluttered and difficult to make out the other signal paths. If you don't see power and ground connected to an IC in a schematic diagram, check the data sheet before wiring your circuit so that you can add it yourself.

This is probably a lot of information to absorb quickly. The best way to sear this into your brain is to read an actual schematic diagram and then build something.

How to solder

Now that you have a basic idea of how to read a schematic diagram, it's time to use this newly won knowledge to build a circuit by soldering the parts together.

You will need several tools before you start: some solder, a soldering iron, solder remover, and all of the parts of the circuit you intend to build. If you are not familiar with these items, refer to Figure I-4. From left to right you can see a soldering iron, solder, and solder wick.

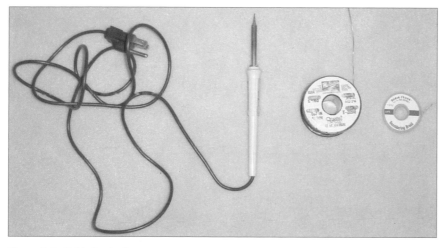

Figure I-4: Soldering tools

I believe in learning by doing, so let's build a simple project to get the hang of soldering. For this mini-project you will need the following items:

- A soldering iron (Weller WM120 or Radio Shack Part #64-2055)
- Solder (Radio Shack Part #64-015)
- Solder remover (Radio Shack Part #64-2090)
- Prototype board (Radio Shack Part #276-147)
- An LED (Radio Shack Part #276-316)
- A 4.7K resistor (Radio Shack Part #271-1124)
- A battery connector (Radio Shack Part #270-324)
- A pushbutton switch (Radio Shack Part #275-618)
- Wire cutters

Solder

I like to use Multicore No-Clean solder (*http://www.multicore.com*) with a 0.5mm diameter. This solder has a built-in flux that does not leave a visible residue. However, there are many brands available, and most of those sold by reputable distributors should work well.

Soldering Irons

For small electronics work, choose a low-wattage, fine-tip iron. I like the Weller WM120 12-watt iron. It comes with a small tip and heats up quickly. There are many different brands of irons: Weller, Metcal (the Cadillac of irons), and Hakko to name a few. You don't need an expensive iron to start out with, but I recommend getting one of these brands. Your soldering iron will (hopefully) get extensive use, and there is no substitute for a quality tool.

I also have a more powerful 75-watt soldering iron from Weller (Model # 7200PK Soldering Gun Kit) for soldering bigger items.

Other Solder Removers

There are other ways to remove excess solder besides solder wick. One alternative tool is called a *solder sucker*. This is a spring-loaded piston that sucks up solder like a vacuum cleaner. One model available from Radio Shack is shown below.

Soldering Hints

There are a few basic things to remember when soldering:

- Make sure the soldering iron tip is clean before soldering. You should keep a small damp sponge nearby for this purpose. Before using the soldering iron tip to melt any solder, gently and quickly wipe its tip on the sponge. The iron tip should become clean and shiny. Solder immediately after doing this.

- Use a solder flux. Most solders have flux built into them. There are times when it is difficult to make a solder joint. Apply a small amount of solder flux to the area you want to solder and proceed.

You will be building the circuit described in Figure I-5. Start off by gently bending the wire leads of the resistor 90 degrees so that it looks like the letter U. Push the two wire leads through two holes in the prototype board. Next, take the LED and push it into the board next to the resistor so that the leads are next to each other. Strip off a few millimeters of insulation from the ends of the battery connector and twist the bare wires so that they do not fray. Gently push them through two holes in the board according to the schematic diagram in Figure I-5. Twist the leads of the components together with your fingers so they are connected, again according to Figure I-5.

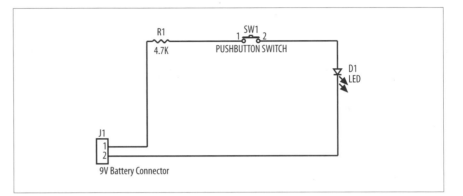

Figure I-5: LED schematic

Now comes the soldering part. The best way to make a good solder connection is to heat the components first. Press the tip of the soldering iron against the items you want to solder together for a few seconds. Now touch a small amount of solder to the components. If it does not melt immediately, touch a little solder to the iron and then back to the components. That's all there is to it! Repeat this procedure for each of the connections in the circuit.

You may occasionally find that you have soldered together the wrong parts. If you do this, your circuit is not ruined—solder can be removed using a number of methods and tools. I like to use a material called solder wick, a copper braid that works like a sponge and absorbs liquefied solder. To use it, place the solder wick against the area with the excess solder and press a hot soldering iron tip against it. The iron tip heats the solder wick and the solder, which then liquefies. Capillary action then causes the liquid solder to be pulled into the wick.

Try this out by removing the solder from the connections you just made. Don't hold the solder wick itself as it will get very hot—hold on to the plastic holder instead. It's a good idea to practice soldering and unsoldering a few times, as you'll likely have to unsolder mistakes made in your first project.

After you have completed building this circuit, connect a 9V battery and test it out. When you press the button, the LED should turn on. If it doesn't work, don't despair. The next section covers how to use a multi-meter to troubleshoot your circuits.

How to use a multi-meter

A multi-meter is often called a Volt-Ohm meter (VOM), a digital volt meter (DVM), or simply a meter. A multi-meter measures voltage, resistance, and sometimes current. Advanced models can also measure the value of capacitors, time, and temperature.

The multi-meter typically has two plastic sticks with metal tips (called *probes*) that are attached by flexible wires connected to two sockets in the body of the meter. The probe wires are removable. In the center of the instrument is a dial that selects the electrical characteristic you will be measuring. The meter shown in Figure I-6 measures resistance, DC voltage, AC voltage, current, diode forward voltage, and battery voltage.

The multi-meter lets you see what is going on inside an electronic circuit. Unless you always build every circuit perfectly, you will be using a multi-meter to find out what is wrong.

We will now use a multi-meter to measure voltage and current in the circuit you just built.

How to measure voltage in a circuit

The multi-meter's dial will usually have two areas marked with the letter V. One will have two straight lines (a solid one above a dashed one), and the other will have a single wavy line.

Overview

When the dial is rotated to the area with the V with the two straight lines, it is set to measure a static or slowly changing voltage such as a battery. There are several different numbers in this area as well, which tell the meter what range of voltages you want to measure. Select the numeric value closest to what you think the signal might be. Touch the tip of the black probe to a point in the circuit that you know to be "ground" (look on your schematic diagram or select the minus terminal of the batteries in the circuit), and touch the red probe to where you want to measure the voltage. You do not always have to touch the black probe to ground in the circuit. The meter will measure the voltage between any two points in the circuit. If the meter reads all zeros or single 1, change the range and try again. Some meters will change the range for you.

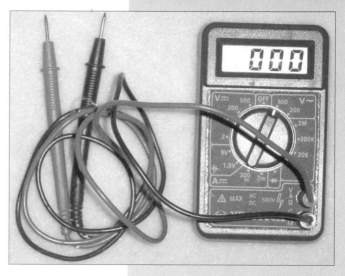

Figure I-6: Multi-meter

Solder Flux

Solder flux is a liquid that makes it easier for two surfaces to be soldered together. It is a solvent (slightly acidic) that helps to clean away oil and residue from the surface of the materials being soldered. Several types are typically available: rosin-based, no-clean, and water-soluble. Rosin-based is one of the oldest types, and may leave an orange residue. This residue should be removed from the circuit board before testing the circuit. Use a flux remover (another solvent) to dissolve the rosin-based flux. No-clean type flux leaves a clear residue that does not need to be removed. Water-soluble fluxes can be cleaned off with water.

I recommend using a no-clean flux, as it requires no action when soldering is complete.

When the dial is rotated to point at the V with the wavy lines, it is set to measure an alternating voltage signal that changes roughly 60 times per second. This setting is used almost exclusively to measure the voltage from a wall power outlet. When used to measure an AC (alternating current) signal from a wall outlet, place the black probe on either of the two power outlet holes and the red probe against the other.

WARNING
Don't touch the metal portions of the two pins together when measuring voltage or current from a wall outlet. Also, never touch the electrical outlet wires or the exposed portion of the plug with any part of your body. You can receive a potentially deadly shock.

Measuring voltage in our circuit

Take out the circuit you built in the previous section and make sure to install a fresh battery. Switch on the meter and rotate the dial to the 20V setting. The display should read "0.00". Touch the metal tip of the black probe to the minus terminal of the battery and the metal tip of the red probe to the location shown in Figure I-7. The display should now show a number between 8.00 and 9.50. Press and hold the button, and the display should show a number between 0.6 and 2.00.

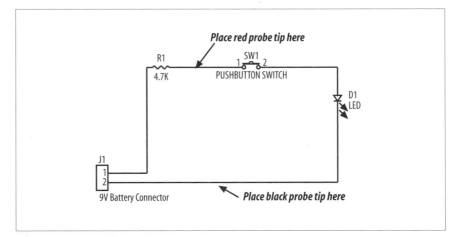

Figure I-7: Circuit probe locations

How to measure current

To measure current, the dial of the multi-meter has two areas marked with the letter A. One will have two straight lines (a solid one above a dashed one) and the other will have a single wavy line.

Overview

When the dial is rotated to the A with the two straight lines, it is set to measure a static or slowly changing current such as that from a battery. There are several numbers in this area as well, which tell the meter what range of current you want to measure. Select the numeric value closest to what you think the signal might be.

When you measure current, you are measuring the current flow through a circuit element or a piece of wire. To measure how much current a circuit is drawing, touch the tip of the red probe to the plus terminal of your battery. Make sure that the minus terminal of the battery is connected to the circuit correctly. Touch the black probe to the point in your circuit at which the plus terminal is normally connected. You are using the meter in place of the wire that normally connects the battery's plus terminal to the circuit. If the meter reads all zeros or 1, change the range and try again. Some meters will change the range for you.

Some meters can measure alternating current (AC), which is the current flowing through a home's current wire. To measure AC, select the function on your meter that has the letter A with a wavy line next to it. The two probes and the meter must be put in the circuit in place of the cut wire. An example of this is shown in Figure I-8.

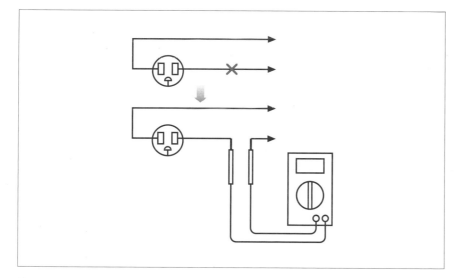

Figure I-8: AC current measurement

Circuit Troubleshooting Tips

Sometimes your electronic circuit doesn't work the way you wanted it to, or it doesn't work at all. Here are some methods I use to troubleshoot or "debug" circuits:

- Check all power and ground connections. Are all grounds connected together? Are all power connections connected together? Is power shorted to ground?

- Use a socket for all ICs. You can quickly replace them if they are damaged.

- Before installing components, power up the circuit with only the power supply in place. Measure the voltage at each power supply point in the circuit to make sure it's connected and the power supply voltage is correct. Add one IC at a time to the circuit and recheck the power supply each time (make sure you power off the circuit before installing parts).

- Check to see that all capacitors are installed according to their specified polarization (the + terminal is where it should be).

- Check that all diodes are installed in the correct direction. The black stripe on the package is the line to which the arrow is pointed in the schematic diagram items for a diode.

- Check all connectors to make sure all pins are soldered and the wiring is correct.

Measuring current in our circuit

Take out the circuit that you built in the previous section and make sure to install a fresh battery. Switch on the multi-meter and rotate the dial to the 200m setting. Some meters may require you to move the red probe to a different socket in the front of the meter labeled with a reference to current or with the letter A—check the instructions included with your meter to be sure. The display should read "0.00". Touch the metal tips of the probes as shown in Figure I-9. The display should now show a number between 2.00 and 5.00, and the LED should light up.

WARNING
When operating in current measurement mode, the meter looks like a short circuit. Do not forget to set the meter back to voltage mode when trying to measure voltage, or it could cause the internal fuse in the meter to blow.

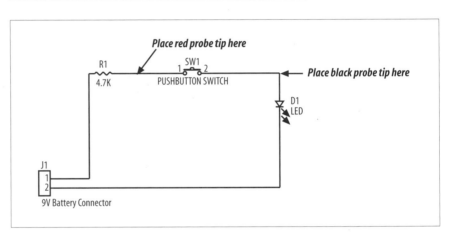

Figure I-9: Measure direct current

How to measure resistance

The Greek character Omega (Ω) is used to represent electrical resistance. To measure the resistance of a resistor or between two points in a circuit, begin by rotating the dial to point to one of the numbers inside the area marked with the Omega character.

Overview

To measure resistance, touch the metal points of the two probes to either end of the resistor or to the two points between which you wish to measure the resistance. The display will show the resistance in the range selected by the dial. The meter has a number of range settings. When set to the 2M setting, the display will show resistance in millions of Ohms (also called mega Ohms). When set to the 200K setting, the display will show resistance in hundreds of thousands of Ohms (also called kilo Ohms). When set to the 20K setting, the display will show resistance in tens of thousands of Ohms. When set to the 2K setting, the display will show resistance in thousands of Ohms. Some meters will automatically adjust the measured range.

Measuring resistance in our circuit

Select the resistance measurement mode on the meter and rotate the dial to the 20K setting. Place the red and black probe tips to the locations shown in Figure I-10. The meter should show a number close to 4.7. If the meter reads all zeros or 1, change the range and try again. Some meters change the range for you.

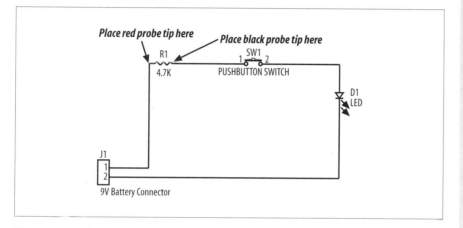

Figure I-10: Resistance measurement

WARNING

Make sure that the circuit that contains the component you are measuring is powered OFF (no power or battery is connected) while measuring resistance. The meter will not produce reliable readings if the circuit is powered ON.

Now that you've worked your way through these exercises, you have the basic skills to successfully begin hacking electronic hardware. However, you will want to read through Part II and practice soldering a number of circuits before tackling some of the more difficult hacks such as Chapter 9, How to Build a Cubicle Intrusion Detection System or Chapter 13, How to Make RC Cars Play Laser Tag.

How to Build a Portable Laptop Power Supply

Cost

$10–25

Time

a weekend

Difficulty

easy

What You Need

- Battery holder for 10 to 12 cells
- Speaker wire
- DC power connector
- Fuse and holder
- D-size batteries
- Tie wraps
- Black electrical tape
- Multi-meter

I've been using laptop computers for a long time, and one of the first accessories I end up buying is an extra battery. These batteries tend to cost anywhere from $100 to $200 and don't provide that much more operating time. I travel by air quite a bit, and the extra battery I carry often does not last even half the flight.

After some thought, I decided to build my own external laptop power extender that would run off of standard alkaline or rechargeable batteries. The battery pack adds anywhere between two and six extra hours of run time. With your laptop fully charged and this power extender packed for backup, you should have enough power to run your applications for as long as you wish on your next transcontinental airplane trip.

Credits

Photographs copyright © 2003 Scott Fullam.

Project Overview

This project uses a set of ordinary alkaline D-size batteries to power a laptop computer.

You will assemble a battery holder and cable and test out the project. The battery pack you assemble will be customized for your laptop model. Before connecting it to another model, you will also need to check for voltage compatibility. When you've completed this project, the battery pack should power your laptop for two to six hours.

Hardware Assembly Instructions

The power extender you build will be customized for your laptop. You will need to check the voltage requirement for your laptop and assemble a suitable pack.

Figure 1-1: Underside of laptop

Figure 1-2: Laptop power jack

1. Determine your laptop's voltage input

Look on the bottom of your laptop computer and locate the input voltage specification. Figure 1-1 shows the location on an IBM model T20 laptop. The T20 specifies 15V DC input at 3.39 amps. (This may seem like a large number, but on average your laptop will not draw this much current.) If this information is not listed on the laptop case, look in the owner's manual or on the AC wall power adapter that came with the laptop.

If the input specification is in AC volts, this hack will not work. AC volts are specified with either the letters "AC" or a wavy line after the voltage specification.

2. Locate a suitable power connector for your laptop

Look at the back or side of your laptop and locate the external power jack.

The IBM T20 external power jack is a yellow plastic jack on the right side. You can see it circled in Figure 1-2. On other laptops, simply look for the jack into which you plug the AC wall adapter.

Look closely next to the power jack and you will also see its polarity. This will tell you how to wire up the power plug from your battery pack. There will be a small inset diagram similar to Figure 1-3.

Radio Shack has a large selection of power jacks from which to choose. Either purchase a few and use the one that fits, or take your laptop into the store and try out several until you find one that fits snugly.

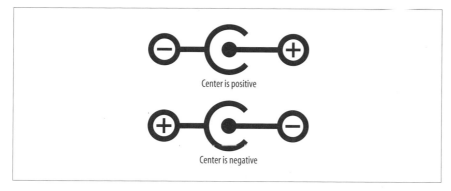

Figure 1-3: Power jack polarity

3. Determine the number of required batteries

In Step 1 you determined the required voltage for your laptop. Divide this number by 1.5 to determine the number of alkaline batteries required to power your laptop. Odd numbered cells should be rounded up to the next even number. Even- and fractional-numbered cells should be rounded up to the closest even number. For example, if you have a 16 volt rating on your laptop, the number of calculated batteries would be determined using the following equation: $16/1.5 = 10.66$. Rounding this number (10.66) up to the closest even number gives you 12. This means you will need 12 batteries to power a 16V laptop. Note that a laptop input power plug can typically withstand a few volts over its maximum rated input voltage. The voltage on the alkaline cells will also drop once the laptop begins to draw current from it.

Rechargeable batteries can also be used. If you want your battery pack to work with both alkaline and rechargeable batteries, you will have to install a switch that selects between the two types. The pack will have to accommodate a larger number of rechargeable batteries since they have a lower voltage per battery. Calculate the number of rechargeable batteries by dividing the required voltage by 1.25 for NiCad or NiMH cells. Round the number up to the closest even number as you did for alkaline batteries.

Types of Batteries

There are several types of popular nonrechargeable and rechargeable batteries that you can use for the battery pack.

Nickel-Cadmium (or NiCad) batteries are a less expensive type of rechargeable cell. They also have less capacity than other types of batteries. Early laptops used NiCad cells, but very few use them today.

Nickel-Metal-Hydride (or NiMH) batteries are a little more expensive than NiCad cells and have 30 to 50 percent more capacity. They are easy to purchase in most electronic stores and through online catalogs.

Lithium-Ion (Li-Ion) batteries are currently the most popular type of battery used in laptop and high-end electronic devices. Each cell has a higher voltage than NiCad or NiMH cells. Special charging electronics are required for Li-Ion cells.

Alkaline batteries are the most popular type of nonrechargeable cells available today. I based this project on alkaline cells because they are inexpensive and easy to find.

Duracell and Energizer are popular brands of alkaline batteries. Depending on your laptop, alkaline batteries may not be able to actually run your laptop, and can only charge its batteries when it is off.

Using our example of a 16V requirement, the calculation is 16/1.25 = 12.8. Rounding this up to the closest even number gives us 14. You can see what this configuration looks like for a 12- or 14-battery pack in Figure 1-4.

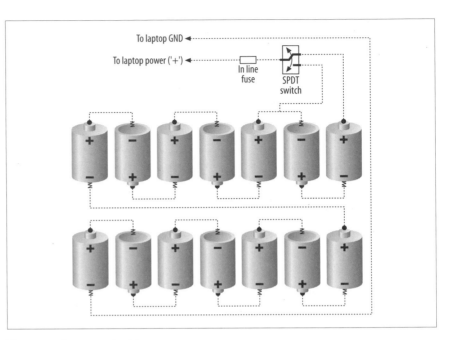

Figure 1-4: Battery pack wiring

Purchase a battery holder for the number of cells you've determined you need. If your pack is going to accommodate both battery types, purchase a holder that fits the larger number of batteries and allows access to the metal contacts inside it. You may need to use two separate battery holders and hold them together (see Step 4 for details on assembling two battery holders). I suggest that you purchase a battery holder from DigiKey or another well-known electronics supplier rather than Radio Shack; I have found that Radio Shack battery holders will break open after a few weeks from the pressure exuded by the springs.

New D-size alkaline cells provide 1.5 volts each. Duracell alkaline D-size cells supply about an amp of current for four to six hours, according to their technical data sheets. This should power your laptop for four to six hours depending on usage (backlight on, hard drive activity, and so on).

New C-size alkaline cells can also be used, but you'll experience a reduction in operating time of 50 to 60 percent. The pack will be lighter, however.

4. Assemble battery holder and connection cable

After you have purchased a suitable battery holder (or holders) and a power jack, you will need two additional items: a few feet of twin conductor speaker cable, and an inline fuse.

If you've purchased two holders, it is time to assemble them. For this step, I drilled four small holes in the edges of the two holders I used and tied them together with small tie wraps. Figure 1-5 shows a top view of the two holders held together with no visible gap between them. Next, insert the number of batteries required for your laptop into the assembled holder, checking to ensure that all the batteries are connected in series.

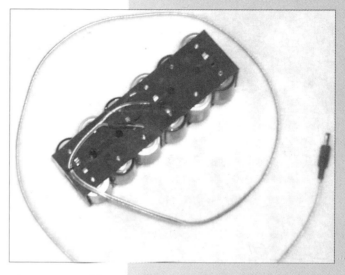

Now, assemble the power cable by taking three feet of 12-gauge twin conductor speaker wire and adding the power plug on one side of it. If the center pin required by the laptop is positive (see Step 2 for how to determine this), make sure that the wire you solder to the center pin of the power plug connects to the positive side of the battery pack. If it is negative, make sure it connects to the negative side of the battery pack.

You will need to add a small inline fuse to the power cable. Clip one of the wires of the power cable and strip the insulation off of it. Carefully solder the wires from the inline fuse holder to the stripped wires from the power cable. Cover over the exposed solder connection with insulated electrical tape or use a piece of heat-shrink tubing. Your power cable should now resemble the illustration in Figure 1-6.

Figure 1-5: Battery pack top view

Figure 1-6: Fuse location

5. Attach power cable to battery pack

After you have connected the battery holders together, determine which of their connection tabs are positive and which are negative. Wire the two packs in a series so that the batteries are all connected in a "line" with the top of one battery connected to the bottom of the next. The positive terminal of one pack will be connected to the negative terminal of the other, leaving one positive and one negative terminal open. You can see what the wiring of the battery pack should look like in Figure 1-7.

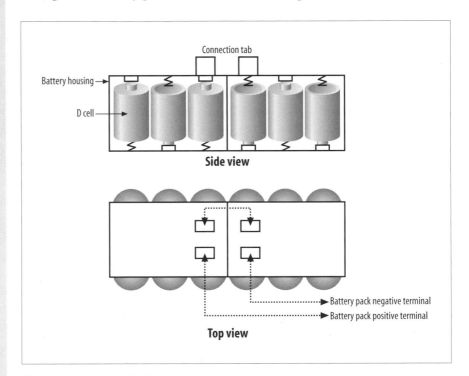

Figure 1-7: Battery pack wiring

For your reference, a schematic diagram of the battery pack is included in Exhibit B.

Carefully solder the positive power cable wire to the positive terminal of the combined battery pack, and the negative wire to the negative terminal.

WARNING
If you accidentally solder the positive wire to the negative terminal of the battery pack and plug it into your laptop, you could damage the laptop.

Drill a small pair of holes in one edge of one of the battery packs. Take a tie wrap, thread it through these holes, and use it to capture the power cable. In the battery pack in Figure 1-8, you can see where I secured the cable on the left side.

After soldering the wire tabs between the pack and the power cable, you will want to cover over any exposed metal. If you have access to heat-shrink tubing and a heat gun, I suggest you use this material to cover over the exposed metal. If you do not have heat-shrink tubing, use black electrical tape.

6. Test out the pack

Install the D cells into the battery holders. Set a multimeter to measure DC voltage and touch the probes to the end of the connector. The meter should read a voltage slightly higher than the number of cells multiplied by 1.5 (newly purchased cells often show a higher voltage than 1.5 volts). If you cannot read this voltage, check your wiring and the installation of the cells.

And your laptop battery extender pack is now complete. You should get anywhere from two to six hours of extra run time for those long plane trips.

Figure 1-8: Completed battery pack

Project Demo

Plug your laptop into the battery pack. The laptop will show that it is plugged into a wall outlet while using the battery pack. This is because the pack is supplying power through the power jack normally used by an AC adapter.

Extensions

If the battery pack included with your laptop no longer holds a charge, you can open up the battery enclosure and replace the dead batteries. You will need to carefully cut open the plastic case and determine the type of cells used; you will likely find either NiMH or Li-Ion cells. Replacement batteries can be ordered from a number of suppliers, including Panasonic and Sanyo.

If you want to use rechargeable batteries instead of alkaline cells in the battery holder, you can purchase the batteries and a charger at Radio Shack.

Exhibit A: Bill of Materials

Item	Quantity	Notes
D-size battery holder	10–12 cells	DigiKey Part #220K-ND, BH4DL-ND
12-gauge twin conductor speaker wire	6-foot length	Hardware store
DC power connector	1	Radio Shack or DigiKey
Fuse and holder	1	DigiKey Part #F062-ND holder and F124-ND fuse
Tie wraps	5	Hardware store or DigiKey
Insulating electrical tape	1 roll	Hardware store
D-size batteries	10–16	Any alkaline or rechargeable batteries
Multi-meter	1	

Exhibit B: Power Pack Schematic

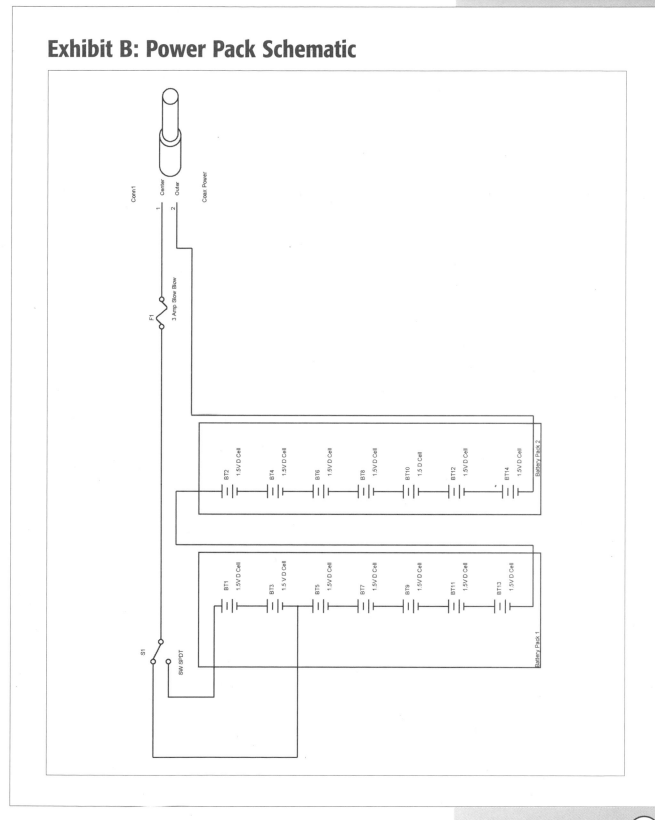

How to Build an Aquarium Inside a Macintosh

Cost

$50–100

Time

a weekend

Difficulty

easy

What You Need

- An old Mac (the "all-in-one" beige box)
- Plexiglas sheets
- Fish tank accessories
- A few hand tools
- Fish
- Other items listed in Exhibit A

One of the best-looking personal computers yet designed is the original Apple Macintosh. It not only had one of the most innovative user interfaces of its time, it also had a very unique and friendly-looking case design. This was a computer that bordered on "art." Well, that old Mac you once used is probably in the garage now or buried in some closet never to be powered on again, so why not turn it into something useful?

In this hack, I'll show you how to turn your old Macintosh into a working aquarium. You'll remove the electronics from the Mac and craft your own Plexiglas fish tank, customized to fit snugly inside the case. When you're finished, you'll have an aquarium and a new use for an old computer. Since you'll be removing all the components from inside the Mac, these plans will work fine even if your Mac is broken.

This hack is easy to complete and should take no more than a weekend to build, once you have all the supplies.

I would like to thank Jim Lower for providing the basic plans from his web site: *http://www.techquarium.com/*.

And, after some research, it appears that Andy Ihnatko was the first to build and document a Macquarium. He is a Mac pundit and runs this web site: *http://www.cwob.com/*.

Credits

Photographs and portions of the text in this chapter copyright © 2003 Jim Lower.

Project Overview

To create your Macquarium, you'll first take apart the Mac and remove the electronics. You'll then prepare the case, removing parts that would interfere with the fish tank and grinding down parts that would scrape it. You'll build the tank, using Plexiglas that you buy at your local hardware store. Finally, you'll assemble the tank, place it inside the Mac case, and populate it with your fish.

Currently, a Mac SE can be purchased on eBay for less than $20.

Hardware Assembly Instructions

The following steps walk you through the construction of your Macquarium.

1. Disassemble the Mac

The first thing you need to do is to carefully take apart your Mac.

Remove all switches and screws

Begin by prying off the sliding programmer's switch with a screwdriver, as shown in Figure 2-1. (Keep in mind that not all Macs are equipped with this switch.) Save the programmer's switch, as it will be put back on later. Mac SEs have a different switch that pries up from the bottom side. The Mac Classics switch is part of the case and does not come off, so you will leave it in place.

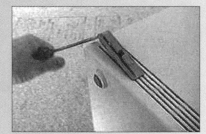

Figure 2-1: Power switch

Now remove the battery door and the Torx screw behind it, as shown in Figure 2-2. (Mac SEs and Classics do not have a battery door, so there is nothing to remove here.) Save the battery door for later reattachment. Torx screws have six-pointed star-shaped sockets that require a special screwdriver, which can be purchased at DigiKey or perhaps a local hardware store.

Look at the back side of the case and remove two Torx screws from the bottom. You can see their location circled in Figure 2-3.

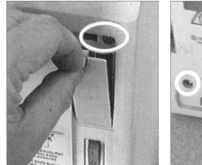

Figure 2-2: Battery door

Figure 2-3: Bottom Torx screws

(On older Macs, you will notice the "Hyperdrive" sticker on the back. This was one of the first internal hard drives for the Mac, with a cable that clipped directly to the processor. It was very cool at the time, but quite expensive.)

Look inside the carrying handle and remove the two Torx screws located deep inside. Their location is circled in Figure 2-4.

Remove the back case. You can do this by laying the Mac on its face and gently slapping the back. Position your hands on opposite corners of the case and slap the sides of the case while pulling upward (see Figure 2-5). If this doesn't work the first time, try again and slap harder.

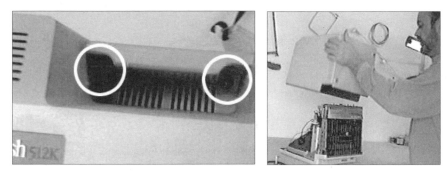

Figure 2-4: Handle Torx screws   **Figure 2-5**: Slide off back case

If this doesn't work, you may need a special tool to crack the case. Try asking an Apple service provider or a repair shop employee. A thin-bladed putty knife may also work, but don't use a screwdriver; its blade is too narrow and will mark up the edges of the case.

Remove all internal connectors

It's now time to get your hands inside the case. Be sure to carefully follow these instructions.

WARNING

There can be high voltages present inside the Mac. These voltages can be dangerous and may be present even on machines that have been turned off for some time. Exercise caution when working on the inside by keeping one hand behind your back when doing so. If both of your hands happen to touch high-voltage parts of the circuit, the high-voltage electricity could flow from one hand to the other across your chest. This high voltage could be enough to stop your heart. Inside the old Macs, you will find the high voltages on the anode cap that touches the picture tube.

Start by removing the plug located at the top of the analog board by pressing the locking tab and pulling outward. This plug is sometimes very hard to remove (extreme heat will weld it in place). If you can't pull it loose, cut the wires. Remember, it's never going to be a computer again. See Figure 2-6 for the location of this plug.

Remove the plug from the CRT to the analog board by pulling the plug that is circled in Figure 2-7. Now remove the grounding screw attaching the analog board to the frame, as shown in Figure 2-8. Next, remove the analog cable from the logic board, circled in the photo Figure 2-9.

Figure 2-6: Power plug location

Figure 2-7: CRT plug location

Figure 2-8: Frame ground location

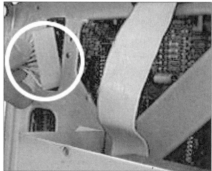

Figure 2-9: Analog cable location

Discharge CRT

WARNING

This task is a potentially dangerous step if your Mac has been turned on within the last few weeks.

You will now discharge the anode on the tube. Put one alligator clip on the shaft of a flat-blade screwdriver and clip the other end to the frame of the Macintosh.

Put one hand behind your back and do not touch the metal part of the screwdriver. With your free hand, slide the screwdriver under the anode cap until it touches the anode wire underneath. If there is still a voltage on the anode, you'll hear a satisfying "pop."

Now push the screwdriver blade against the anode wire and work it loose from the CRT. The freed anode wire and cover should look like Figure 2-10.

Remove analog parts

You will now remove the screws holding the analog board to the frame. You can see two of these screws in Figure 2-11. There may be others, depending on the model, along the front of the circuit board, which also must be removed. Lift this side circuit board out of the frame.

Mac SEs and SE/30s have a large power supply screwed to the analog board and located partially under the frame. You'll have to pull back on the logic board frame to get it clear (see Figure 2-12). Mac Classics are similar to Mac SEs in this respect.

Figure 2-10: CRT connector

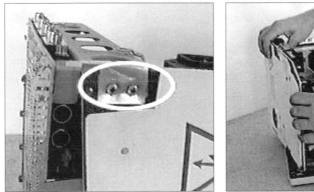

Figure 2-11: Analog board screws   **Figure 2-12**: Pull back logic board

Pull the brightness knob circled in Figure 2-13 off the analog board and set it aside. (This knob is not present on Classics.) It will be put back later for cosmetic purposes.

Remove the floppy cables, CRT, and logic board

Remove the floppy cable from the logic board. For Mac SE and Classic models there may be two floppy cables and/or a hard drive cable.

Mac SEs and SE/30s may have an expansion card installed. It's located on the opposite side of the logic board from the analog board and must be removed before removing the logic board. Mac Classics may have a RAM card installed on the right side of the logic board. Remove the two plastic clips and pull it up and out.

Figure 2-13: Brightness knob

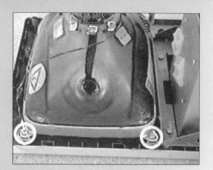

Figure 2-14: CRT screws

Figure 2-15: Logic board

Figure 2-16: Logic board screws

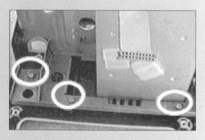

Figure 2-17: Top frame screws

Remove the four Torx screws that hold the CRT in place. Two of the screws are circled in Figure 2-14; the other two are on the top of the case and are hidden behind the tube. Now lift the CRT out.

If you plan to throw the CRT away, you should release the vacuum from the tube. To do this, place the neck of the tube in a box and hold it so the box is between you and the tip of the tube. Reach in and break off the tip with a pair of pliers. You should hear a hissing sound that lasts for several seconds.

Now that the CRT is out of the way, pull the logic board out of the frame. An unmodified Mac 128/512/Plus board pulls straight out. A board with an accelerator or other upgrade installed can be removed by prying one guide rail aside and releasing the board. Mac SE and SE/30 boards pull up until notches in the board match tabs in one side of the frame, then pull outward. Remove the speaker wire after freeing the board. The Mac Classic board is about half the size and pulls straight up and out. You can see how an unmodified logic board pulls out in Figure 2-15.

To release the remaining metal frame, remove the two Torx screws holding the bottom of the frame to the bezel, as circled in Figure 2-16. Next, remove the three Torx screws that are holding the top of the frame (see Figure 2-17), and lift the frame assembly from the bezel.

The Mac case should now be completely stripped of all metal parts and components. In the next step, you will clean out the inside of the case to ready it for a waterproof tank.

2. Prepare the case

Since the Macintosh case is built from two separate halves with many protruding bits of plastic, you'll need to cut the two halves up and remove all of the plastic protrusions so that the largest possible tank can fit inside the case.

Remove all plastic protrusions from the front case

WARNING
It is very important that you wear safety goggles while using the rotary cutting tool to protect your eyes from flying bits of plastic.

First, cover the Apple logo on the front of the bezel with masking tape to keep it from getting scratched while you work. The Mac Plus, SE, and Classic logos are recessed far enough to prevent scratching, but you should cover the printed name with tape to protect it anyway.

Almost everything that sticks up, out, or down must be cut off and ground smooth. You can see what a finished cutting job looks like in Figure 2-18.

The curve of the inside of the bezel opening shown in Figure 2-19 will have to be reduced to allow the tank to fit closely to it, but we'll deal with that later.

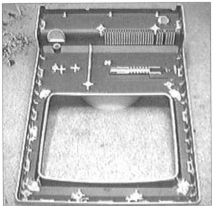

Figure 2-18: Cleaned front case

Figure 2-19: Front case close-up

Also leave the socket for the brightness knob, circled in Figure 2-20. You will put the knob back in later.

Cut the plastic structures in two passes. During the first pass, use the cut-off wheel to remove as much material as possible without cutting into the bezel frame; you can see what this looks like in Figure 2-21. Next, use one of the small stone-grinding wheels to bring the structures all the way down, as shown in Figure 2-22.

Figure 2-20: Brightness knob location

Figure 2-21: Front case cleanup

Figure 2-22: Front case plastic removal

Cut out the lid

This is the most cosmetically important cut of the whole process because it will be the most visible on the finished fish tank. Be extra careful and make the cuts as cleanly as possible. A small, round metal cutting bit should be used to cut through these structures.

The first cut will be on the top of the base of the case. Follow the white lines as shown in Figure 2-23.

Then, an easy way to draw these lines is as follows: use a ruler and pencil to make a line along the seam on each side, as shown in Figure 2-24. Draw a line about halfway between the vents and rear edge along the back. Draw another line at the same width down through the handle depression. When you are done sketching these lines, step back and see if everything looks symmetrical. Remember, you will have to look at this handiwork for as long as you have your completed tank.

Figure 2-23: Lid cutout pattern

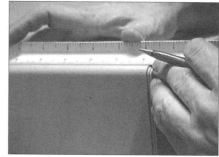
Figure 2-24: Lid cutout lines

After you are satisfied with your lines, cut a shallow trench along them as shown in Figure 2-25. You should not let the cutting wheel go all the way through the material on this first cut. Push the tool against the direction of rotation to prevent the cuts from filling in with melted plastic.

WARNING
If you see smoke coming from the cutting wheel, you are cutting too quickly. Let the cutting wheel and the trench cool for a few seconds, then resume more slowly. Remember that it should take several passes to cut all the way through.

You can cut straight across the handle, but don't try to cut on the line yet, as seen in Figure 2-26. After the lid is removed, go back and trim the handle hole on the case.

Figure 2-25: Cut top of lid

Figure 2-26: Finish cutting top of lid

There are two braces on the inside of the Mac case that serve as guides for the analog board, as seen in Figure 2-27. Cut them from the inside so that the top will come off.

Now pull the top free, as shown in Figure 2-28. You will be saving the majority of the top of the case, except for the handle. It is best removed in chunks.

Clean the top and remove the handle

Cut out the open part of the handle, as shown in Figure 2-29. Don't worry about how these cuts look. Leave a little bit (1/8 of an inch or so) sticking up from the underside of the handle; it will be smoothed out later. Next, cut off the two screw receivers, as shown in Figure 2-30.

Now cut a line across the middle of the screw receivers and across the vents at the front and remove the next chunk of handle, as shown in Figure 2-31.

Cut down the inside of each side of the remaining piece, and continue cutting out the plastic across the front. Cut away any plastic edges protruding from the inside and smooth it out, as shown in Figure 2-32.

Figure 2-27: Remove inside braces

Figure 2-28: Pull away top of case

Figure 2-29:
Pull away handle

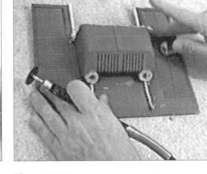

Figure 2-30:
Remove remaining handle material

Figure 2-31:
Cut away material under handle

Figure 2-32:
Smooth out bumps

Chapter 2, How to Build an Aquarium Inside a Macintosh

3. Prepare the back case

You must now remove the plastic structures inside of the back case. This process is simple and quick.

The circled structures in Figure 2-33 should be removed. Use the cut-off wheel to remove most of the pieces and then follow up with a barrel stone to grind them flat.

Now remove the raised lip around the battery door. Be careful not to cut too deep, or it will show on the outside and keep the battery door from fitting correctly when you're done. This is a tricky cut, so take your time. You can see the area to be cut in the lower left corner of Figure 2-34. Cut off the other circled protrusions as well.

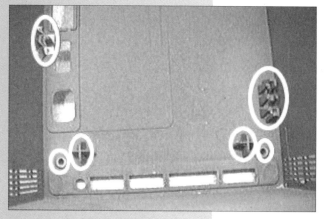

Figure 2-33: Back case structures

Figure 2-34: Additional back case structures

Figure 2-35 shows the edge of the case after one pass with the cut-off wheel. Switch to the steel cutter and carefully ream out the gap.

4. Build the tank

Now that you've cut and cleaned the outer case, you need to build a water-proof tank to hold your fish. In this step, you will be cutting and bending the plastic components that will make up the tank.

Cut out the tank components

Clamp a sheet of Plexiglas to the bench and draw an outline of each of the three pieces you'll need (see Figure 2-36).

The first piece measures 221mm by 810mm. It is a simple rectangular part that sits in the middle between the two sides. The second and third pieces are the sides or legs of the tank. They have the shape of the Mac case so that they can fit inside the newly hollowed-out case, and are cut into two pieces from a rectangular sheet measuring 255mm by 328mm.

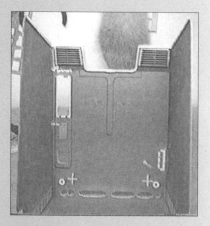

Figure 2-35:
Back case after one cutting pass

Take each of the side panel plates and draw lines between the coordinate points shown in Figure 2-37 and in the table below. The "zero-zero" point is the upper-left corner; the X axis is horizontal and the Y axis is vertical. All measurements are in millimeters.

Point	X	Y
1	0	63
2	21	23
3	227	0
4	255	268
5	215	273
6	215	328

Figure 2-36:
Plexiglas material

Clamp the marked sheet to a bench, as shown in Figure 2-38, and cut along the lines with a jigsaw. Cut out the second plate in the same way.

If you are using a computer case other than the Macs described here, you will need to design and measure a custom insert for your particular machine. If you decide to design your own tank, make sure that you leave enough clearance between your tank and the case you are planning on using. Give yourself at least half an inch on all sides.

Bend the Plexiglas

The tank is constructed by placing a bent piece of Plexiglas between the two sides. The bends that form the tank are created by heating the acrylic with a propane torch. You will use a medium flame and move the flame back and forth across the acrylic at a moderate pace. The goal is to soften the Plexiglas without actually melting it. If you see a lick of flame from the Plexiglas after you move the torch away, it's getting too hot and the Plexiglas may bubble. This doesn't ruin the piece, but it is unsightly.

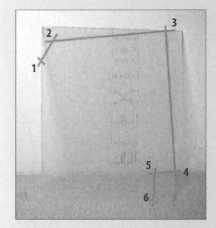

Figure 2-37:
Side of tank pattern

WARNING

After the Plexiglas is soft enough to bend, you'll have a couple of minutes to adjust the angle. Be careful removing the clamps and positioning the piece. Don't try adjusting a bend after it begins to cool; if you do, the Plexiglas will crack. After the piece is completely cooled, there will be enough flex in the bends to allow minor last-minute adjustments to the tank.

Begin this step by first cleaning up bits of plastic and dust from the area to be heated. Remove the protective film from both sides of the long center piece of Plexiglas. Take as much care as possible to avoid scratching it once the cover is removed.

Figure 2-38:
Clamp down side

Use a square and a permanent marker to draw a straight line across the Plexiglas, about 192mm from one end. This will be the face of the tank. Clamp the Plexiglas over a piece of aluminum foil folded over the edge of the bench, as shown in Figure 2-39.

Ignite a flame on the torch and move the flame back and forth across the Plexiglas above the place where you are bending, as shown in Figure 2-40. Try to heat evenly.

Alternate heating the top and bottom sides of the sheet. When the Plexiglas starts to sag, support it with your hand until it's soft enough to make the entire bend as shown in Figure 2-41. Allow the sheet to drop, and make sure the bend is the same on both ends.

As soon as the Plexiglas has bent at an angle of 30 degrees or so, remove the clamps and stand the sheet on its side on one of the end pieces (see Figure 2-42). Adjust the bend angle to match the side of the tank. The area you just heated with the torch will be very hot, so be careful when handling it.

Figure 2-39:
Prepare for first bend

Figure 2-40: Heat area to be bent

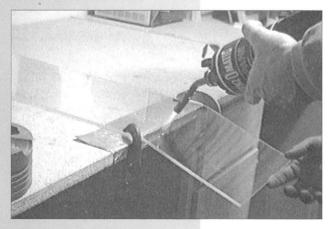

Figure 2-41:
Material bending under heat

Figure 2-42: Two complete bends

Now place a piece of scrap acrylic under the far end of the unbent portion of the sheet (see Figure 2-43). With the acrylic properly positioned on the side piece, make a mark about 10mm from the bottom.

Use a square to draw a straight line across the Plexiglas at the location of the mark (see Figure 2-44).

After the Plexiglas has hardened, lay the sheet back on the bench with the bent part hanging over and downward (see Figure 2-45).

Use the torch as described earlier to heat the area along the line until the piece is soft. Bend it to about the angle shown in Figure 2-46.

Stand the bent piece on the side piece and adjust the angle so that the bottom of the tank is parallel to the bottom the side piece (see Figure 2-47).

Now mark a spot 10mm from the back edge and use a square to draw a line along the mark as you did previously. Clamp the plexiglas, heat the edge until it is soft, and bend it to the angle shown in Figure 2-48.

Once again, stand the bent piece on the side piece and adjust the bend to fit inside the edge (see Figure 2-49). Place the other side piece on top of the tank and make sure that everything lines up (see Figure 2-50).

You now need to cut off the excess material sticking out. Place the tank on the table with the open end facing up. Draw a line across the two pieces

Figure 2-43: Level the Plexiglas

Figure 2-44: Mark bend location

Figure 2-45: Prepare for second bend

Figure 2-46: After second bend

Figure 2-47: Mark third bend

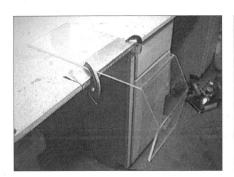

Figure 2-48: Prepare for third bend

Figure 2-49: Secure center piece to one side

Figure 2-50: Secure other side

that are sticking up above the other two edges to make all of the top edges the same height. Before starting to cut, mark the line with masking tape (see Figure 2-51).

Finally, clamp the bent piece back on the bench and cut the excess acrylic along the line (see Figure 2-52).

Figure 2-51: Mark excess material   **Figure 2-52**: Remove excess material

5. Assemble the tank

You now have all the components needed to assemble the tank. The next step is to assemble those components.

Check the piece for a good fit

Put the side and the center tank pieces in the case to make sure they fit. You can see how this works in Figure 2-53.

Clamp the pieces together and apply solvent to seams

Using three woodworking clamps, press the side against the center piece. The tank should be even at the top and flush along the front of the side pieces, as shown in Figure 2-54.

Figure 2-53: Completed tank   **Figure 2-54**: Clamp the tank

Stand the tank up and place another clamp at the top rear of the tank. Line up the back of the tank with the tops of the side pieces (see Figure 2-55).

Make sure the sides both sit flat on the bench before continuing. Loosen the clamps and adjust the parts if they do not.

Lay the tank on its face, being careful not to jar the alignment of the parts. Take a small amount of the acrylic solvent and put it into the applicator bottle with the syringe. Follow the seams and apply the solvent to the seam along each side of the front of the tank (see Figure 2-56).

WARNING

Before you apply the solvent, make sure that everything is in place. The solvent will actually dissolve a small amount of the plastic on both sides of the bond and fuse them together. Once bonded, you will not be able to take the two pieces apart without breaking the plastic.

Flip the tank on its back and apply solvent along the other side of the edge. Move the first two clamps to the bottom of the tank and apply the solvent to both sides of the bottom seams (see Figure 2-57).

Now move the clamps to the locations illustrated in Figure 2-58 and apply the solvent to the seams on the back. If you have designed your own tank and/or cut out your own parts, make sure that the edges that meet are smooth and straight. If there are any gaps or chips, you can use RTV Silicon sealant to fill them.

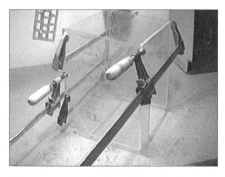

Figure 2-55: Apply solvent for seal to bottom

Figure 2-56: Apply solvent for seal to sides

Figure 2-57: Applying solvent close-up

Figure 2-58: Let solvent set

Chapter 2, How to Build an Aquarium Inside a Macintosh

Remove all the clamps and see if the tank fits inside the hollowed out Mac (see Figure 2-59). Next, take the pieces of the case you previously trimmed and make sure everything fits together (see Figure 2-60).

Figure 2-59: Check tank fit   **Figure 2-60**: Check all pieces for fit

How to Read the Born-On Date from the Mac

Here's some interesting trivia about the serial number on the side of the Mac: it contains a date code. The "F" in the figure below mean it was produced at the Fremont, California plant. The "6" indicates 1986 as the production year, and the "23" means it was manufactured in the 23rd week.

6. Build the filter

In order to have a healthy environment for your fish, you will need a filter at the bottom of the tank. Since this tank is a different size than a standard fish tank, you will need to cut the filter to fit inside your custom tank.

Mark out the new tank size

The filter plate used for this project was part of a kit for a 55-gallon aquarium and is larger than necessary for your tank. Any filter should work as long as it is at least 6 inches by 8 inches.

Measure the space available in the bottom of your new tank (see Figure 2-61). The width should always be about 8 inches, but the depth will vary between 4 inches and 6 inches depending on how you made your tank.

Mark these dimensions on the filter (Figure 2-62) and cut along those lines with a hacksaw (Figure 2-63).

Figure 2-61: Cut down filter   **Figure 2-62**: Measure filter   **Figure 2-63**: Cut filter

Cut the edges from the piece of filter material you have left over. You will be using these two pieces to replace the sides to the filter you cut for your tank.

Take some of the acrylic solvent and attach the side edges to your filter. Use masking tape to hold the pieces in place while gluing.

The finished plate should fit in the bottom of the tank with about half an inch to spare on each side. See Figure 2-64.

7. Add accessories

The tank and case probably look pretty good at this point, but adding back the programmer's switch and the contrast (or brightness) knob will make it look even better.

Add back the brightness knob

Put some glue (thickened acrylic cement works very well) on the shaft of the knob and put it in the hole (see Figure 2-65).

After the glue sets, use the cut-off wheel to cut away most of the knob. The extra plastic inside the case may interfere with the fit of the tank (see Figure 2-66).

Add back the programmer's switch

The reset switch, or programmer's switch, can be modified so that it can be reattached to the outside of the case. Remove the plastic "finger" behind the switch with the cut-off wheel (see Figure 2-67).

Glue the modified reset switch back to the outside of the case. When complete, it should look like Figure 2-68.

Figure 2-64:
Check filter fit

Figure 2-65:
Replace brightness knob

Figure 2-66:
Cut away brightness knob material

Figure 2-67: Progammer's switch pieces

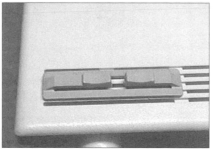

Figure 2-68: Replaced programmer's switch

Figure 2-69:
Completed Macquarium

8. Test the aquarium

Before adding fish and a water pump, you will need to ensure that the tank is water-tight. Take the tank to your sink and fill it up with tap water, watching for leaks. If you see any, note their locations with a marker. Dry out the areas in question for 30 minutes and then add more solvent. Retest after you've fixed the leak.

Project Demo

If there are no leaks, install the filter plate and add gravel to the bottom of the tank. Install an air pump and fill the tank with water. Treat the water according to the directions on the treatment package. Add fish and enjoy your creation! You should have something that looks like Figure 2-69.

Upon first seeing your new fish tank, most people will probably do a double take. They might even comment, "I don't recall the Mac SE having a color screensaver."

Clean and maintain the tank just like a regular fish tank. And don't forget to feed your screensaver!

Extensions

- In this hack we concentrated on the Macintosh, but it is quite simple to use the same techniques to modify an old monitor. You will need to figure out for yourself how to take apart the case. Please be very careful when handling the electronics and the tube inside the monitor. Follow the same precautions as were described for discharging the Mac's picture tube.

  You will have to design your own Plexiglas enclosure following the same methods outlined in this hack. Get a little extra acrylic plastic to practice with before starting on the final project.

  These tanks can be quite striking when complete. Figure 2-70 shows a tank that fits inside a large monitor case.

- To add some realism to your monitor/tank, you could add a blinking LED to the power lamp of the monitor.

- In Chapter 15, How to Build an Internet Coffeemaker, you will hack together a web-based temperature and water sensor. You could easily use that hack with your new fish tank to allow you to monitor the temperature and maintain a satisfactory water level for your fish tank from anywhere in the world.

- If you want to give your fish some company, you could mount the screen from an old laptop computer in the back and run a fish-tank screensaver. Any color laptop should work. Simply separate the screen from the base of the laptop, taking care to protect the thin connection cables between the two. Repack the main CPU board and keyboard in an enclosure behind the tank, and you are ready to go. If the laptop has a free USB port, you could even add a web camera and watch the fish.

- If you want to be able to remotely feed your fish, an inexpensive fish feeder can be hacked to allow web-based control. The same mini-web server used in Chapter 15 could be used to trigger a relay that switches on the feeder.

Figure 2-70:
Large monitor aquarium

Exhibit A: Bill of Materials

Item	Notes
A Macintosh computer	These plans will work without modification on a Mac 128, 512, Plus, SE, and SE/30 computers. With slight modification, the plans will work for Mac Classic and Classic II computers.
Plexiglas brand acrylic sheets	There are other brands that may (or may not) work as well. A 3' x 6' sheet of 1/4" Plexiglas costs about $45 at Home Depot and is large enough to make about three aquariums. Buy a smaller sheet if you like, but if this is your first time working with acrylic you may ruin a sheet or two, so the extra material could come in handy. Do not use Lexan—it may be harder to scratch or break, but it's almost impossible to glue together.
Acrylic solvent	Sold under various trade names and found at plastics supply houses; check your Yellow Pages under "Plastic Supply" for more info. Get both the liquid and thick-ened versions. You won't need a lot, so buy the smallest can and tube you can find. This stuff isn't really a cement or glue; it's a solvent that melts the acrylic pieces together. Once bonded correctly, the pieces will never come apart. It also creates seriously toxic fumes, so follow the warnings on the can and tube and avoid breathing the vapors.
A plastic squeeze bottle with a needle-like tip	Pick one up at the same place as the acrylic cement. Note: when you're done cementing pieces together, pour the remaining solvent back into the metal can it came in. The solvent will quickly evaporate from the plastic bottle, even when capped.
Undergravel filter (UGF) kit	A UGF kit designed for a 5- or 10-gallon aquarium should cost $5 to $8 and is more than large enough. Easily found at WalMart or aquarium stores.
Goggles	These are very important. When you start cutting and grinding on the Mac case and the acrylic, the pieces are going to fly and you will need protection.
Dremel Moto tool (or other rotary tool)	You'll want the variable-speed model (although the single-speed model will work) with the flexible neck attachment.
Dremel accessories	You will want the cut-off wheel, the large and small barrel stones, and the steel cutting bits.
Hand tools	Flat, square, and round files; masking tape; C clamps; T-15 sized Torx screw-driver; Phillips screwdriver; flat screwdriver; hand or power jigsaw; propane torch; black or red marker; four bar clamps.
Air pump	Purchase from a pet/fish store.
Water filter	Purchase from a pet/fish store.
Fish	Purchase from a pet/fish store.
Gravel	Purchase from a pet/fish store.
Alligator clips	From your toolbox or purchase at Radio Shack.

How to Hack
802.11b Antennas

3

Cost
`▓▓▓▓░░░░░░░░░░░░░░░░░░░░░░░`
$10–20

Time
`▓▓▓▓░░░░░░░░░░░░░░░░░░░░░░░`
a few hours

Difficulty
`▓▓▓▓░░░░░░░░░░░░░░░░░░░░░░░`
easy

What You Need

- 802.11b network card
- Computer (Windows, Linux, Mac)
- A Primestar dish
- Soldering iron
- N-style RF connector
- A chassis-mount N connector
- Low-loss coaxial cable (optional)
- A "pigtail" connector
- Other items listed in Exhibits A and B

I've been using a wireless Ethernet card in my laptop for several years. The change from wired networking to wireless was an amazing shift. I was no longer tethered to a thick cable. I could wander around my office or my home and connect to the Web. However, in many situations I found that the range of the built-in antenna in the PC card was limited, and I desired additional range.

In this hack, I will show you how to build two different range-extending antennas for your wireless LAN card. The first design is made from a used soup or coffee can. It is inexpensive and easy to implement, and will send and receive a signal in one direction that's up to 16 times more powerful than the built-in antenna on your wireless card. The second design uses a discarded Primestar satellite TV dish antenna. It is highly directional and can theoretically send and receive data to another dish up to 10 kilometers away under ideal conditions.

Credits

All photographs (except Figure 3-4) copyright © 2003 Rob Frohne.

Project Overview

This project uses the Lucent Orinoco 802.11b card, but any brand of 802.11b network card will do. Whichever design you choose to build, you'll need a "pigtail" connector that has the proprietary Lucent connector (for the PCMCIA card) on one end and an N connector on the other. The pigtail can be obtained from a number of online stores for $35 to $40.

You'll also need to know the basics of soldering for this project. The construction of either range-extending antenna for your wireless LAN card can be completed in a few simple steps.

WARNING

Before attempting either of these hacks, you need to be aware of the FCC regulations on maximum allowed power output from an antenna at the frequencies that the 802.11b cards operate. Read FCC part 15.247 at *http://www. access.gpo.gov/nara/cfr/waisidx_00/47cfr15_00.html.*

Hardware Assembly Instructions for Recycled Can 802.11b Antenna

This hack is quick and can be very useful. I put together a can-based antenna in about two hours. I then took it to a local café that offers a pay 802.11b service. After powering up my laptop and connecting the antenna, I slowly moved the antenna around, scanning for other networks. Within one minute, I had located another network and "borrowed" access instead of having to use the pay service.

If you are interested in using these antennas at other radio frequencies, the dimensions can be scaled appropriately.

It is quite simple to take an ordinary metal can and transform it into a directional antenna for your 802.11b network card in four simple steps. See Exhibit A for a complete list of materials you'll need.

802.11b/g and 802.11a Radio Frequencies

The 802.11b and 802.11g wireless network cards operate at a frequency of approximately 2.4 GHz. This antenna was designed with that frequency in mind. 802.11a operates at 5.8 GHz; if you shrink the can assembly parts by 50%, it should work at that frequency.

1. Select and prepare the can

Locate a metal food can that is between 3 inches and 3.25 inches in diameter. A longer can is better. Be sure the can is clean and dry, and that the open end is free from any ragged metal edges.

2. Measure and punch holes in the can

Drill a hole approximately 2.5" from the closed end of the can for the N connector. You can find this connector from DigiKey, Radio Shack, and ham radio stores. Depending on where you buy it, the exact dimensions may be different from those shown in Figure 3-1, so check the dimensions of your connector. Also drill several smaller holes for the mounting screws. Figure 3-1 shows where the connector will be mounted on the can.

3. Build and install the antenna probe

Next, take the N connector (see Figure 3-2) and add a short piece of 12-gauge wire so that the wire sticks up 1.21" above the edge of the connector.

Mount the N connector to the hole you drilled in the previous step. Figure 3-3 shows a cut-away view of the completed antenna. On the left you can see the N connector with added wire "stub." Hold the N connector in place with four 4-40 screws and nuts.

4. Add a connection cable and test

The radio signal from your 802.11b wireless card must now be connected to the antenna. The Lucent Orinoco PCMCIA card has a tiny (and proprietary) connector at the end of the card. A small plastic cap usually covers this connector. Remove the cap.

You will now need to either locate an adapter connector cable that changes the tiny Lucent connector to a standard N connector, or open up your PCMCIA card and solder a wire to the antenna inside.

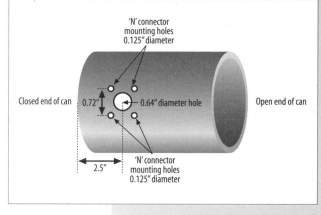

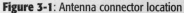

Figure 3-1: Antenna connector location

Figure 3-2: N connector (back and front)

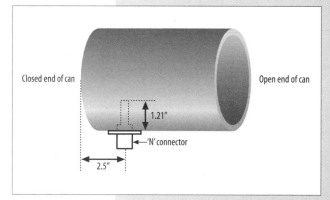

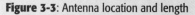

Figure 3-3: Antenna location and length

Signal Loss in Cables

Loss can vary from 1-2db to over 16db per 100 feet. The "db" stands for decibel and is a logarithmic unit of measure. Each 3db of gain represents a linear doubling and each 3db of loss represents a 50% decrease. By way of example, a 6db loss represents a 75% loss from the original signal (50% x 50% = 25%). A 12db loss represents 93.75% loss.

signal gain (loss) = log (strength of signal 1 / strength of signal 2)

If you choose to purchase a connector, do a quick web search for "Orinoco Pigtail" or try these online stores:

http://www.hyperlinktech.com/web/orinoco_accessories.html
http://www.wifidirect.com/products/orinocopigtail.html

I cannot personally vouch for either of these stores, but they carried the appropriate part at the time this book was written.

It is possible for you to open up your Orinoco card and solder a thin length of microwave coaxial cable directly to the connector internally. See *Building Wireless Community Networks* by Rob Flickenger (O'Reilly) for more details.

Try to keep the length of the cable between the antenna and the wireless card as short as practical. At the frequencies at which your 802.11b wireless card operates, the cable will exhibit loss of your signal.

Project Demo

You have now completed construction of the antenna. Connect it to the wireless card and start up your computer. Aim the open end of the can toward another wireless-enabled computer or an access point (Figure 3-4). Make note of the signal level as reported by the wireless software on your computer. Remove the antenna and make another note of the signal strength. The antenna should make a noticeable improvement. Because the signal it emits is polarized, you may need to rotate the can to get the best signal strength.

WARNING

You should never look into the open end of your antenna when it is operating. Although the signal levels from the built-in antennas in your wireless card have been deemed safe by the FCC, your antenna focuses the signal to levels that could be harmful.

Figure 3-4: Using the can antenna

Hardware Assembly Instructions for Primestar Dish 802.11b Antenna

The Primestar antenna hack described here is the brainchild of Rob Frohne, who details some of the steps at *http://www.wwc.edu/~frohro/Airport/ Primestar/Primestar.html*.

First, a little background. Primestar (a satellite TV company) was recently purchased by DirecTV (another satellite TV company), which is phasing out all the Primestar equipment. This means the dishes are being abandoned and are available for other uses such as the one described here. If you can't locate a Primestar dish, you may be able to use a DirecTV or other satellite TV system dish antenna. A little experimenting will be required to get them to work. Primestar antennas can be found at tag sales, local newspaper classifieds, or on the Internet.

It is easy to transform a surplus Primestar dish into a highly directional antenna for the very popular IEEE 802.11 wireless networking. The resulting antenna has about 22 db of gain (this means that the signal is amplified in one direction about 128 times) and is fed with 50-Ohm coaxial cable. Usually LMR400 or 9913 low-loss cable is used if the source is more than a few feet from the antenna. (See the sidebar on low-loss cable.)

The resulting range of your wireless system using two of these antennas with a line-of-sight path should be close to 10 miles at full bandwidth. I must stress the line-of-sight path, though. Leaves and trees weaken the signal significantly, so you will want to make sure that the path between antennas is clear. Even rain and fog can limit the range.

The long-range link you will create can connect remote homes to the Internet or allow retrieval of audio/video data from remote locations. Imagine being able to set up a web camera on the side of a mountain to monitor wildlife or connect to a hard-to-reach local network with full bandwidth.

In the following easy steps, you will construct and set up a highly directional antenna. See Exhibit B for a complete list of materials for this project.

Your resulting hacked dish should look something like Figure 3-5. You can see the can antenna at the bottom of the figure.

Low-Loss Coaxial Cable

Low-loss cable can be expensive and stiff, making it hard to install and work with. A cable with reasonably low loss for a decent price is the LMR-400 cable from Times Microwave Systems *(http://www. timesmicrowave.com)*. The company has information on distributors. If you buy this cable, it will not have any connectors on the ends; you will have to add them yourself. This will require you to purchase the male termination connectors and solder them in place. You may also want to purchase a few female-female adapters to make sure that everything connects together. Ham Radio Outlet also carries these parts *(http://www.hro.com)*.

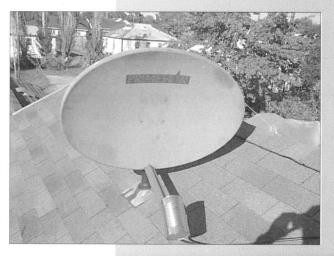

Figure 3-5: Mounted dish antenna

1. Decide where to mount the antenna

Decide on a place to mount your antenna (which hopefully has a line-of-sight path to the access point or to another 802.11b site) and remove the apparatus at the feed position of the dish (the end of the arm sticking out from the dish). Save the mounting hardware for later.

Finding a good location can be time-consuming if you have to crawl up on your roof, but it is important for good performance.

2. Prepare a can

Locate and prepare a metal can with dimensions close to those described in Step 1 of the last hack.

3. Solder wire to the N connector

Solder a 1.15" length of stiff wire onto the center conductor of the chassis mount N connector. The 1.15 inches should be measured from the wall of the can to the tip of the wire. You can see what this looks like in Figure 3-6.

4. Mount the N connector to the can

Using a punch or whatever other tools you deem necessary, mount the N connector so that it is about 1.2 inches from the closed end of the can, as shown in Figure 3-6. It is also a good idea to put a drip hole at the lowest point of the can to insure that water doesn't build up inside. In fact, you might want to put a plastic lid on the open end of the can. If left exposed to the rain and the elements, the inside of the can will likely rust and lose some sensitivity (and therefore range).

Alternate Dishes

You may use any satellite dish, but if it is much bigger than the Primestar shown here, the gain might be higher than that allowed by the FCC rules for use within the United States.

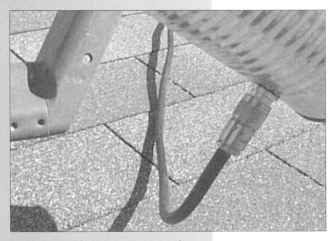

Figure 3-6: Dish antenna connector close-up

Figure 3-7: Inside the dish antenna

If you look inside the can at the N connector with the short wire sticking out, it should look like Figure 3-7.

5. Mount the can to the dish

If you are certain of the polarization you will need, mount the can so that that polarization is achieved. (You want the antenna you are communicating with to be lined up with yours.) If you don't know the polarization, you can set everything up and experiment to get the maximum signal strength by rotating the can around its axis before mounting the can. Most commercial antennas I've seen use vertical polarization (the orientation of the antenna). Figure 3-8 shows this orientation.

You want to mount the can so that the opening is just at the focus of the dish. You can see what this looks like in Figure 3-8. Even without a perfect alignment and with a long run of cable, you will likely have a decent signal. The easy route is to mount the can as far back as you can, punch two holes through the can, and bolt it in. The best way would be to find the best feed place (which I found to be just a little farther back), and use some PVC tubing or other material that allows you to extend the mount so the feed is in the perfect position. In some installations, every decibel of extra signal will count, and this should be considered.

6. Align the antenna

This antenna is very directional; therefore, you must have it aligned very carefully, or you will lose a lot of signal. It also needs to be mounted securely so that the wind doesn't blow it out of alignment. Even a few degrees of movement will make a big difference.

This antenna is an offset feed dish, which means that the feed horn (the can) is not positioned in the way of an incoming signal and doesn't shadow the dish. This makes the aiming a bit tricky because it actually looks like it is aimed down when it is aimed at your target antenna. Figure 3-9 shows an antenna aimed just a few degrees above the horizon. Most dishes have an angle scale on the side that can be used to determine the approximate angle. The dish isn't as directional in the vertical direction as it is in the horizontal direction. This is good, because without turning the mounting upside down, you can only set it a few degrees above the horizon. You will lose a little signal by not mounting the antenna upside down, but is it much easier to mount on a roof.

Figure 3-8: Can mounting

Figure 3-9: Pointing the dish

Polarization

You've probably heard this term used when looking for sunglasses. You may have even taken two pairs of polarized sunglasses and placed the lenses back to back while rotating one of them. The lenses will turn completely black at one angle and will be clear at an angle 90 degrees later. This is because the light that passes through one of the lenses becomes polarized or oriented in one direction. The other lens, when oriented 90 degrees from the first, blocks the polarized light.

Radio waves behave the same way. If you want two radios to communicate, their antennas must be pointed in the same direction.

You can mount the antenna on an old roof TV antenna mount or on a roof vent pipe. You will probably need an assistant to help you align the dish toward your target. One person will need to be on the roof (or wherever the dish is mounted), and the other at the computer with the wireless card. Most of the card utilities include a signal strength meter.

Start by pointing the antenna in from the bottom to the top position. Move it a little bit to the right and repeat this sweep. Now move it a little to the left and repeat. Have the person watching the signal strength meter report its reading frequently. Stop moving the antenna when you have found the best location. Tighten down all screws and check the signal strength again.

The alignment process can seem tedious and sensitive, but do not give up. Make small alignment adjustments in direction and elevation. You are trying to align two tight radio "spotlights" over great distances without the luxury of being able to see the beam with your eyes.

But the reward is that you should now have a working, highly directional 802.11b antenna!

Exhibit A: Bill of Materials for Recycled Can

Item	Quantity	Notes
Metal can 3" to 3.25" in diameter and 4" long	1	Metal soup or veggie can works well
N-style RF connector	1	DigiKey Part #ARF1005-ND
4-40 screws and nuts	4	Hardware store
12-gauge copper wire	3"	Hardware store
A "pigtail" connector that has the proprietary Lucent connector on one end and an N connector on the other	1	The pigtail can be obtained from a number of online stores for $35 to $40
Low-loss coaxial cable	20–50'	Time Microwave Part #LMR-400
Soldering iron		

Exhibit B: Bill of Materials for Primestar Dish

Item	Quantity	Notes
Primestar dish	1	eBay or yard sale
Metal can about 4" in diameter and at least 8" long	1	Metal soup or veggie can works well
Chassis-mount N connector	1	DigiKey Part #ARF1023-ND
A "pigtail" connector that has the proprietary Lucent connector on one end and an N connector on the other	1	The pigtail can be obtained from a number of online stores for $35 to $40
Low-loss RF cable	20–50'	Times Microwave Part #LMR400 or 9913
Soldering iron		
12-gauge wire	2"	DigiKey or hardware store

How to Build a PC Water-Cooling System

Cost

$50–75

Time

a weekend

Difficulty

moderate

What You Need

- A home PC with an AMD or Intel CPU
- 1mm thick sheet of copper
- Fish tank pump
- Vinyl tubing
- Rubber bands
- Other items listed in Exhibit A

Over the last few years, it has become a popular hobby to run your PC's CPU at a rate faster than the factory default rate. This practice is known as *overclocking*.

The Pentium or AMD processor inside your PC runs its software based on an internal heartbeat known as the clock. The clock speed determines how fast your system operates. AMD and Intel shamelessly flog their products (for example, the Pentium 4 2GHz and the AMD K6II-400) based on this clock number. Many processors that have a similar megahertz rating are actually the same part with a different clock, potentially reducing your ability to overclock that particular processor.

Running the clock faster than what the CPU manufacturers recommend has certain side effects. One such effect is that the CPU gets hotter than it should. Many recently manufactured CPUs with clock speeds over 1GHz have a temperature sensor and circuit built in, which allows the CPU to monitor its temperature and slow things down if it gets too hot.

Many of the overclocking "pioneers" used big fans and metal-finned heat sinks to transfer the heat generated by the faster clock rates away from the CPU. These fans moved the air past the heat sink where a heat exchange took place. The fans were usually noisy, and the heat sink provided only limited cooling to the CPU. (The CPU in your PC probably has a heat sink built in already.)

Air cools the CPU reasonably well, but other substances pick up or exchange heat from the CPU even better. Many liquids, including water, are excellent.

The benefits of exploiting liquid cooling can be enormous compared to passive cooling. More often than not, mainframe makers turn to liquid cooling to achieve levels of heat dissipation unmatched by any number of fans. However, due to size restrictions and because water cooling is dangerous to implement in home PCs, it has never caught on in the home users' market. Yet over the last year, a few companies have sprung up and begun producing kits that allow you to make your own water-cooled PC. Unfortunately, these kits, which range from $60 for just a water block to over $200 for the whole cooling system, can become a very expensive setup. In this hack I will show you how to build your own water-cooling system for your home PC, which will allow you to overclock the CPU with less chance of damage.

Project Overview

This hack is based on work from Rob Dickinson, who designed and built this very effective and inexpensive CPU cooler. All photos in this hack are courtesy of Rob.

The project is targeted at single Socket7 CPU computers, but with some careful planning it can be adapted to other types of processors. (A Socket7 processor looks like a square ceramic slab with many metal pins sticking out the bottom.)

You will construct this water-cooling system using a waterproof metal can connected to a water pump that attaches to your PC's CPU.

You can find most, if not all, of the necessary parts in your local hardware store. You will need a few hand tools such as a hacksaw, a bench vise, a pair of pliers, and a soldering iron.

Before You Start

Putting water inside your PC can be risky. If the water cooling system you build has any leaks, the water will likely damage or destroy parts inside of it. Water and electricity are also a potentially dangerous combination, so take extra care when building and testing your work.

Before you start, you need to figure out whether your CPU and motherboard can actually be overclocked. First, determine the exact model and clock speed of the processor. This information is shown when your PC first boots up. You can also look under Control Panel → System Properties → General (see Figure 4-1). Next, check the motherboard manufacturer and model number by opening up the computer case and examining the main circuit board. Check this data against the lists of CPUs and motherboards found on web sites such as *http://www. hardocp.com/* and the others listed at the end of this chapter.

You can also check for overclocking compatibility by restarting the PC into the BIOS screen. To do this, press the F4 key just after the PC starts up. Look through the various options for the one that lets you change the clock speed. Most Pentium and AMD processors rated for 200MHz-plus installed in the motherboard and made in the past four years can be overclocked. Search the forums in the web sites listed at the end of this chapter for confirmation of your hardware.

Hardware Assembly Instructions

Follow these six steps to build your overclocked PC with water-cooled processor.

1. Build the water block

The water block is a waterproof metal can connected to a water pump that is attached to the CPU in your PC. Water is pumped through the water block, which removes the excess heat from overclocking. You'll then need to test the water block for leaks and, finally, install it on top of the CPU and connect the water piping.

This specific water block was designed with a few simple rules in mind: the space inside of a PC is limited, so the system should easily fit; it should cool an AMD or Pentium CPU; and it should be easy to secure the cooler to the CPU.

In this step, you will construct a copper box that will be attached to the CPU in your PC using cotton thread. This box will pull heat away from the CPU and transfer it to the water that will flow through the box. You will need a sheet of copper, a 75-watt soldering iron, the copper tubing, and solder (see Exhibit A for more details on the parts you need).

Before you begin construction of the water block, look inside your PC and locate the main processor. Look at the space around and above it. Make sure that you have 1 to 2 centimeters of space around it for both the water block and water tubing. You may need to modify the design presented here to accommodate your specific motherboard and CPU if you do not have this extra space. There are seven tasks you need to complete to build the water block.

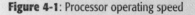

Figure 4-1: Processor operating speed

Task 1: Cut out the box parts from the metal sheet

Obtain a sheet of copper with the dimensions noted in the Bill of Materials. You should be able to purchase the material from a local hobby shop or online (*http://www.onlinemetals.com/*). Draw the design shown in Figure 4-2 onto the sheet.

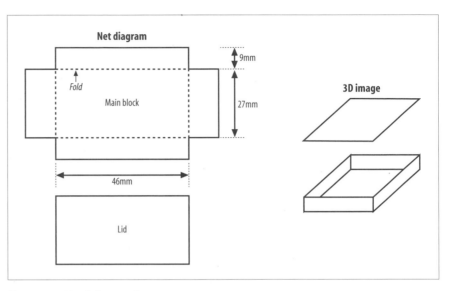

Figure 4-2: Metal sheet cutting pattern

Place the copper sheet into a bench vise and cut out the design using the hacksaw. The photo in Figure 4-3 shows the metal sheet being held in place. The best way to cut the pattern is to first cut out a rectangle of the overall outline. You'll cut out the corners in the next task.

Next, the copper has to be cut into shape. Begin by cutting the outline of the box shown in Figure 4-4; then, cut out the shaded corner areas.

The cutting process will be easier if you hold the piece to be cut off with a set of pliers while you use a saw to make the cut. See Figure 4-5.

Figure 4-3: Secure the metal sheet

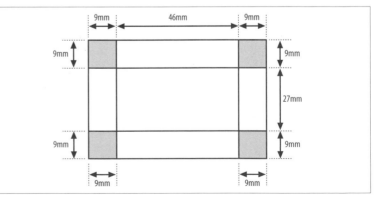

Figure 4-4: Metal sheet cutting area

Task 2: Cut out corners and bend the box sides into place

The corners now have to be cut out and the metal has to be bent into shape. Place the rectangular metal plate you've cut in Task 1 in the bench vice. Bend one of the sides as shown in Figure 4-6.

Next, part of the bent copper needs to be cut off in order for the next wall to be bent into shape. Use either a Dremel with a cutting disc or a small hacksaw to make the cut. Rotate the plate from the position shown in Figure 4-7 and remove a corner square to make the cut.

Repeat this bend-and-cut procedure for the second and third walls (Figure 4-8).

Once the second and third walls have been bent, the last one becomes tricky. The fourth wall is impossible to bend in the bench vice without damaging the other walls.

To overcome this, use one small piece of metal cut into the shape of the water block minus the walls, and one long bar to allow you to bend the last wall into position (Figure 4-9). You may want to use wood instead of metal, as it's easier to cut into the shape required.

Figure 4-5: Bend the metal sheet

Figure 4-6: Bend box sides

The 9mm square cut out

Figure 4-7: Bend second wall

The next 9mm wall to be bent

Figure 4-8: Bend second and third walls

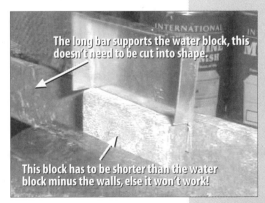

The long bar supports the water block, this doesn't need to be cut into shape.

This block has to be shorter than the water block minus the walls, else it won't work!

Figure 4-9: Bend fourth wall

Once mounted in the vice, push the last wall into place so that it looks like the box in Figure 4-10. This was the hardest part of building the water block. Next you will solder the corners to prevent leaking, install the piping, and seal the lid.

Task 3: Solder the seams of the box

Soldering the corners of the water block should be easy if the gap between each wall is small enough. If you find that the solder doesn't close the gap, use a hammer to tap the walls together tighter.

Heat the metal surface to be soldered for a few moments and then touch the solder to the hot metal, as shown in Figure 4-11. This should produce the most reliable and watertight solder connection.

Once all four corners are sealed, pour water into the block and look for leaks. Figure 4-12 shows how this is done. If water seeps through any of the corners, repeat the soldering procedure until the leak is stopped.

Figure 4-10: All walls bent

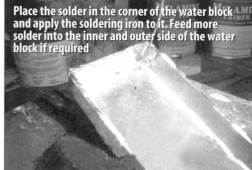

Place the solder in the corner of the water block and apply the soldering iron to it. Feed more solder into the inner and outer side of the water block if required

Figure 4-11: Solder edges shut

Water

Sealed water block

Figure 4-12: Test box for leaks

Drill two 4mm holes into the side of the water block.

Figure 4-13: Drill hole locations

Task 4: Drill holes for tubing

Drill two holes for the copper tubing. (see Figure 4-13). Using a Dremel drill greatly helps to drill the holes without damaging the water block itself, but a regular drill may also be used. You may want to use a center punch to mark where the 4mm holes will go. The exact location of the two holes is not important as long as they do not interfere with the internals of the motherboard when the water block is installed.

Task 5: Cut the tubing

Cut the 4mm copper piping into the desired length for the water block (two 40mm lengths should do the trick). Place the piping in the vice (very gently, or else the wall will collapse) as shown in Figure 4-14, and make a clean cut with either the small hacksaw or Dremel disc cutter.

When you place the cut copper pipes into the 4mm holes of the water block, you will find them too loose for even solder to seal. To overcome this, use a center punch to increase the bore of the copper piping at one end, which should tighten things up. This procedure is shown in Figure 4-15.

Task 6: Connect the tubing

Place a 4mm drill bit inside the cut 4mm copper pipe and clamp it in place using the bench vice (the drill bit will stop the copper pipe walling from collapsing).

Next, use the center punch placed on top of the copper piping and hammer it. This will further lengthen the end of the copper pipe to about 5mm to 7mm bore. Repeat for the second pipe. Once both have been modified, slide them into the holes from inside so that the larger bore end is stuck inside the water block.

Seal the area around the piping on both the inside and the outside of the water block. This should form a very strong bond between the water block and the piping itself and should look like Figure 4-16.

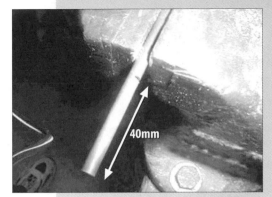

Figure 4-14:
Fit pipe snugly into box holes

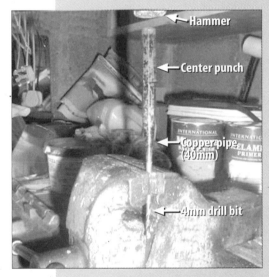

Figure 4-15: Cut metal pipe

Figure 4-16: Seal the piping

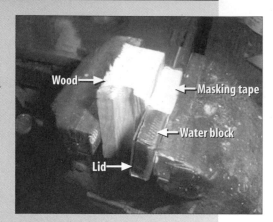

Figure 4-17: Solder the lid

Figure 4-18: Completed box

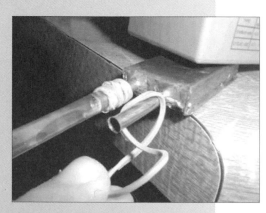

Figure 4-19: Rubber band hose clamps

Task 7: Add a lid to the box

The final step is to solder on the lid of the water block. This lid will be the side that sits on the CPU, so keeping it undamaged and free from dents is important.

Use masking tape and some wood on the lid side to hold it onto the water block itself, and use a vice to clamp it together (see Figure 4-17). Now, with the soldering iron, solder around the edges where the lid meets the water block. Once you've soldered the area that is not covered in masking tape, allow it to cool for five minutes, unwrap the tape, and place new tape over the area you just soldered. Now solder the rest of the unsoldered area to complete the seal of the lid to the water block. When you are done, it should look like Figure 4-18.

2. Connect water tubing to the box

It is very important to seal the tubing to the copper box. Water leaks may permanently damage components. You will need two pieces of tubing to connect the box to the pump, rubber bands or hose clamps, and a water basin. There are several types of tubing that you can use; clear vinyl tubing is the least expensive and most easily found.

Two possible methods for connecting the plastic tubing to the copper tubes are rubber bands and hose clamps. Rubber bands can work well if you wrap them as tightly as possible around the plastic tubing and piping (see Figure 4-19).

An alternate method is to use hose clamps obtained from a hardware store. Buy the smallest size available. You may need to add a layer of rubber bands or other flexible material to fill in any gaps. Place the hose clamps over the plastic tubing and tighten them. Be careful not to overtighten, or you could crush the copper tubing.

3. Connect pump and water pan

In this step you will connect the water block to a pump and water pan using clear plastic tubing. You will need a fish tank pump (the EHEIM Model 1046 available at *http://www.premiumaquatics.com/* works well). You can find the hose at most hardware stores.

Connect the water block, water pump, and water pan as shown in Figure 4-20.

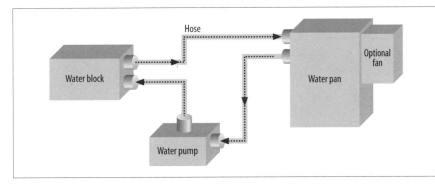

Figure 4-20: Cooling system with water pan

Use more rubber bands and hose clamps as described in the previous step to seal the hose to the various other components. Fill the water pan with water and place the water block on a piece of paper towel. This will allow you to easily see any leaks. When connected, it should look like Figure 4-21. You can see the water block on the paper towel at the bottom of the image and the water pump at the top. The paper towel will show water leaks more clearly.

4. Test for leaks

Fill the water pan with tap water and run the system for at least 10 minutes, looking for leaks on the paper towel. If there are none, run it for another 6 to 10 hours. It is important that the system be leak-free, as it will be installed semipermanently inside your PC.

If you find leaks, you may want to reseat the hose clamps and add additional filler between them and the copper tubing.

5. Attach water block to the CPU

The water-cooling block must touch the CPU because it cools by conducting the heat away from the CPU to the water in the water block.

Begin by carefully removing the CPU from the motherboard. Place it on a piece of aluminum foil to prevent damage from static electricity.

Mount the water block against the top of the CPU. A simple way to attach the water block to the CPU is to use cotton thread or string. Before wrapping the string around the CPU and water block, you may want to put a small amount of heat-sink grease between the two. Wrap the thread around the water block and CPU tightly until it holds by itself with very little movement. Use a double knot to stop the thread or string from coming

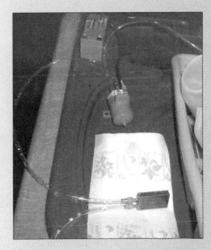

Figure 4-21: Test for leaks

undone and use only cotton material. You can see what this looks like with a Socket7 CPU in Figures 4-22 through 4-24.

Carefully plug the water block tied to the CPU back into the CPU socket of the motherboard (see Figure 4-25). You may want to initially install the water block with the motherboard removed from the case to make installation easier. Once you have things securely installed, you will need to locate an opening in the back of the PC to allow the hoses to exit. Be careful not to kink the tubing, as this will prevent water from flowing.

You can use tap water to fill the system, but you may want to use deionized water instead. This water has had all of the impurities removed and has very low electrical conductivity, and is therefore less likely to cause damage if a little water leaks out.

Figure 4-22: Block tied to CPU

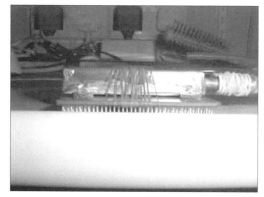

Figure 4-23: Block side view

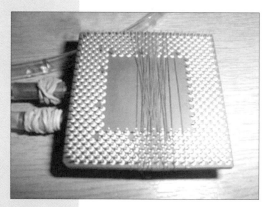

Figure 4-24:
Bottom view of CPU with string

Figure 4-25:
Block and installed CPU

6. Set the CPU clock

Once you are sure that the system of pipes, water pan, and water block does not leak, it is time to increase the clock speed of your PC. This is usually accomplished by changing the setting in your PC BIOS setup; check your PC owner's manual or look in *http://www.overclockers.com/* for details. If your motherboard does not support CPU clock or front-side bus clock rate changes, you may need to change a set of jumpers instead. Consult the owner's manual that came with your PC's motherboard to determine what you need to do.

The amount of speed that you can overclock in your CPU will also depend on the speed of the other components in your system, such as the DRAM, video card, and PCI bus chipset. Your CPU will draw extra power when overclocked, so make sure your PC has a power supply of at least 300 watts (400 watts if you have an AMD Duron CPU).

WARNING
Overclocking your CPU voids its warranty and may burn up the CPU. I strongly suggest that you install a monitoring and shutdown utility before you begin, and review up-to-date information available on any of the overclocking web sites listed at the end of this chapter. Do not make large jumps in speed, and watch the temperature of the CPU carefully. Even with these precautions, you may damage or destroy your processor.

Here are the names of a few useful CPU monitoring, shutdown, and bench-marking utilities as of the writing of this book:

- ShutDown NOW (*http://www.dworld.de/*)

- WCPUID (*http://www.h-oda.com/*)

- Mother Board Monitor (*http://mbm.livewiredev.com/*)

- 3Dmark2001 (*http://www.madonion.com*)

- SuperPi (*http://www16.big.or.jp/~bunnywk/superpi.html*)

Overclocking may not give you a huge increase in clock speed. You may only see a 10 percent increase or less depending on the exact CPU and mother-board you have.

The method you use to set the new clock speed for your CPU will differ depending on whether you have an Intel or AMD processor, as described in the following sections.

Intel CPUs

Beginning with the Pentium II series, Intel has blocked direct access to the CPU clock speed. In a system with an Intel CPU, you will be increasing the clock speed for the front-side bus (FSB). This will not only increase the speed of the Pentium processor, it will also increase the speed at which the DRAM and all of your PCI devices run. If you do not have high-quality DRAM, video card, and PCI devices, overclocking may not work.

Since there are different kinds of motherboards, the actual procedures you undertake may differ from what is described here. Check one of the over-clocking web sites listed at the end of this chapter for more specific information.

When you boot to the BIOS settings, look for a setting that says CPU Speed and set it to Manual. CPU Speed may be listed under Frequencies or Soft Menu.

Locate the settings for the CPU voltages. Increase the core voltage to the maximum value.

Next, look for System/PCI Speed or CPU Host/PCI Clock. The number listed here will be much lower than your CPU speed. Don't worry about this, as the CPU speed will be altered automatically when you change this number.

Increase this PCI bus speed by 5 to 10 MHz, exit the BIOS setup, and save all changes. Start the water pump so that the CPU will be cooled, and reboot the system. If it successfully boots to Windows, run a benchmark utility such as 3DMark2001 to insure that the system is stable. Run one of the CPU monitoring utilities as well and look at the temperature. If everything is stable, reboot back to the BIOS setup and increase the PCI bus another 5 to 10 MHz, repeating this procedure until the PC is no longer stable. At this point, reduce the PCI clock speed by 10 to 20 MHz and re-verify system stability.

AMD CPU

If you have an AMD processor, the system BIOS should allow you to directly alter the CPU clock speed. You can also alter the front-side bus speed settings the same way as for Intel.

Some AMD CPUs are locked so that their clock speeds cannot be directly changed. You should check with one of the web sites at the end of this chapter for detailed instructions on how to unlock your specific AMD part.

After unlocking the CPU, boot to BIOS as described in the previous section and locate the CPU Core Voltage. Increase this value by 10 percent.

Next, locate the CPU Clock Multiplier. Increase this multiplier a small amount, save the BIOS changes, and reboot the system. Switch on the water-cooling system and boot the system to Windows. Run one of the CPU monitoring utilities as well and look at the temperature. If everything is stable, reboot back to the BIOS setup and increase the CPU Clock Multiplier a little. Repeat this procedure until the PC is no longer stable. At this point, reduce the CPU Clock Multiplier a little and re-verify system stability.

You should now have an overclocked PC with a water-cooled processor!

Project Demo

Figure 4-26 shows a 650 MHz Intel PII system that has been over-clocked to 1 GHz. Note the 1,000 MHz at the top of the screen.

Check the CPU temperature and core voltages from the BIOS. You should see that the cooling system keeps the temperature in the seventies to low eighties.

Extensions

What you've seen so far is a very basic water-cooling setup, which can be somewhat clumsy for everyday use because it uses an open pan of water. In this section I describe how to add a small radiator and water reservoir, another method to cool the water. Space doesn't permit a complete step-by-step set of instructions, so I'll just give you some loose guidelines to follow if you're interested in pursuing the radiator on your own.

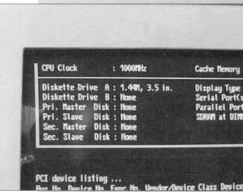

Figure 4-26: Overclocking results

Add a radiator and a closed flow system

Purchase a standard automobile oil radiator from an auto parts store. These radiators are rather small and lightweight. Get a few different hose diameter adapters so that the input and output tubes from the radiator match the hose to the CPU cooler and water reservoir.

Because the system will become a closed circulation system, you need a way to prevent air bubbles from forming inside it. Air bubbles will disrupt operation and need to be removed. A reservoir will allow you to add water and bleed the system of air. A 4-inch-square underground plastic electrical box from a local hardware store should work well. You will need to drill two holes in the top and add brass hose barbs for connection to the water system. You can see a schematic diagram of this in Figure 4-27.

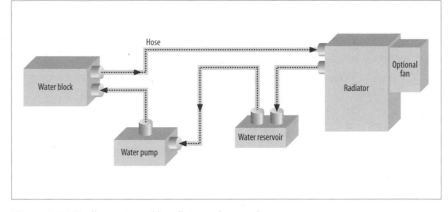

Figure 4-27: Cooling system with radiator and reservoir

If you do decide to add a radiator, note what type of metal it is made of. If the water block and the radiator are made of different materials, such as aluminum and copper, you have the basic elements of a battery. Over time, these two dissimilar metals will react through the water and begin to break down. There are several things you can do to prevent this. One, use de-ionized water. Two, add a small amount of Water Wetter from Red Line Oil Inc *(http://www.redlineoil.com/)*, which will slow and prevent any corrosion.

As mentioned previously, it is important to ensure that the water-cooling block be in contact with as much of the CPU as possible. If you want to get a good thermal connection, you may want to use a small amount of thermal grease. This material is often called heat-sink grease and is available at Radio Shack.

Water flow through the system will be limited by the diameter of the tubing. Once you have built one or two water blocks, you may want to experiment with designs that use larger-diameter hoses. You may even want to add quick disconnect couplings to allow easy assembly and disassembly of the hoses from the PC case.

Cooling other components

The system CPU is not the only component that can be overclocked for increased performance. The chip on the graphics card can also be run faster than normal with a water-cooling system. You will need to change the size and possibly the shape of your water block to fit onto the other chips, but this is easily done.

Other coolants

If you want a liquid that has better thermal performance than plain water, try automobile radiator coolant. Pick up a gallon jug from an auto parts store.

Resources

Below is a list of web sites with information about parts, water cooling, and PC overclocking in general.

http://www.premiumaquatics.com/
http://www.tomshardware.com/
http://www.water-cooling.com/
http://www.hardocp.com/
http://www.dangerden.com/
http://www.redlineoil.com/
http://www.onlinemetals.com/
http://www.petswarehouse.com/
http://www.overclockers.com/
http://www.overclocked-hardware.com/
http://www.h-oda.com/
http://mbm.livewiredev.com/
http://www.dworld.de/

Exhibit A: Bill of Materials

Item	Quantity	Notes
Copper board, 1mm thick, 30cm x 30cm	1	Hardware store
Copper tubes, 4mm diameter, 30cm length	2	Hardware store
Hacksaw	1	Hardware store
Bench vise	1	Hardware store
Pliers	1	Hardware store
12" x 8" x 3" plastic pan or automobile cooling radiator	1	Hardware or auto parts store
25-watt soldering iron	1	Hardware store
Solder	1	Hardware store
75-watt soldering iron	1	Hardware store
Vinyl tubing, 4mm diameter, 10 feet	2	Hardware store
Rubber bands	4	Office supply store
Fish tank water pump (submersible)	1	Pet supply store
Thermal grease (also called heat-sink grease)	1	Radio Shack Part #276-1372
Plastic tubing	1'	Hardware store
Silicone sealant	1 tube	Hardware store
Cotton string	4'	Hardware store
Tie wraps	5	Radio Shack or hardware store

How to Hack a Furby (and Other Talking Toys)

5

Cost

$100–125

Time

a weekend

Difficulty

very difficult

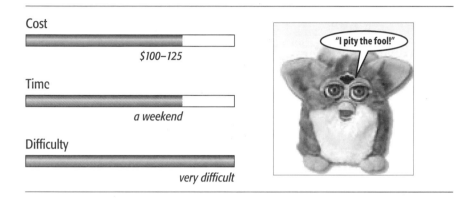

"I pity the fool!"

What You Need

- One un-hacked Furby
- A soldering iron
- Solder wick
- Electronic hand tools
- A multi-meter
- 36 inches of 30-gauge insulate wire
- Other items listed in Exhibit A

In 1998, a subsidiary of Hasbro Toys called Tiger Electronics introduced Furby, a cloth-covered robotic toy controlled by microprocessor. Furby had a microphone, an infrared receiver/transmitter, a speaker, and a set of gears to make its eyes, mouth, and features move. Furby responded to its sensor inputs and would speak phrases in English, Spanish, or Japanese (depending on where the toy was purchased), as well as its own language, "Furbish." Furby was an instant hit. However, after playing with the toy for a short while, the built-in phrases ceased being cute and began to annoy its owner (me).

In this hack I will describe one method of hacking a Furby to allow complete control of its actions and output phrases. After modification, the Furby will be fully programmable in either C or assembly language. I will also describe how to hack more basic talking toys to allow you to change what they say.

Project Overview

To perform this hack, you'll first take apart the Furby and remove several of its circuit boards. Next, you'll assemble your own circuit boards and install them. (This can be tricky, as you will be soldering some very small surface mount components to a board.) Finally, you'll reassemble the Furby and surprise your friends with its new vocabulary.

Figure 5-1: Tie wrap holding fur

Figure 5-2: Peel back fur

Figure 5-3: Remove fur

This project may take a couple of weekends to complete if you don't have any soldering experience. You will be soldering very small parts, so you might want to practice your techniques on a simpler project first.

The Furby hack described in this chapter is the brainchild of Andrew Staats and Jeff Gibbons. They detail some of the steps of their Furby hack at *http://www.appspec.net/products/UpgradeKits/FurbyUpgrade/root.html*.

Hardware Assembly Instructions

The cost of materials for the hardware you need for this project will include $25 for the Furby, and $75 or so for the kits or the parts. You can order a complete kit that includes a printed circuit board and all the required chips and connectors from *http://www.appspec.net/index.html*.

After you've assembled the hardware, you will have a chance to program your creation. I've included several sections outlining the software structures available for this hack under Software Setup Instructions, including a description of the tools and of an API (applications programming interface).

1. Skin the Furby

Before you begin, remove the Furby's batteries. Inside the battery compartment, remove the FCC tag; it won't be FCC-approved after this. You may also want to remove the "Tiger" tag from the Furby's side.

Now it's time to remove your Furby's skin. Feel underneath the fuzzy little tail and find the bump. This is the closure of a nylon cable tie. The cloth is sewn shut there. Use the printer's knife or your wire cutters to cut the thread holding the seam shut (see Figure 5-1). Pull back the cloth. Use the wire cutters to cut the nylon cable tie—a white plastic strip. Beware of flying plastic when you cut the cable tie.

Now feel the upper edge of the Furby's ears. You're looking for the plastic rods that make the ears move. The cloth ears are sewn to these rods at their tips, about two-thirds of the way up the ear. Cut those threads. Pull the cloth ears off the metal rods that keep them in place. The cloth ears will still be attached at the bottom edge. Figure 5-2 shows the partially removed cloth covering.

Pull the fur over the head. It will seem sort of like peeling off a sweater (see Figure 5-3). Depending on the revision of your Furby, you may find some screws that hold the plastic faceplate; on some Furbys the faceplate is held on with glue. The fur is also held in place around the eyebrows and forehead with glue. Some revisions of the toy have plastic hooks at the base of the ear canal, which keep the fur from blocking the ear rod slot.

Use the printer's knife to carefully cut or pry the fur loose. Lift the fur over the ear rods. The ear rods are attached to the white tab shown in the lower right corner of Figure 5-4.

Some revisions of Furby have a hook on the top of the forehead, which retains the top of the faceplate. You can see this hook clearly in the middle of Figure 5-5.

Figure 5-4: Fur and ear rods

This project calls for a medium- to low-wattage soldering iron. If you can, buy an iron with temperature control, and set it to 800 degrees Fahrenheit. Be sure to buy an iron with a fine tip.

---

2. Remove the circuit boards inside Furby

In this step, you'll use solder wick and a soldering iron to remove the electronics responsible for making the Furby utter its canned phrases. You will be following these steps as per the instructions given with the kit.

Figure 5-5: Ear rods exposed

Wedge a pen between the base board and the top of the battery case. This will give you enough room to get at the solder joints at the bottom of the two processor cards. You'll be removing these cards, the connector labeled SP/S2, and the resistor labeled R2 on the base board (directly behind the SP/S2 connector). The cards may be held in place with silicone adhesive—pry this stuff off before continuing. It melts at a low temperature, is a bit messy, and smells bad when it burns. Figure 5-6 shows the two boards you will be removing using this technique.

Apply flux to both sides of the solder wick. Solder wick, or braid, is a narrow bunch of copper wires woven into a thin metal ribbon. It is used as a "sponge" to absorb molten solder. Place the braid on the far end of one of the sets of solder joints at the bottom of the processor cards, as shown in Figure 5-7. Touch the soldering iron against the solder wick and hold it in place for a moment. You will see a little smoke, and then the solder will "magically" get sucked up into the braid.

Figure 5-6: Boards to be removed

Now, slowly drag the braid and the iron across the solder joints. The melted solder will run up into the braid, freeing the processor board. Repeat as necessary with fresh solder wick. Once the braid absorbs the solder, it cannot be "wrung out" and must be discarded. Expect to use about two inches of solder wick, cutting off a quarter inch of braid per attempt. As you trim off braid, reapply flux to the braid so the solder "wicks" into the braid. If you've done this correctly, the braid will make a squeaking noise as you pull it across

Figure 5-7: Using solder wick

Figure 5-8: Remove R2

the connections. You should not have to force anything. The boards you just desoldered should slip out of their slots in the base board. Tidy up the solder joints and make sure the solder hasn't found its way into places where it doesn't belong. Use a multi-meter to check for shorts.

Desolder the SP/S2 connector whose location is circled in Figure 5-8. Cut the wires leading to the connector; one pair is for the speaker, the other for the tummy switch. Strip the ends of the wires and solder the tummy switch (red and black—verify if you're unsure) into S2. The speaker leads (orange and brown—verify if you're unsure) will be attached to the microcontroller unit (MCU) board. We'll talk about that in a later step.

Remove resistor R2 using the side of the iron tip. You can see its location in Figure 5-8. Place the iron parallel to the resistor and hold it in place for a moment. Take a pair of pliers with your other hand, grab the wire you are heating, and gently pull this wire out of the board. Don't use your bare fingers—this resistor lead is now very hot. Rock the iron back and forth so both ends of the resistor are heated. The resistor should come loose from the board and may stick to the iron tip. Wipe off the tip of the resistor using a small sponge moistened with water.

As described in Part I, electronic components are referred to with a letter and then an ID number. Capacitors are referred to with the letter C, resistors with the letter R, transistors with the letter Q, and integrated circuits with the letter U.

Locate the capacitor labeled C6 (just to the right of the capacitor labeled C20) and remove it. Remove resistor R31 and replace it with a 1.5K Ohm resistor (the new resistor is labeled "152" in the kit. If you are unsure, measure its value with the multi-meter). Replace C6 with the new part included in the kit, ensuring that the new part has exactly the same orientation as C6 did.

Remove resistor R11 (just to the left of the back switch) and replace it with a short piece of wire across the pads.

Remove capacitor C20 (located to the right of the back switch) and *remember its orientation*. You will be putting it back in exactly the same way. Remove resistor R28 (just behind C20) and replace it with a short wire. Put the C20 you just pulled out back in place.

Place a 1K Ohm resistor (this part may not be included in the kit, depending on version) between the top lug of the ball switch and ground (the pad of the removed R2 resistor closest to the front of the Furby works well). Verify that you have correctly chosen a ground using your multi-meter before you begin soldering.

You've now emptied your Furby base board of the factory-installed board, and it is ready to accept the new hacked ones.

3. Prepare and assemble the add-in circuit board

It's now time to assemble the replacement circuit board to control the Furby's actions. You'll be inserting the new board into the Furby you just disassembled.

Cut out the new circuit boards

Cut out the printed circuit boards (PCBs) using a Dremel tool or a printer's knife. (The uncut boards should look like Figure 5-9 if you have purchased the kit.)

If you use a printer's knife, score the board along the perforation holes on both sides. Be patient—it will take some time to cut out the boards without damaging the delicate wire traces etched on the front and back.

If you're using a Dremel tool, use the cutting wheel and be careful—the cutting wheel goes through the boards easily. In either case, beware of copper traces on the other side of the board when cutting. You can clean up any rough edges with a small file after you have cut the circuit board free.

Figure 5-9: Blank PCB

Clean any fingerprints from the PCB using rubbing alcohol. Oil from your fingers can make it harder to solder.

After cutting the boards apart, they should look like the boards in Figure 5-10.

If you choose not to use the kit, you will need to build the board yourself. Look at the example circuit board in Figure 13-1 in Chapter 13. Purchase a piece of blank circuit board and sockets for the integrated circuits. Where possible, use dual inline package (DIP) parts. They will be larger than surface mount (SMT) parts, but are much easier to work with on a circuit board of your own construction. DIP parts have thick plastic bodies with pointy metal legs coming out the sides. SMT parts have plastic bodies with small flat legs coming out the sides. (See the sidebar for more information.) If you're building your own board, solder all of the connections according to the schematic diagram in Exhibit C.

Your hand-built board will be larger than the SMT kit, so you will need to make some modifications to make it fit within the Furby skin.

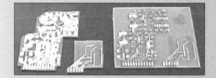

Figure 5-10: PCBs cut apart

Orient the circuit board

Using sticky tape, fix the board to the workbench with the location for the part labeled U2 facing up. You can see what this looks like in Figure 5-11.

Figure 5-11: Holding a PCB in place

You'll be working on the upper right quadrant of the board. Be aware that when soldering, the heat will go through the board and may damage the surface of the workbench.

Attach the MAX883 integrated circuit

Apply flux to the PCB pads of U2 (the large square integrated circuit) and to the bottom of the pins of the MAX883 chip (this chip has "MAX883" in small print on its top). Place U2 onto the PCB, making sure to align pin 1 of the MAX883 with pin 1 of the PCB. Pin 1 of U2 is located next to the small dimple on its plastic package.

Pin 1 is denoted on the PCB by a square pad, and on the MAX883 by a dimple on the case. Align the pins on the pads as well, and center the MAX883 up and down so as not to short any traces that run beneath the IC. Use the flat side of the tip of the printer's knife to place the MAX883 chip. Press the chip down onto the board. The stickiness of the flux should help keep the chip from sliding around too much.

WARNING
Once you've soldered a component into place, it is almost impossible to remove. So get it right before soldering all of the component pins into place.

Wipe the tip of the iron on the damp sponge to clean off excess solder and any oxidation. After a few moments of exposure to the air, the tip of the soldering iron will turn a slight gray color. This is oxidation that needs to be cleaned off to allow the solder to easily stick to the iron. If you do not clean the iron tip before you attempt to solder, it is nearly impossible to get the solder to even melt against it.

Heat one of the corner pads with the tip of the iron, being sure not to bump the chip. Apply solder to the pad; the solder should flow up to the pin/pad joint. Remove the iron, and the solder will fix the chip to the board. Repeat on the opposite corner of the chip. The chip should be solidly attached to the board so that the rest of the pins can be soldered in a normal manner. Be sure to reheat the two corner pins to ensure a good electrical connection.

Add resistors and capacitors

For each of the parts listed below, add flux to the PCB pads and the components and use the printer's knife to place each one:

R2a. Resistor labeled 474 (47 + 4 zeros = 470K Ohm).

R2b. Resistor labeled 105 (10 + 5 zeros = 1M Ohm). Place as you did R2a.

R3. Resistor labeled 104 (10 + 4 zeros = 100K Ohm). Place as you did R2a.

DIP and SMT Parts

DIP parts have larger packages and metal pins meant to be placed into holes in the PCB or a socket. If a socket is used for a DIP part, it can be removed if the part fails or if the part has programmable memory. Care must be taken with DIP parts to avoid bending the pins too much.

SMT parts have much smaller packages and small flat metal pins that sit on the surface of the PCB. In general, SMT parts are not placed in sockets and are only soldered to the board.

SMT parts are used when space is at a premium on a board. They can be harder to solder and replace. DIP parts are bigger and easier to install.

R18. Resistor labeled 104 (10 + 4 zeros = 100K Ohm). Place as you did R2a.

C2. The caps are unlabeled. They are the same size as the resistors and are normally a kind of brownish-beige in color.

Do not place C1 at this time. Its height makes it difficult to solder other components. When you have completed placing the parts, the circuit board should look like the one in Figure 5-12. Once all the other parts have been placed and soldered, put C1 on the board.

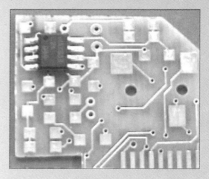

Figure 5-12: MAX883 in place

Connect power wire

In the kit you will find a power wire similar to the one shown in Figure 5-13. Connect this single conductor wire to the connection hole labeled VBAT. The other end will connect to the positive lead of the battery compartment later on. For now, use a length of 30 gauge wire or other scrap wire to connect the positive lead of the battery compartment. Use the multi-meter to verify which lead is positive, then remove the batteries. To check the lead, set the meter to measure DC voltage, touch the black probe to one of the battery wires, and touch the red probe to the other side. If the meter shows a negative number on the display, the wire you touched with the black probe is the positive side and the red is negative (sometimes referred to as ground).

Solder a short length of 30-gauge wire to pad 24 of the edge connector; this is the ground lead. In some cases, the ground lead (or your power wire) may be colored red. These traces can be confusing in later steps.

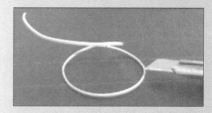

Figure 5-13: Power wire

Test the board

You should now test out this part of the circuit before proceeding. Connect pad 24 to the ground lead of the battery compartment. Connect the power wire to the positive lead of the battery compartment. Use the multi-meter to check for 5 volts between ground and the location labeled TP1.

Add remaining ICs

Place U6 as you did U2. The spacing between the pins of this part is very small, so take your time with this one.

Add flux material to the board and the part, ensuring that pin 1 is lined up correctly. Solder the corners pins first and then the rest of the pins after everything is correctly aligned. Re-solder the corners. After you have finished soldering U6, the board should look like Figure 5-14.

When you solder the corners, the excess solder remaining on the tip of the iron should almost be enough to hold the pin in place. You may use the printer's knife to hold the chip down while you run the tip of the iron along

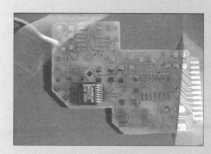

Figure 5-14: MAX221 in place

the edge of the corner pins. The rest of the pins can be soldered to the board using the excess solder on the iron. Lightly reload the solder on the iron tip every 2 or 3 pins. The solder should bubble up around the pin edges and be smooth and shiny.

Be very sparing with the solder—the pins are so close together that you could solder a batch of pins together if you're not careful. If you do happen to apply too much solder and two or more of the pins get stuck together under a blob of solder, don't despair; you can use the solder wick to absorb the excess. Apply a little flux to a clean bit of braid and place it over the blob. Briefly hold the iron to the top of the braid and wait until it absorbs the excess solder.

Using the same technique you used before to solder the other SMT components, place components C3, C4, C5, C6, and C7. These are the beige 0.1uf capacitors. After you have completed this step, the board should look like Figure 5-15.

Figure 5-15: Capacitor soldered in place

WARNING

For C5 and C6, do not mistake the pads of the resistor for where the capacitors go; it's easy to place them incorrectly. Check twice before soldering the parts in place.

---

4. Add the connectors

The new circuit boards are programmed through a serial interface. In this step, you will mount and test these connectors and cables.

Add earphone jack

Flip the board over. Place the earphone jack and press it toward the top of the board, away from the edge connector. Use a fair amount of solder, since this is what mechanically holds the plug in place. Make sure that the jack's plastic base nubs are resting in the two larger holes you've drilled, as shown in Figure 5-16.

Figure 5-16: Earphone jack in place

Build serial cable

Use the wire cutters to strip the ends of the ribbon cable by separating the individual conductors in the valleys between wires. Once the wires are separated by about an inch, use the 30-gauge wire strippers to remove one-eighth of an inch of insulation from the ends of the wires. Do this to both ends.

Select a wire to be wire 1 (some of kits will have a red wire for this). Other wires are then numbered in order up to wire 5.

Wires 1, 3, and 5 are the ground wires. They are all connected together at either end of the cable, as shown in Figure 5-17. At one end, connect the ground group of wires to pin 5 of the DB9 PC serial connector. There are numbers on the plastic housing of this female DB9 serial connector. If you solder the ground group together and trim them to one-sixteenth of an inch before soldering them to pin 5 of the connector, the soldering will be easier and the wires won't fray.

Solder wire 2 to pin 2 of the DB9 serial PC connector, and solder wire 4 to pin 3. The final soldered connections should look like Figure 5-18.

Now make the following connections on the 9-pin PC connector itself. Solder a small wire from pin 7 to pin 8. (These are the RS232 Clear To Send and Ready To Send signals. Some PC software needs the signals connected in this way to work correctly.) Solder pin 1 to pin 4 and pin 4 to pin 6. (These are the RS232 Data Set Ready, Data Carrier Detect, and Data Terminal Ready signals.)

On the other end of the cable, thread the ribbon cable through the hood and then start soldering on the 3.5mm stereo plug, as shown in Figure 5-19.

Solder wire 2 to the large ground lead of the plug; the lead is connected to the base part of the plug shaft. (Use the multi-meter to check continuity if you're not sure.)

Solder wire 4 to the tip/center lug of the 3.5mm plug; that lead is connected to the very tip of the plug shaft. (Use the multi-meter to check continuity if you're not sure.)

Solder wires 1, 3, and 5 to the ring lug of the 3.5mm plug; that lead is connected to the ring between the tip and base of the plug shaft. (Use the multi-meter to check continuity if you're not sure.)

Thread on the plug hood. Place the DB9 connector on one half of the black plastic hood, as shown in Figure 5-20. Fold the two halves together so that the hood "snaps" together. Don't worry about the cable retaining bolts; the ribbon cable is too small to hold.

Using the multi-meter, check for continuity from pin 5 of the DB9 connector to the base of the plug shaft. Set the multi-meter to measure resistance or continuity. Typically, when the two meter probes are connected to a circuit at zero resistance, the continuity test settings cause the meter to make a beeping sound; this signifies a properly connected printed circuit-board trace. Check these traces:

- Pin 2 of the DB9 should be connected to the tip of the plug shaft.

- Pin 3 of the DB9 should be connected to the ring of the plug shaft.

- Check for shorts between the ring, tip, and base of the plug. These three pins should not be connected.

Figure 5-17: Serial cable wire

Figure 5-18: DB9 wire

Figure 5-19: 3.5mm plug wiring

Figure 5-20: DB9 cover

Tips for Soldering Surface Mount Components

The resistors are contained inside a strip of paper tape and are stored inside a small pocket. Use the printer's knife to cut the paper on all four sides of the resistor. Be careful when using the tip of the knife to remove the resistor from the paper tape—the resistor can fly pretty far. (It's not easy to find them in shag carpet.)

Place the resistors with the labeling facing up and the metal pads facing down onto the board.

These components are so small that the surface tension of the solder can move the component while you are soldering. They'll also stick to the iron. The trick around this is that the PCB is already pre-tinned with some solder.

Place the component and press it down onto the PCB using the tip of the printer's knife. Run the tip of the soldering iron along the metal edge of the resistor/capacitor and the PCB pad. The solder already on the PCB should lightly affix the component to the board.

Once you've stuck one end of the component in place you can solder the other end in a normal manner, but you must be quick to keep the other end from melting.

(continued)

Insert the data cable plug into the jack on the circuit board and test for good connections between these locations:

- DB9 pin 5 and pad 24 of the edge connector
- DB9 pin 2 and U6 pin 13
- DB9 pin 3 and U6 pin 8

When connecting the plug, wiggle it until the connector loosens up. It will be tight on the first try.

Check the circuit

Follow the traces from pins 9 and 11 of U6; they go to a pair of holes in the circuit board inside the outline of pads comprising U4, then along to pins 11 and 13 of U1. Place a length of 30-gauge wire between pads 11 and 13 of U1. These are the RS232 Transmit Data and Receive Data signal paths; by connecting them you will loop back any serial data sent to the board.

Connect the cable to a standard PC running a terminal program such as Hyperterm. Set the terminal software to run at 19200 or 38400 bits per second. Insert the batteries and be sure that polarities from the battery compartment are correct. Now fire up your terminal program, and verify that whatever you type is visible in the terminal software window.

Once the board has passed this test, remove the test wire. Remove excess solder from U1 pads 11 and 13 with fluxed braid.

If the board did not pass this test, examine the circuit board for cuts in the traces or improper solder joints.

5. Add the oscillator and test the serial port

In this step you will add the system oscillator—the part that provides a heartbeat to the processor—and test out the complete serial port hardware.

Solder the oscillator

Add flux to the circuit board pads and the legs of U3. Put the part on the board and heat a pad. Allow the solder to liquefy and flow onto one pin. (Be careful not to bump a chip.) Heat and solder other pads as usual. Re-solder the first pin. Be sure pin 1 of U3 (the dimple in the lower left corner) is on pad 1 (the square pad).

This part is an oscillator in a large metal can. The can has a very large thermal mass, which means it is a large part that can absorb a lot of heat. Use enough solder to bubble the pad. Drag the iron tip up into the side notches of the oscillator to ensure a good connection. When you've completed this step, your board will look like Figure 5-21.

Power up the board. Connect the logic probe to ground and the +5V test point.

Set the logic probe for TTL and Pulse Detect mode. Connect the tail of the probe to the battery group. Touch the tip of the probe to pad 3 of U3 to ensure that the oscillator is outputting a 20 MHz signal (or is at least oscillating). One of the lights on the probe should be blinking.

If no oscillation is detected, place a wire across R24. Otherwise, leave R24 open.

Add the main processor

Place U1 and ensure that pin number 1 is aligned properly. Pin 7 of U1 is a rounded pad. Pin 1 is along the side between the 25 pad edge connector and U3 (the MAX883 that was placed in a previous step).

Heat the pad and flow solder onto one pad. Repeat with a pad on the opposite side of the integrated circuit. Now solder the other pins.

The soldering iron tip has a much smaller thermal mass than the LCC (leadless chip carrier) pins, so be sure to flow solder onto the PCB pad first and then bring the iron vertical so the side of the iron tip drags upward onto the PLCC (plastic leadless chip carrier) pin. This will draw some of the solder up onto the pin and make a good connection. When you have completed this step, the soldered part will look like Figure 5-22.

Now place U4, a 74HC04 inverter. Ensure that pin 1 (the square pad) is aligned first. Use the same technique as was used with MAX883 in an earlier step. Pin 1 is in the lower left corner when reading the label of the part. See Figure 5-23.

Figure 5-21: Oscillator in place

Figure 5-22: Main processor in place

Figure 5-23: 74HC04 in place

Tips for Soldering
(continued)

Once you've properly soldered one end, go back and properly solder the end that you preheated onto the board.

Use small dabs of solder flux on the PCB pads where you will be soldering the part. This will make the part soldering much easier. You can also try solder paste instead of thin braid solder. Solder paste is a mix of tiny balls of solder mixed with flux. To use it, place a small dab on the PCB pads, gently place the part to be soldered on top of the pasted pads, and heat each lead to cause the solder paste to reflow and make a connection.

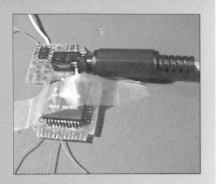

Figure 5-24: Testing the serial port

Place R4 (labeled 104, 10 + 4 zeros = 100K), using the same technique as in previous steps.

Next, test your work so far.

Solder a 30-gauge wire to pads 19 and 20 of the edge connector. Use another short wire to temporarily connect both of these wires to ground. Plug in the data cable if it's not already there.

Power up the board as you did in the first test. Move the wire on pad 19 to the +5V test point 1 (a small lead from the TP location). Use a large 100K-leaded resistor (not included with kit) between pad 19 and +5v. Use some sticky tape to hold the board and the growing number of test leads and wires, as shown in Figure 5-24.

The MCU (microcontroller unit) should be in program mode and now out of reset.

Run the ICP (in-circuit programming) program from either Temic or Philips, depending on which part you have. Be sure that no other program has the COM port already open (for example, your Palm's Hot Sync). Select the CPU and 20 MHz clock from the onscreen menus in the software.

Do a "blank check" on the part using the ICP software. If the program comes back with "part blank" or "part is not blank," all is well. If you get "part must be reset" or "invalid response to U," then double-check the oscillator and solder connections, and look for shorts on the board due to solder blobs or misaligned pins.

If you want, you can test the current consumption. Connect your meter in series with the positive power connection to the circuit board. Set the meter to measure current (put it in the milliamp range). The circuit should draw about 37 mA in reset and 80 mA in program mode. This is not a required step, but might be interesting to do.

Install the digital-to-analog converter

Place R5, a resistor labeled 102 (10 + 2 zeros = 1K).

Place U5 as you did U6 earlier. This part has tiny pins and may be difficult to solder. Take your time. Place R15, a resistor labeled 102 (10 + 2 zeros = 1K). When you've completed this step, the board will look like Figure 5-25.

Figure 5-25:
Digital-to-analog converter placement

The DAC (digital-to-analog converter) is a QSOP (quad small outline package). You will need to take special care in soldering this part.

When you solder the corners, the excess solder on the tip of the iron should almost be enough to hold the pin in place. You can use the printer's knife to hold the chip down while you run the tip of the iron along the edge of the corner pins. Be sparing with the solder, as the pins are very close together. If you do accidentally solder multiple pins together, use the solder wick to remove excess solder as outlined earlier.

The balance of the pins can be soldered to the board using the excess solder on the iron. Lightly reload the solder on the iron tip every 2 or 3 pins. The solder should bubble up around the pin edges and be smooth and shiny.

Now, test the DAC. Assemble and load the test code: *super_lf.asm* (available from *http://www.appspec.net*). Use the multi-meter to measure for voltage between GND and the non-U5 side of R15 (or better, the empty pad of C9).

The multi-meter should show a voltage that goes smoothly from 0V to +4.5V over about 5 seconds, then repeats (0 to 5V, jump to zero, 0 to 5V, and so on).

6. Add the rest of the integrated circuits

You will now add the remaining ICs to the boards.

Install the audio amplifer

Place C9 (the beige 0.1uf capacitor) using the same method used for the other SMT capacitors.

Place U7 (the part with the letters MAX4168 on top of it) using the same technique you used on U3 earlier.

Place R7, R8, R9, R19, R13, R14, and R1 (label 104, 10 + 4 zeros = 100K). Place R10, R11, R17, and R23 (label 103, 10 + 3 zeros = 10K). Place R12 (label 224, 22 + 4 zeros = 220K).

Using the same soldering techniques as before, place C8 and C11. When you have completed this step, the board should look like Figure 5-26.

On the Furby, detach the front speaker but retain the screws. Remove the speaker. Strip speaker lead wires and solder them to speaker holes on your new PCB. Figure 5-27 shows what this will look like.

Figure 5-26:
Digital-to-analog converter PCB size

Figure 5-27: Speaker wires

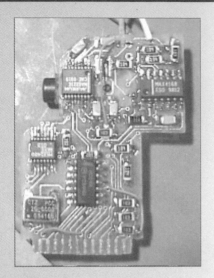

Figure 5-28:
Digital-to-analog PCB completed

Figure 5-29:
Digital-to-analog PCB capacitor locations

Figure 5-30: Install new PCB

Next, test that the DAC and audio amp work together. (Skip ahead to the software setup section for details on how to do this.) Locate the files *sine. hex* and *sinewav.hex* on the web site *http://www.appspec.net/index.html*, and load these into the CPU. Reboot the CPU and listen for a sound from the Furby speaker. If you don't get any sound, check C8. One side is connected to ground, the other should be +2.5 volts. Check pins 6 and 9 of U7; both should show +5 volts when measured with the multi-meter. If you don't receive these readings, power off the system and check for opens and for shorts.

Install the capacitors

Place R20, R21, R22 (labeled 103, 10 + 3 zeros = 10K).

Next, install jumpers J1, J2, J3. (Jumpers are made using 30-gauge wires. The pads look like slightly enlarged holes in the new circuit board with slightly larger drill holes.) Add a jumper to U4 pin 11; cut the exposed wire short enough so that the jumper wire "drops" onto the board (i.e., so the tip of the wire doesn't bottom out on the underside of U1 on the other side of the board). The jumpers attach to these pins; the pad is a through-hole so they can be soldered on either side of the board. Solder to whichever side is easiest, and flux the exposed wires and solder. After adding these parts and jumpers, the board should look like Figure 5-28.

Now place C1 and use the multi-meter to check continuity to pad 24 of the edge connector (this is the ground point). The negative polarity is the pad toward the edge connector. The gray negative stripe should be toward the edge connector. Flux the leads and tape down the board after inserting the cap; the leads will poke through, and you'll get the cap snug against the PCB. When done, it should look like Figure 5-29.

Test out the serial connection to the circuit board again. You will soon be installing the board inside the Furby case, and it would be a real pain to unsolder the board from this point forward.

Install the board you just built

Jam a pen into the hinge of the Furby base to hold it open while you are soldering. Insert the MCU board, label U1 facing outwards—use tape to keep the board vertical in the slot while you solder it into place. Watch for protruding bolts touching the PCB around the audio amplifier U7, and use electrical tape to insulate the bolt if it is there. Trim edges as necessary and flux the edges. Align pads with the pads of the base board. Place the iron tip in the corner where the board pads intersect so as to heat both the PCB pad and the base board pad; the solder will bridge and make a connection. Solder into place. You soldering job should look like that in Figure 5-30.

Be sure that the batteries have been removed before working on the board. Thread the power wire up behind the ears and around the cable bundle running down the right side of the Furby, then around the front and back along the side of the battery compartment to the positive battery compartment lead. Solder it there. Be sure that the wire will not be caught in the gears. Keep the wire snugly wrapped around the cable bundle to avoid it getting crunched in the mechanical works after the shell is replaced. When you have completed this step, it should look like Figure 5-31. Check that the power wire is clear of the gears and doesn't impede the up/down bounce of the Furby. Double-check for shorts, opens, and missed pins that should have been soldered.

It's time again to test your work so far. Replace the batteries, close the battery door, and push the reset button if necessary. It should play the same sound test (if you haven't overwritten the flash). Make sure all of the connectors are plugged back in, as shown in Figure 5-32.

Figure 5-31: Clear wiring from gears   **Figure 5-32**: Check completed assembly

Hold the tummy switch while you push and release the reset button; check that MCU is in program mode.

Load *no_ram.asm* (a file used to test the system with no RAM installed) by attaching your favorite terminal program, and use these settings: 9600 bps, 8N1, flow control off.

When you have completed these steps, your Furby should look something like Figure 5-33.

Install new flash memory

If U8 is an Atmel part, place pin 1 on the square pad, close R25 with wire, and leave R26 open. If U8 is a Nextflash part, place pin 1 on the square pad, close R26 with wire, and leave R25 open.

Figure 5-33:
Completed installation of first PCB

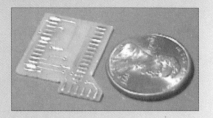

Figure 5-34: Memory PCB

Figure 5-35:
Memory chip installed on PCB

Figure 5-36:
Reassembled Furby

The empty flash board is a little bigger than a penny. You can see a picture of the board without the flash part in Figure 5-34.

Place the board in the slot flash label facing outward. Flux the edge and solder it in place. Installed, it will look like Figure 5-35.

Test this board by loading the *post_final.asm* file. You will need to first assemble it and then download the resulting *post_final.hex* file with terminal program (9600bps, 8n1, flow control off) attached. After downloading this code and starting the PC terminal software, it should say whether or not the serial flash is readable and writeable.

7. Reassemble the Furby

To reassemble your Furby, hold the left side of the shell in place and mark the location of the jack with the printer's knife. Take the shell off and drill a hole at the mark you just made. Place the half shell back on and adjust the size of the hole so that the plug fits. Your Furby will look like himself again (see Figure 5-36).

Software Setup Instructions

You will now need software tools for programming your new Furby.

Furby has been upgraded to use the venerable 8051 processor, which has been around since 1980 and has the widest range of variants of any embedded controller on the market. Freely downloadable software tools abound for the 8051. It has a small package, modest power requirements, and is inexpensive.

The hacked Furby is currently programmed in either 8051 assembler (most efficient) or C (complete with an API), so you will need to be (or become) familiar with one of those. The 8051 is a simple 8-bit CPU with a single accumulator; if you know any assembly language you can quickly pick up the 8051. Some resources to help you are listed in the following sections. All of the source code is in the public domain, and I hope that other Furby-hacking enthusiasts will write their own code and release it onto the Internet.

By virtue of the hardware design of the hacked Furby, there is no external memory. This means that MOVX commands and the like will not work. The hacked Furby has two 128-byte blocks of memory. The lower block is directly and indirectly accessible; by default, the registers and stack occupy this memory. The upper block is also 128 bytes and is indirectly accessible. There is also 1028 bytes of external RAM, which can be accessed with MOVX commands.

You will need software to program the new Furby boards. You can download a copy of this software from *http://www.appspec.net/index.html*.

Must-have software

There are a number of software utilities and packages that you will need in order to develop for your hacked Furby.

- The Small Device C Compiler allows you to write your software in a high-level language. A copy can be obtained at *http://sdcc.sourceforge. net/*.

- You will also need an 8051 assembler (*mlasm51.exe*) to assemble the code produced by the C compiler, or if you want to write everything directly in assembly. A copy can be found at *http://www.atmel.com/ atmel/products/prod74.htm*.

- The Atmel flash update utility (WinISP) that allows you to program the chip via its serial port can be found at *http://www.temic-semi. com/upload/dev_tools39dd839562c61.zip*. The Phillips ISP can also be used, but the two chips are different enough that some functions of the Phillips ISP don't react normally. Beware.

- All sound-file conversion and manipulation can be accomplished with the SOX utility. A copy can be found at *http://www.spies.com/Sox/*.

- You will need to convert between hex and binary file formats for the sound files. For this, I suggest you use the Bin2Hex and Hex2Bin utilities. Copies can be found at *http://www.atmel.com/atmel/products/ prod74.htm*.

Nice-to-have software

Although not required, there are a number of software tools that can make development easier. You may want to run your software on a simulator to debug the basic logic before running it on the real hardware platform. A few 8051 simulators for Windows can be found here:

http://www.atmel.com/atmel/products/prod74.htm
http://www.hte.com/html/8051sim.htm
http://www.dontronics.com/8051sim.html

Useful information

If you want to learn more about the processor for the system and its architecture, you can look at the "8051 chip FAQ" here:

http://www.landfield.com/faqs/microcontroller-faq/8051/

If you need a reference to the 8051 Instruction Set with details, take a look here:

ftp://download.intel.com/design/MCS51/applnots/01502a01.pdf

If the 8051 is new to you and you wish to start with a basic tutorial, take a look here:

http://www.pjrc.com/tech/8051/

Like most things on the Web, these links can change. If you cannot locate them, simply do a web search at *http://www.google.com* to find their latest locations.

A Quick Overview of Assembly Language and C for the Hacked Furby

The hacked Furby can be programmed in C and assembly language. We'll step through how to do this now.

If you want to program your newly modified Furby in C, a set of APIs will allow you to control most of the basic functions of the hacked Furby. The code for these APIs is at *http://www.appspec.net/index.html*.

Learning 8051 assembler code

The *mlasm51.exe* download mentioned earlier is a self-installing executable for Windows. When you run it, it unpacks the free assembler and an excellent manual, as well as code samples and figures. Print them all out and read them to learn 8051 assembler. If you have any assembler knowledge, 8051 is not hard; it just takes an investment of time. The CPU does have one or two architectural curiosities, and is limited by its 8-bit architecture. On the other hand, those provide some simplifications too. The 8051 in the new Furby rips along at 20 MHz, more than four times faster than the original IBM PC (4.77 MHz).

Coding in C

This is perhaps the simplest solution for most people, though it doesn't allow you the most efficient use of the Furby's resources. It does, however, allow you to use the nice little C API that handles most of the basic functionality you'll want out of your Furby.

A good C compiler for the 8051 is the Small Device C compiler or SDCC; it's available at *http://sdoc.sourceforge.net*. Follow the instructions included with SDCC for its operation. A treatment of its general usage is beyond the scope of this chapter; reference the Temic documentation for the T89C51RD2.

Preparing code for download

Make sure you have downloaded and installed your chosen development tool, either an 8051 assembler or SDCC. Once you have written your code, compile or assemble the source file according to the directions given for that particular package. That generates a *.hex* file from your source. The *.hex* file is an ASCII file in S-record format, which is a printable ASCII format consisting of an optional header, any number of data records (each representing a start address and any number of content words), and a trailer record.

You will also want to bin2hex any sound samplings. See the example under Sound files for your Furby.

You can use either of the simulators to test or step through your code before you download it into Furby. Of course, you cannot check that sounds or movements play correctly until you run on the actual hardware.

Downloading and using the software

You will be downloading an ASCII file of hex content into the hacked Furby's flash memory using the WinISP software. WinISP transmits a file from the serial port of your Windows PC into the hacked Furby's flash PROM. Plug the adapter cable from the kit into the hacked Furby's socket at one end and into the serial port of your PC at the other. Plans are in the works for a freeware, open source version of the ISP program. (It should be an easy task with something like Perl.)

Make sure you have downloaded and installed the WinISP program onto your PC. You can find it at *http://www.temic-semi.com/upload/dev_tools39dd839562c61.zip.*

Start WinISP

The software requires three parameters. Consult the table below for the appropriate value to be entered into each. Use the values in this table for the following three parameters on this screen.

Parameter	Value
Chip	P89C51RD2
Port	COM1 (or whatever PC port you are using)
Osc (MHz)	20 (this is the MHz speed of the CPU)

If all is well, the status display will read "Comm Port Opened (19200 bps)." Initial code loads and debugging are done via the serial port at a speed of 19.2K bps. The impatient will love the high-speed downloads, while Unix fans will be thoroughly at home with the character-oriented console access.

Power on your hacked Furby

Hold down the belly button (the microswitch on the front of the hacked Furby, about an inch under the beak) and use a ballpoint pen to press the switch marked "reset" on the base of the hacked Furby. It presses in about 1/8 of an inch. Release the reset, then release the belly button. This procedure puts the hacked Furby into ISP (in-system programmer) mode, where it can accept file downloads into flash ROM.

WARNING

Everything gets downloaded into flash ROM: code and WAV file sound effects. You turn the content into ASCII S-records and download the files (there will typically be several files to put into memory) using WinISP. See the later section Sound files for your Furby for information on how to prepare a WAV sound effect file for downloading.

WARNING

It is possible to overwrite the ISP program in the chip's flash. The ISP sits in the last few bytes of the 64K flash provided, which will disable further programming via ISP. The only remedy to this is to remove the MCU from the hacked Furby and reprogram it using an eprom burner. So be careful never to change the Vector value; it should always be set to "FC". If you change this value, you will permanently disable the ISP code. Do not set any of the "security bits."

Program the Furby

The "S-record" format is used by the WinISP software to load flash memory. Here is a typical set of commands to do that:

1. Select your S-record file to load. There can be several of these (up to 64 KB). Memory is cleared as the file is written into flash.

2. Initiate the programming/data transfer. The files are transferred into memory, which is erased before the data is written.

3. Verify your data.

Note that the S-record format tells WinISP where to load that block. An example of what these S-record files look like is listed below:

```
table.hex:
:10010000808183848687898A8C8E8F91929495973B
:1001100098999B9C9E9FA0A2A3A4A6A7A8A9AAACBD
:10012000ADAEAFB0B1B2B3B4B5B6B6B7B8B9B9BA8F
```

```
short.hex:
:208000008080808080808080808080808080808080808080808080808080808080808080
8060
```

```
:20802000808080808080808080808080808080808080808080808080808080808080
8040
:20804000808080808080808080808080808080808080808080808080808080808080
8020
:20806000808080808080808080808080808080808080808080808080808080808080
8000
:20808000808080808080808080808080808080808080808080808080808080808080
80E0
:2080A000808080808080808080808080808080808080808080808080808080808080
80C0

sinwave.hex:
:03000000020200F9
:1002000075A80075D9825380DF4380205390FB434B
:1002100090045380F34380005380FD4380027B10A1
:100220001202B41202A71202A71202A77B1A12022C
:10023000B45390FE4390005380F34380041202A70E
:100240001202A71202A77B1A1202B45380F3438052
```

Sound files for your Furby

Furby comes with a power-on self-test subroutine called "SND" (sound) that can play files in a particular WAV format. The format is mono WAV files recorded at 8 KHz. There will be 8 KB of data for each second the sound plays, so these files can get large pretty quickly. You can download sound effects from many places on the Web; do a Google search or go to *http://ultimatesoundarchive.com/*.

As an example, we will prepare the "Microsoft sound" for downloading into the hacked Furby. First, make a Furby directory on your PC and copy the file into it:

```
mkdir c:\Furby
cd c:\Furby
copy c:\windows\media\themic~1.wav noise.wav
```

Next, run the sox utility with the -V option to see the sampling rate of this file, and convert it into 8 KHz 8-bit mono:

```
sox  -V  noise.wav  -r 8000  noise2.wav
```

The -V option is not required and can be omitted without affecting the command. (There is some great information on audio file formats at *http://www. textfiles.com/programming/FORMATS/audiof23.txt*, written by Guido van Rossum, who created Python.)

Now, convert the binary WAV file into an ASCII form that can be edited and uploaded using WinISP. The bin2hex utility will do this.

Chop off the 52-byte ASCII header and footer from the sound file, using the binhex option or your favorite binary editor. Emacs will also do this, or you can download the hex-edit shareware file. Or you can just ignore the header and footer—they introduce a little bit of noise, but not much. Give it a starting address where the sound file won't interfere with anything else in memory (perhaps at 0x8000, the top 32 KB of memory). Remember that bin2hex expects its arguments in decimal!

Use bin2hex to turn your chopped file into ASCII file ready to be uploaded. Use this command:

```
bin2hex   /I 52  /M 32768   file.wav   file.hex
```

Controlling the Furby motors and other output devices

The Furby output devices and their corresponding hardware actions are shown in the following table:

Output device	Hardware action
Speaker	Sound is played.
Motor	Motor does stepped rotation. This controls the eyes, ears, mouth, and "bounce" of the Furby.
Infrared out	Infrared is emitted.

The same cam drives all your hacked Furby's ear, eye, and beak movements. That means that any possible movements are limited by the position of the cam. If you want to open the eyes, you may be in a cam position that requires Furby to open and close the mouth to get there. This is a limitation of the original design.

Input devices on the Furby

The Furby input devices and their corresponding hardware actions are shown in the following table:

Input device	Pin	Hardware action
Back button	CEX4	Interrupt vectors to 0x33
"Feed" button	P0.6	Polled
Tummy button	P0.0	Polled
Attitude inversion sensor	P1.1 / T2EX	Polled
Tilt sensor	INT1	Interrupt vectors to 0x13
Sound Rx	CEX2	Interrupt vectors to 0x33
Infrared in		Polled
Light clock (cam position counter)	CEX1	Interrupt vectors to 0x33
Cam home	CEX0	Interrupt vectors to 0x33
Light Rx	CEX3	Interrupt vectors to 0x33

Some of these are cleared by hardware after interrupting. When the interrupt occurs, the CPU will jump to the location shown. You need to write the code to handle that interrupt and place it at that address. If the code is more than a few bytes, you will need to put a jump instruction in the vector and put the interrupt service routine somewhere else where there is room. See the following table:

Input device	Priority	Interrupt vectors to
External 0	1	0x0003
Timer 0	2	0x000B
External 1	3	0x0013
Timer 1	4	0x001B
PCA interrupt	5	0x0033
Serial port (PC)	6	0x0023
Timer 2	7	0x002B

The last instruction in your interrupt service routine is always "RET" to return to whatever was happening when the interrupt arrived (that's why it is called an "interrupt"). More specific information can be found on page 19 of the Phillips P89C51 data sheet.

Project Demo

Your new Furby hardware should now be up and running. All you have to do is code some simple (or complex) Furby applications. The web site *http://www.appspec.net/index.html* has a few examples from which to start.

Extensions

Not only can you change the vocabulary and voice of the Furby, you can use the sensors in interesting ways. You could, for example, turn the Furby into a simple motion-sensing alarm system that spouts off amusing phrases when it sees movement.

How to Hack a Generic Talking Toy

In 1989 a group calling itself The Barbie Liberation Organization purchased 300 talking Barbie and GI Joe dolls and switched the voice chips. They then placed these "hacked" toys back on toy-store shelves to be purchased by unsuspecting children. The hacked GI Joe dolls said things like "I love school. Don't you?" and "Let's sing with the band tonight." The hacked Barbie said phrases like "Dead men tell no lies." Newspapers across the country picked up the story and an urban legend was born. This "act of sabotage" (according to a few of the Mattel and Hasbro people I worked with) occurred when I was working as a toy designer.

A year or two later, a talking Barbie playset that I designed hit the market. At about the same time, Mattel released a new talking Barbie, one of whose phrases included "Math class is tough." The story of the non–politically correct Barbie hit the press and sent my product to an early grave. (I think Mattel pulled all talking Barbies for a while after that.)

However, the talking Barbie playset I designed was much cooler than a simple doll that said inane things. My playset could read special tags on the doll's clothing to determine where the doll was and trigger short dialogs that included the location and clothing. And it never said anything about mathematics...I swear!

In this section I'll show you how you can hack a small talking toy so you too can sow a little subversion of your own.

Finding the Sound Electronics

Most talking toys have a backpack of some sort where the electronics are hidden. If there is no backpack, look inside the chest cavity of the toy.

Figure 5-37: Toy figure packback

Project Overview

First you will disassemble the voice box backpack—included with most small action figures—that holds the manufacturer's phrases. Next, you will modify a voice-recording module from Radio Shack and install it in place of the original. The following steps will walk you through the modification process.

Hardware Assembly Instructions

This project requires taking apart the simple electronics from a small talking toy and replacing them with a set of electronics from Radio Shack. I used a military action figure. Locate the materials in Exhibit B before you start.

1. Disassemble the backpack

Remove the screws that hold the two plastic halves of the pack together, as shown in Figure 5-37.

2. Desolder the speaker and battery wires

Remove the two screws that hold the small circuit board connected to the speaker and batteries. Carefully desolder the speaker and battery wires from the original audio board.

3. Modify the audio recording board

First, think of a clever audio phrase that you want your talking toy to say. For my military figure I spoke the phrase "Let's go shopping" in the highest falsetto I could manage. The Radio Shack board has instructions on how to record audio onto the board. Follow these instructions before modifying the board, since you will be removing the record button from the board to allow it to fit inside the small backpack.

After recording the phrase on the board and testing to make sure it sounds acceptable, you will modify this new audio circuit board. Before modification, the new board should look like that shown in Figure 5-38.

Remove various components

Remove the battery's plus and minus wires, both record button wires, and both speaker wires. Remove the white rubber button on the main board by removing the metal ring that holds it in place.

Remove capacitors

Now you need to remove several capacitors on the board so that it will fit inside the toy's original backpack. Next, remove the capacitor marked C in Figure 5-39 (the small blue can-shaped object) and move the capacitor marked D to the new position indicated. Make sure that the wire from the capacitor originally in location B is connected to location F, and the wire originally at A is moved to E. I had to carefully bend the two metal wires on the bottom so that they faced the opposite direction. The minus terminal (you will see a minus symbol if you look on the side of the part) of the capacitor should be connected to the same wire as before it was moved. I also had to solder a small piece of wire so that this minus terminal would reach to the board in location F. Finally, remove the black plastic components in location G.

Trim the board to fit

Trim the board so that it will fit inside the toy's backpack. You will also need to trim some of the plastic from the inside of the case. Cut the board as indicated by the lines in Figure 5-39. Trim a little at a time until the board fits inside the case.

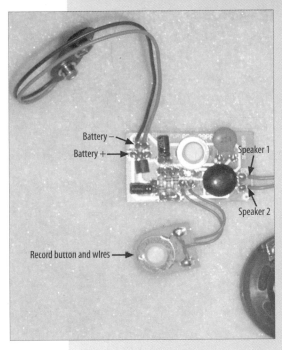

Figure 5-38: Sound board

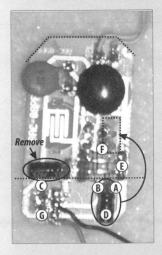

Figure 5-39:
Sound board before modification

Figure 5-40:
Sound board after modification

Figure 5-41:
Covered and modified sound board

Make your connections

When you trimmed the board, a required circuit board trace (the shiny metal strips on the circuit board) was cut. Take a short piece of wire and connect it between point B and point A, as shown in Figure 5-40. You will also have to unsolder the black wire and move it to point A. Two of the switch leads should be hanging over the edge of the circuit board at locations E and F. Make sure that they are not touching any of the traces on the circuit board. Now connect these two leads to locations C and D with two short pieces of wire.

Test your work

Take the small pushbutton and determine which two of the four leads (the metal legs that come out the sides of the switch body) are shorted together when the button is pushed using the multi-meter. Set the meter to measure resistance and hold each test probe against one of the metal leads. Press the button and observe the meter display. When the display reads 0 or 0.001, you have found the two leads to use. Place the button on the back of the board as shown in Figure 5-41. You can see that two of the unused metal legs have been trimmed in Figure 5-40. The switch can be held in place with a small drop of super glue.

Place a small strip of insulating tape on the back of the board, as shown in Figure 5-41.

4. Test the modifications

Before you put the circuit board back into the backpack, be sure to test it out. Take the metal clip attached to the black wire and replace it into the battery area of the backpack; it should fit back into the slot from which you removed it. Do the same with the metal clip attached to the red wire. Place the three small button batteries back into the case, making sure that the plus terminal points toward the clip with the red wire. Tap the button, and you should hear the phrase you recorded. If you don't, review your work, looking for bits of solder that may have dripped on the board or poor soldered connections that come loose if gently pulled.

5. Reassemble your toy

Put the modified circuit board into the case and put the screws back in. You're done!

Project Demo

Leave the modified toy solder for an unsuspecting child and watch their reaction. Or leave it on your desk at work and see what your coworkers say.

Extensions

You can use just about any talking (or non-talking) toy for this hack. I chose a model that had a backpack that could accommodate the Radio Shack audio circuit board. You could also choose a stuffed animal and add a small activation switch to the front or on a paw. If the toy does not have batteries and has the space for the entire circuit board, you can use a 9-volt battery that the Radio Shack board normally uses.

The simple recording chip from Radio Shack will hold only a single phrase. You may want to build a system that has several phrases triggered by different events. There are a number of ways to go about this—you could use a microcontroller or basic controller, and a Chipcoder IC from Winbod Electronics (you can buy these from DigiKey).

A remote control could also be fun. If you wish to buy a ready-to-use solution, Parallax Inc. offers a number of simple one-way radio control board sets that can be used to trigger the sounds from the toy.

Exhibit A: Furby Bill of Materials

Item	Quantity	Notes
Furby	1	
Ceramic capacitor, 0.1uf	9	C2, C3, C4, C5, C6, C7, C8, C9, C11
Resistor, 100K Ohms	10	R1, R3, R4, R7, R8, R9, R13, R14, R18, R19
Resistor, 10K Ohms	7	R10, R11, R17, R20, R21, R22, R23
Electrolytic capacitor, 100uf	1	C1
Resistor, 1K Ohms	2	R5, R15
Resistor, 105 mega Ohms	1	R2b
Crystal oscillator, 20 MHz	1	U3
Resistor, 220K Ohms	1	R12
Resistor, 514K Ohms	1	R2a
Integrated circuit, 74HC04 Hex Inverter	1	U4
Integrated circuit, AT45D081 1 MegaByte Serial Interface FLASH Memory	1	U8
Integrated circuit, MAX221 +5V RS-232 Interface	1	U6
Integrated circuit, MAX4168 Precision Operational Amplifier	1	U7
Integrated circuit, MAX5480 Digital to Analog Converter	1	U5
Integrated circuit, MAX883 Low Dropout Linear Voltage Regulatro	1	U2
Phone jack	1	JK1
Integrated circuit, T89C51RD2 FLASH Memory Micro Controller	1	U1
Circuit board	1	PCB
Soldering iron	1	
Solder	1 roll	No-clean solder
Solder wick	1 roll	
Printer's knife	1	
Hand tools (small pliers, wire cutters)	1 of each	
PC (for programming)	1	
Multi-meter	1	

Exhibit B: Talking Toy Bill of Materials

Item	Quantity	Notes
Talking action figure	1	
Voice recording module	1	Radio Shack Part #276-1323
Momentary button	1	DigiKey Part #SW400-ND
Small Phillips screwdriver	1	
Wire cutters	1	
Soldering iron	1	
Solder	1 roll	No-clean solder
Thin wire	4"-6"	
Small tube of super glue	1 roll	
Insulating tape	1	

Exhibit C

Exhibit C: Schematic for Building Your Own Board

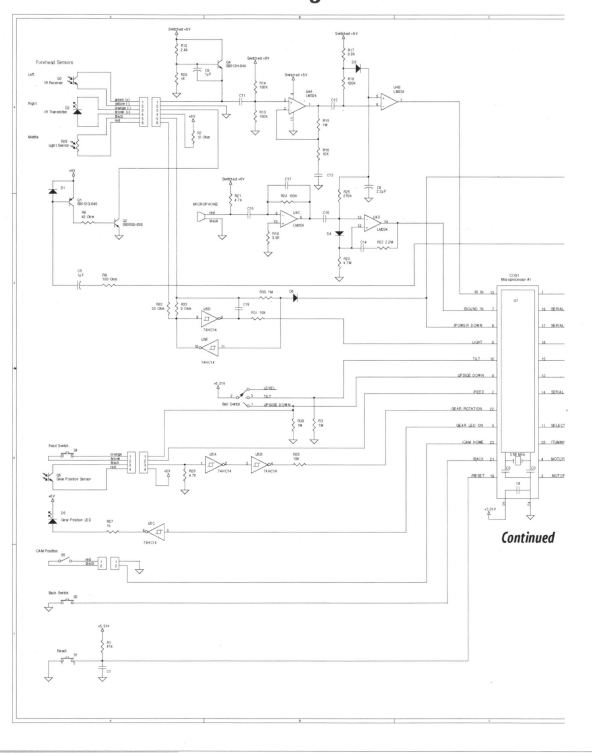

Continued

Exhibit C

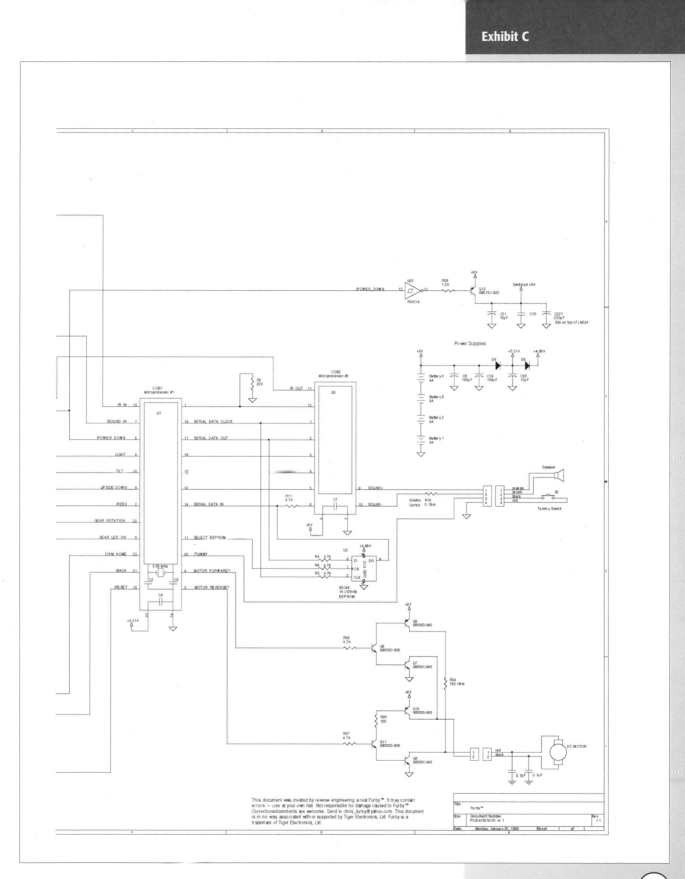

Chapter 5, How to Hack a Furby (and Other Talking Toys)

How to Hack a Video Periscope for Your Car

Cost
$100–200

Time
a weekend

Difficulty
moderate

Have you ever been stuck in traffic and wondered what was happening up ahead, but could not get out of your car to look?

When backing into a parking space, have you ever wanted to see exactly how far the bumper of your car was from the curb or from the car behind you?

Have you ever been concerned about people walking behind you while you're backing out of a parking space?

Have you ever wanted to peek over the giant SUV you're stuck behind?

When caravanning with friends, have you ever wanted to look out over traffic to see where they are?

Build your own video camera periscope and these problems can be solved. In this project, I will show you how to build a weatherproof housing for a small, color video camera and how to mount it on the outside of your car. When you're done, you will be able to orient the camera to see what's ahead or behind the car. You will hopefully never dent your bumpers again!

What You Need

- Color video camera
- LCD TV set with video input
- RTV sealant from local hardware store
- Other items listed in Exhibit A

Project Overview

When I began this hack, I looked at a number of inexpensive color video cameras. One of the first I experimented with was the X-10 wired color video camera, which has been advertised extensively on the Web.

I purchased one of these cameras and connected it to see the image quality it produced. After connecting the camera to a small LCD television, I was immediately disappointed with the results. The images had little color and would often break up if the lighting levels changed even slightly. It was clear that I needed a better solution.

A quick search in the DigiKey catalog yielded the answer: a small color video camera made by Panasonic. After a quick test of image quality, this camera looked right for the project.

You will assemble this camera and mounting hardware in a few simple steps. The camera will be connected to a small LCD monitor that you will install inside the car for viewing the video images. The camera will be protected inside of a Pactec plastic case.

Hardware Assembly Instructions

For this project, you will need to know how to solder and how to read a schematic diagram.

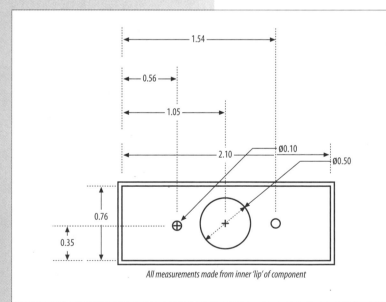

All measurements made from inner 'lip' of component

Figure 6-1: Camera cutouts

1. Assemble the camera housing

To begin, you will need the Pactec plastic housing, the Panasonic color video camera, two 2-56 screws (1 inch long) and nuts, and a small piece of clear Lucite. You will be drilling and cutting holes in the plastic case to hold the camera and protect it from the elements.

Drill holes in front of the plastic enclosure

You will need to make several holes for the camera lens and mounting points on one side of the Pactec housing, as shown in Figure 6-1. Note that the measurements are in inches. If you use a different housing, you will need to adjust these measurements.

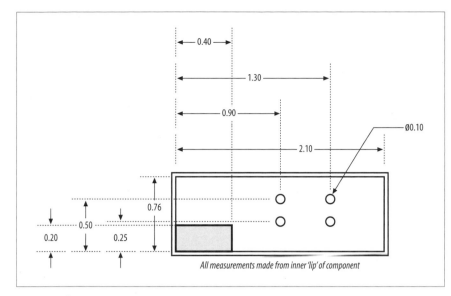

All measurements made from inner 'lip' of component

Figure 6-2: Camera enclosure back diagram

Cut exit hole for wire

Next, cut several holes in the back of the plastic enclosure to allow the video and power cables to exit. You will also need to cut holes that allow you to capture the cables inside the enclosure with tie wraps. Cut holes in the pattern shown in Figure 6-2. You do not need to be exact about these dimensions.

Mount the camera

The Panasonic camera has two holes on either side of the lens. These holes will easily fit a 2-56 threaded screw. Use two 1-inch-long, nylon 2-56 screws to hold the camera to the front plate you cut in the previous task. You can see what this looks like in Figure 6-3. Do not tighten the screws too much, as you will later need to adjust the focus of the camera by rotating the front lens on the camera.

2. Assemble the power supply

The camera requires a 5V power supply to operate, and the LCD TV set I used requires just over 6 volts. The cigarette lighter socket in your car supplies 12 volts, and the circuit converts it to the required 5 and 6 volts. You can easily build this circuit in about an hour.

Build the simple power supply according to the schematic diagram in Exhibit B. This circuit can be built in a small piece of perforated board and placed inside a small insulating enclosure. When you are done, it should look similar to what you see in Figure 6-4.

Figure 6-3: Camera mount

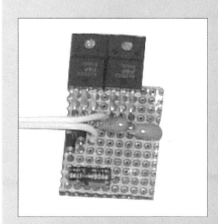

Figure 6-4: Power supply PCB

Purchase a small enclosure from Radio Shack or DigiKey. I used DigiKey Part #SCR4TL-ND, but any small enclosure will do as long as it covers all of the exposed wires.

Connect the 12V cigarette adapter, 5V camera power wire, and LCD monitor wire to the board. Cut appropriate holes in the enclosure to allow the wires to exit.

Attach a 3/32" jack to the camera power supply wires to allow easy disconnect from the camera.

After assembly, test out the power supply with a multi-meter. Make sure that the camera power supply generates 5 volts (within 5 percent) and that the LCD monitor power supply generates 6.2 to 6.4 volts. (If your LCD TV set does not accept 6V input, purchase a separate car adapter from Radio Shack.)

You should add a heat sink to each of the voltage regulators. Radio Shack and DigiKey both offer a large selection (the DigiKey part #HS189-ND will work for the TO-220 package for the voltage regulators used in this project). Make sure you leave room for the heat sink, as it is larger than the chip to which it attaches. The heat sink usually bolts onto the back of the regulator with a metal 4-40 screw and bolt.

After all the cables have been attached, the open power supply should look like Figure 6-5. When it is closed, it should look like Figure 6-6. (The white wire is the LCD TV power.)

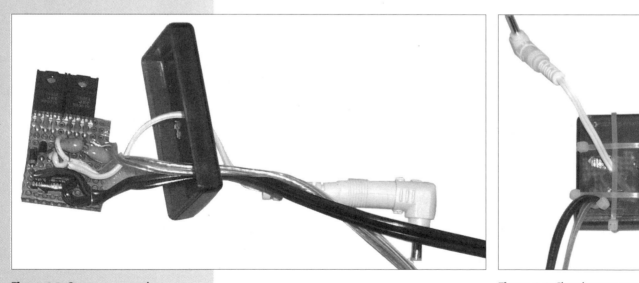

Figure 6-5: Open power supply   **Figure 6-6**: Closed power supply

3. Assemble car mounting hardware

The camera can be mounted in a number of locations on the outside of your car. In this example, the camera is mounted at the end of a four-foot-tall PVC pipe attached to the left rear side of the car.

The Madol antenna mount is a well-constructed trunk-mount assembly that is made for amateur radio antennas. It is very adjustable and has a hole in the center that is perfect for a six-inch-long bolt. You can see these components in Figure 6-7.

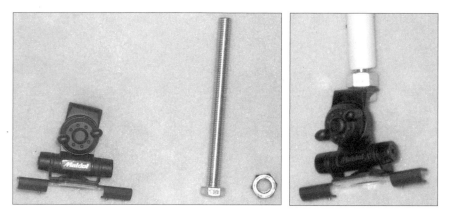

Figure 6-7: Car mount components

Figure 6-8: Car mount assembly

The mounting assembly needs to be able to hold the PVC pipe and camera in place on an automobile traveling at 80-plus mph. The components should be as tough as possible.

Thread the bolt through the hole in the Madol mount and secure it with a nut, as shown in Figure 6-8.

4. Wire the mount pole and camera

In this step you will install the video and power cables into the PVC pipe and connect the camera to these wires. Wiring can be somewhat boring, but doing it neatly will ensure that it does not get tangled after you have it installed.

Measure the wire path

Take a look at the car on which you'll be mounting the camera and locate a convenient place on the back trunk. Measure the path that the power and video cables will travel from that point to where you wish to have the monitor inside the car. Add 7 feet to this number, and cut out that length of video and power cable.

Power Supplies and Heat Sinks

When I was experimenting with these power supplies, I neglected to add the heat sink. The camera and TV worked on my lab bench when I first tested them out, but when I installed them in the car, the camera power supply overheated and shut down after two minutes.

Cut PVC pipe to length and drill mounting holes

Locate the length of PVC pipe you will use for the camera mount and cut it to the desired length. Try to make the length as short as is practical for your requirements, and make sure that the ends are smooth and flat. Drill a set of five holes in the top, as shown in Figure 6-9. Tie wraps will be threaded through these to hold the camera housing in place. The dimensions are approximate; you may adjust as you see fit. The fifth hole near the top will be used to thread the video and power cable through the interior of the pipe. The holes at the bottom will be used to hold the pipe to the car mount and to thread the video and power cables.

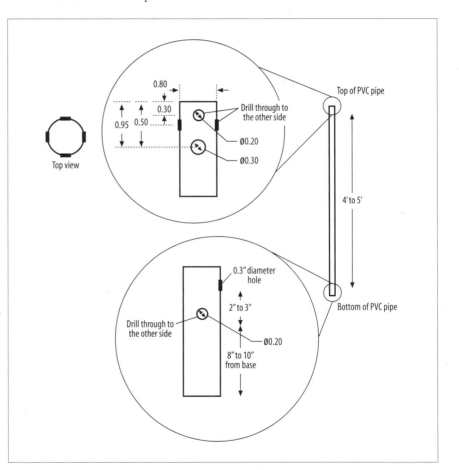

Figure 6-9: Pipe mounting holes

Thread wire through the PVC pipe

Thread the power and video cables through the 0.3" diameter holes in the pipe. It should look something like Figure 6-10 when you have completed this step. Leave 5 to 6 inches of each cable outside of the top hole.

Figure 6-10:
Threaded cables

Connect camera cable to video and power cables

The camera has a very small connector for its power and video signals. The wires from the camera connector cables need to be connected to the larger video and power cables. The most reliable and easy-to-assemble method I found was to take a small piece of perforated board, solder the connectors to each side, and then bridge the appropriate signals together. Figure 6-11 shows a diagram of the connections for the Panasonic camera and connector cable. Figure 6-12 shows a completed connection board. The two unconnected wires are unused for this project.

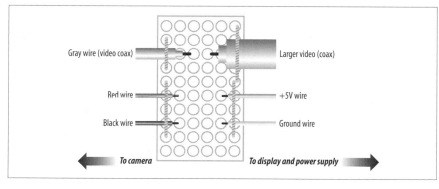

Figure 6-11: Camera connector diagram

Figure 6-12:
Completed camera connector

This delicate cable assembly should be secured against the back side of the camera enclosure. Use two tie wraps to hold the large cables in place, as shown in Figure 6-13. The notch in the corner allows the cables to escape.

Connect the power supply to the power cable and measure the voltage at the small camera connector circuit board to ensure that everything is connected properly.

Assemble the enclosure walls and plug in the camera.

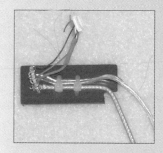

Figure 6-13:
Enclosure back wall

Add connectors to ends of video and power cables

Add a 1/8" two-conductor plug to the end of the power cable and a 1/8" three-conductor plug to the end of the video cable. Figure 6-14 shows how I wired my video cable to a 1/8" plug. You should test this cable out before you install the plastic cover.

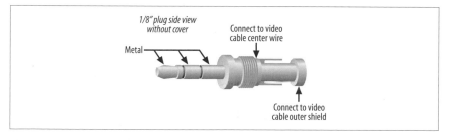

Figure 6-14: Video plug wiring

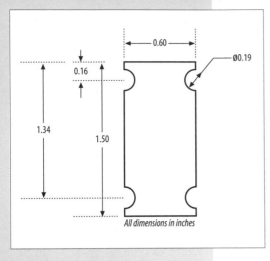

Figure 6-15: Lens cover

5. Install the camera and monitor

You now need to connect all the parts and test them out. In this step you will temporarily mount the camera enclosure to the PVC pole and mount it on the trunk of your car to ensure that everything fits. You will be using tie wraps to hold things together, but they will be replaced with semipermanent sealing in Step 6.

Construct a camera lens cover

The camera lens that comes with the Panasonic was not meant to withstand any severe conditions, so you will need to add a cover to it. Purchase a small piece of Lucite and cut it out according to the pattern in Figure 6-15.

Use a number of tie wraps to secure the lens cover to the front of the camera lens.

Secure camera housing to PVC pole

The holes that were previously drilled into the top of the PVC pipe will now be used to mount the camera. Thread through several large tie wraps and loop them over the camera case. Figures 6-16 to 6-18 show three views of the camera as it should look when you've completed these steps.

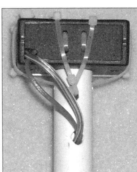
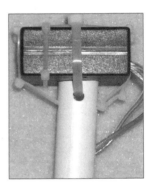

Figure 6-16:
Camera mount front view

Figure 6-17:
Camera mount back view

Figure 6-18:
Camera mount side view

Install the car mounting hardware

Clamp the Madol car mount to the trunk of your car according to the instructions enclosed with it. Place the camera pole onto the 6-inch bolt.

After you seal the camera case closed, use several large tie wraps looped through the holes at the bottom to hold the pole down onto the mount. There should be a space under the mount to loop the tie wraps through. These ties will be cut off later to allow sealing of the case. When you're done, the mounted camera should look like Figure 6-19. You can see a close-up in Figure 6-20.

Figure 6-19: Camera in place

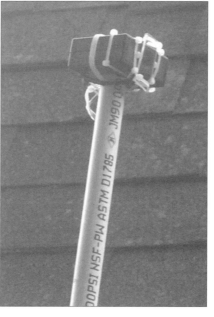

Figure 6-20: Camera close-up

It is very important that the pole be firmly secured to the car mount. If the camera assembly comes loose when you are driving, it can become a hazard to both you and other drivers.

You can also easily mount the camera on a shorter pole and facing toward the back of your car, as a backing-up warning system.

Pull wires from camera mount to front of car

Pull the power and video cable to the front of the car (or wherever you intend to place the LCD TV monitor). In my car, a Toyota Corolla, I threaded the wires around the sides of the back seats through to the area between the front passenger and driver's seat. The fact that my back seats fold down made it easy.

6. Seal the enclosure with RTV silicone

Remove the PVC pipe and enclosure from the car. In a well-ventilated room, apply a thin bead of RTV silicone sealant along all of the enclosure's seams and holes. Be somewhat liberal with the sealant at the holes. Also apply a thick bead around the camera lens opening. This will seal against the lens cover to protect it. Install the screws that hold the case together and let the RTV cure according to its enclosed instructions. Inspect the seals after the curing period and add more RTV if needed.

Reinstall the camera on top of the pole and reattach all of the wiring. You now have a video periscope that will allow you a unique view of traffic!

Test out the camera assembly

Take the entire assembly out to the car, but do not attach the trunk mount—you first want to see if everything works. Plug in the video camera to the LCD TV set and plug the power cable into the power supply. Connect the power supply to the 12V cigarette lighter and see if there is a video picture on the LCD TV.

Close the trunk of the car over the cables and connect the camera. Plug in the cigarette adapter and look for video. Don't go for a ride just yet—you will need to check the weatherproofing at the enclosure and tighten all of the tie wraps.

Adjust the Madol antenna mount to give you the view you want. It can be oriented forward to get a peek at traffic up ahead, or backward to see what (or who) is behind you.

Extensions

Once you have the camera working, you may want to experiment with different configurations. Here are four examples.

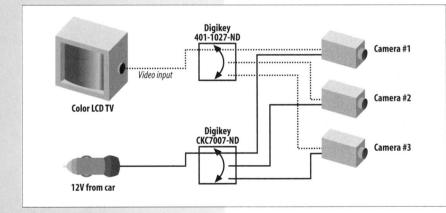

Figure 6-21: Multi-camera setup

Multiple cameras

Multiple cameras can be attached around the car. Simply purchase and build additional cameras and housings and add a multi-pole switch to rotate the power and video among the different cameras. Figure 6-21 shows an example of how multiple cameras can be connected.

Motorized mount

If you want to be able to rotate the camera left and right, you can use a model airplane servo. Pick up a medium-size servo and mount it to the pole and the camera. You will need some sort of control circuit to send position information to the servo; a simple circuit that accomplishes this is shown in Exhibit C. The circuit consists of an LM55 timer IC, a few resistors and capacitors, a transistor, and a potentiometer. Build the circuit and mount it in a small box with a large potentiometer sticking out. Add a knob that allows rotation of the camera to be controlled from the front seat of the car.

If you feel ambitious, you can build a microprocessor-based servo controller and have the camera pan automatically. I will leave this as an exercise to you.

When mounting the servo, you will need to build a small cover to prevent water from getting inside the case. (This cover is not needed if you only want to use the camera inside the car.)

Battery-powered version

If you want to use the camera as a portable periscope, you could use six D batteries to power up the set. Put them in a small case, and you can now look over fences and walls without being detected.

Connect a video recorder

You have probably seen the television programs "COPS," "Dangerous Car Chases," or similar real-life highway patrol programs. Much of the video from these shows is from in-car video cameras and recorders. Using the video periscope and an old VCR, you can set up a similar system for yourself.

Locate an old but functional VCR, a 12V to 120V voltage converter (available at Radio Shack and many auto-supply stores), and a basic microcontroller. Connect them as shown in Figure 6-22. You will need to connect the controller to the remote control so that the Record button is pressed 10 to 20 seconds after the system is powered up. I will leave the details of this project up to you.

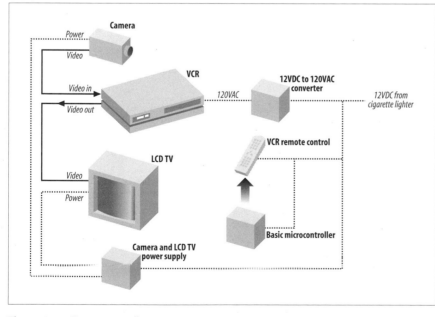

Figure 6-22: Camera recording system

Exhibit A: Bill of Materials

Item	Quantity	Notes
Color video camera	1	Panasonic GP-CX161-53P, DigiKey Part #P9505-ND
Camera connection cable	1	DigiKey Part #P9507-ND
LCD TV set with video input	1	eBay is a good source
Thin video cable RG179 B/U 75 Ohm	15'–20'	DigiKey Part #A317-100-ND
16-gauge speaker wire	15'–20'	Radio Shack Part #278-117
Plastic enclosure	1	Pactec Part # JM22 (*http://www.pactecenclosures.com/*) (Newark Electronics carries it)
External antenna mount	1	Madol Antenna Trunk Mount #PRM-T, Ham Radio Outlet carries these
Schedule 40 0.5" diameter PVC pipe	5'	Hardware store
6"x 0.5" long carriage bolt and nut	1 set	Hardware store
5V linear regulators	2	Radio Shack Part #276-1770
4.7uF capacitors	2	Radio Shack
12V cigarette lighter power plug	1	Radio Shack Part #27-1509
Dual or single conductor shielded wire	10'–30'	Radio Shack
Power connector for color TV	1	Radio Shack
RTV sealant	1 tube	Hardware store
Assorted tie wraps	1 box	Hardware store
Two-conductor 1/8" plug and jack	1	Radio Shack Part #274-283
Three-conductor 1/8" plug	1	Radio Shack Part #274-284
3" x 3" x 1/8" clear Lucite or other clear plastic	1 sheet	Hardware or plastics store
Blank printed circuit board (PCB)	1	Radio Shack Part #276-158
Heat sink	1	
Multi-meter	1	
Wire cutters	1	
Drill	1	
1/4" drill bit	1	
3/8" drill bit	1	
Rotary cutting tool	1	
Cutting wheel	1	
Grinding wheel	1	

Exhibit B: Schematic Diagram for Power Supply

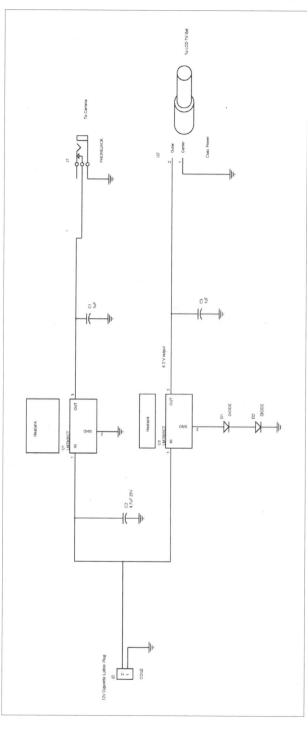

Exhibit C: Schematic Diagram for RC Servo Driver

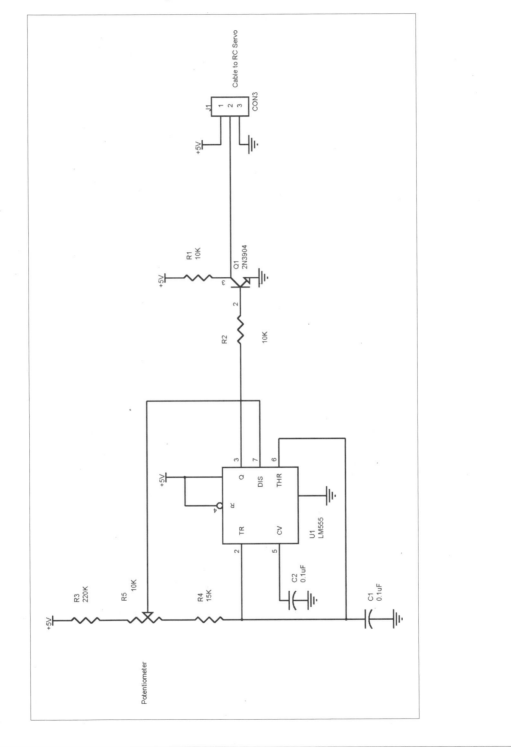

Advanced Hacks, Tools, and Techniques

II

Now that you've got a few hacks under your belt, it is time to add some skills to your repertoire that will allow you to tackle the more advanced projects coming up.

Some of the projects in this section require that you be able to identify the value of resistors and capacitors, know what a transistor looks like, identify integrated circuit packages, and be familiar with several different connectors. In addition, you will need to know how to read a component manufacturer's data sheet to determine how the part should be installed in a circuit and where to make the connections specified by a schematic diagram.

How to Identify Resistor Values

One of the more common electronic components is the resistor. You can see what one looks like in Figure II-1.

Figure II-1: Resistor

A resistor reduces, or resists, the flow of electrical current. Think of it as a dam that holds back water, letting only a certain amount flow through.

A resistor has its resistance value in Ohms marked with color bands on its side. Each color band represents a number you can plug into the equation illustrated in Figure II-2. The values for the colors are given in Table II-1.

Combining Resistors

Resistors can be combined to change the net value. If two resistors are combined in series, their values are added. If they are combined in parallel, their values are determined by the equations depicted below.

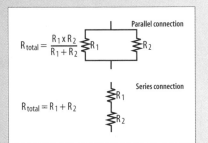

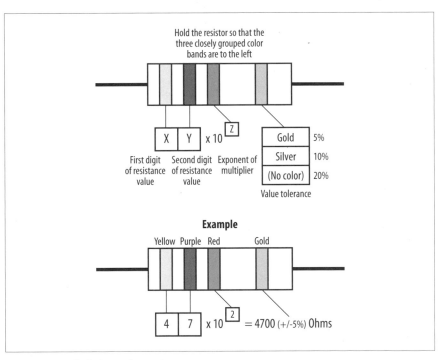

Figure II-2: Calculating resistor values

Table II-1. Resistor color values

Color	Numeric value
Black	0
Brown	1
Red	2
Orange	3
Yellow	4
Green	5
Blue	6
Purple (Violet)	7
Gray	8
White	9

Resistors are rated for how much power they can handle. Typical power ratings for small resistors are 1/8, 1/4, and 1/2 watts. Do not exceed the wattage rating: doing so causes the resistor to heat up and fail.

Each resistor is rated for how close its actual value is to the markings on it. This accuracy is specified either by the vendor or by one of the colored bands displayed on the resistor. A silver band means that the actual value is guaranteed to be within 10 percent of its marked value. A gold band means that the actual value is guaranteed to be within 5 percent of its marked value.

How to Identify Capacitor Values

Capacitors store electrical energy and are similar in some ways to small batteries. A capacitor contains two metal plates and some sort of solid or semiliquid chemical. Figure II-3 shows some of the different shapes and sizes of capacitors. From left to right are electrolytic radial lead large value, axial lead electrolytic, standard electrolytic radial lead, tantalum radial lead, ceramic radial lead, stacked metal film radial lead, and miniature polyester metalized film radial lead.

Capacitance is measured in Farads, with the letter F after the value used as shorthand. The value of the capacitor can be from a trillionth of a Farad (referred to as a pico Farad with the shorthand pF) to whole Farads.

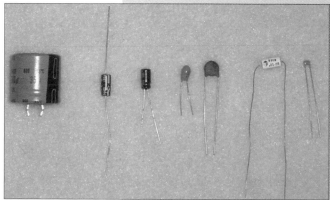

Figure II-3: Capacitors

Capacitors in Series and Parallel

A capacitor stores electrical energy. Capacitors can be combined to increase or decrease the capacitance value. You can see how the net capacitance is calculated through series and parallel connections below.

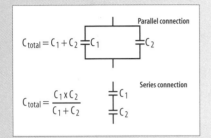

Capacitor Values and Polarization

The capacitance value is typically marked on the outside of its package. Tantalum and electrolytic parts are usually polarized, with either a plus or a minus symbol printed on the side of the part with an arrow pointing to that terminal. It is very important to pay attention to this and install the part according to the schematic diagram. If a polarized capacitor is installed backward, it may smoke and pop off your circuit board when power is applied.

Prefixes are often added to the capacitance value, so that you can avoid writing out large numbers. Table II-2 gives the common prefixes and their value multiplier.

Table II-2. Capacitance value prefixes

Prefix	Symbol	Value multiplier
Pico	p	10E-12
Nano	n	10E-9
Micro	μ	10E-6
Milli	m	10E-3
Kilo	K	10E3
Mega	M	10E6
Giga	G	10E9

For example, if a capacitor has a value of 10 pico-Farads (10 pF), it has a value of 10 x 10E-12 Farads (10E-12 is scientific notation for 1 divided by 10 to the 12th power).

Types of capacitors

There are a large number of capacitor types. Each type has different characteristics and is used for different applications. A few of the more common types are listed here with their general characteristics.

Electrolytic

The electrolytic capacitor is most like a regular battery. It contains layers of metal foil surrounded by an electrolyte paste (thus the name "electrolytic").

These capacitors are generally used for low-frequency filtering such as with power supplies and audio circuits. They can have values from a few tenths of a micro-Farad to over one Farad. The value tolerance of electrolytic capacitors is typically large; plus or minus 20 percent is not uncommon. The values of these capacitors vary greatly with temperature. When a high-frequency signal is applied to this type of capacitor, it ceases behaving as a capacitor.

Electrolytic capacitors are very small for the amount of capacitance they contain and are relatively inexpensive.

It is important to note that most electrolytic capacitors are polarized; they have plus and minus terminals. They must be installed with the plus terminal connected to a positive signal, and the minus to ground or to a negative signal. Electrolytic capacitors also exhibit some charge leakage; if one is charged up and left on its own, the charge will drain off.

Ceramic

A ceramic capacitor has the simplest design structure, consisting of two metal plates with a chemical coating between them. A ceramic material coats and protects the metal plates.

Ceramic capacitors can be used for a variety of applications. They are typically very stable over a wide temperature range, have a tight tolerance, and retain their capacitance over a wide frequency range. They are available in values from a few pico-Farads up to a few micro-Farads.

Ceramic capacitors are non-polarized; they can be placed in a circuit without concern for which terminal is connected to the positive signal. They also have very low leakage; once charged, they will hold that charge for a relatively long period of time.

Tantalum

Making this type of capacitor involves placing a tiny pellet of tantalum, a rare element, on a wire, growing an $MnO2$ layer, and attaching another wire. The package is covered in plastic or ceramics. The tantalum element can store a large amount of charge in a small space.

This type of capacitor exhibits low leakage current, a small size for relatively large capacitance, and good temperature stability. However, it has a low operating voltage (50 volts maximum depending on the part), and it is polarized. If the plus side is connected to a negative voltage, the capacitor will likely be permanently damaged and make a nice pop or bang when it dies.

Which capacitor for which job?

Electrolytic capacitors are typically used as power supply filters where the capacitance value is not critical but large capacitance is needed, up to the Farad range. This type of capacitor's value can vary 20 percent or more from the value marked on the package.

Ceramic capacitors are typically used for timing circuits where a tight tolerance value is required. These capacitors are generally available only in small values, typically less than 1 uF.

Tantalum capacitors are typically used for power supply filtering where the size of the capacitor package needs to be small. These capacitors can have capacitance values close to electrolytics but are much smaller and can cost more.

Transistor Types

There are two basic types of transistors: Bipolar and Metal Oxide Semiconductor Field Effect Transistor (MOSFET).

Bipolar: The first types of transistors developed were called bipolar, referring to the type of semiconductor used. Bipolar transistors typically have three connections: a collector (an input), an emitter (an output), and a base (a control). Current in a bipolar transistor flows from the collector to the emitter and is controlled by the current flowing into the base. Unlike MOSFET transistors, bipolar transistors are not sensitive to static electricity.

MOSFET: Metal Oxide Semiconductor Field Effect Transistors were invented after the bipolar transistor. There are typically three connections in a MOSFET: a drain (input), a source (output), and a gate (control). These transistors work differently from bipolar transistors in that you can control the current flow between the drain and the source by a voltage applied to the gate. MOSFETs are sensitive to static electricity and should be handled carefully to avoid damage. MOSFETs belong to a family of transistors that include P-channel and N-channel FETs and JFETs (Junction Field Effect Transistors).

How to Identify Transistors

Transistors are switches that control the flow of current in a circuit. Depending on what type it is, either voltage or current can control these switches. Transistors are made from materials that change their resistance based on a control voltage or current. They are typically made from pure silicon with trace amounts of other elements added in. Figure II-4 displays different examples of transistor packages.

Most transistors have three connections: an input, an output, and a control. These connections are referred to differently depending on the type of transistor.

Figure II-4: Transistor packages

How to Identify Integrated Circuit and Component Packages

Throughout this book, I mention two types of packages for the components you'll use: surface mount (SMT) and through-hole (also called DIPs). The following are brief descriptions for these two circuit-packaging technologies.

Surface-mount components

Surface-mount (SMT) components sit flat on top of a circuit board. Connection pins are spaced more closely than in through-hole components, and SMT parts are much smaller than through-hole parts. Several examples of SMT parts are shown in Figure II-5. From left to right are a surface-mount inductor, a 0603 surface-mount resistor, a surface-mount SOIC logic gate, a 1206 surface-mount tantalum capacitor, and a surface-mount SOT-23 transistor.

Figure II-5: Surface mount parts

Through-hole components

Though-hole components are an older circuit-packaging technology. As the name implies, the connection pins of the parts fit in holes that go through the circuit board. The dual inline package (DIP) is used for through-hole integrated circuits. You can see an example of DIP components in Figure II-6.

Figure II-6:
Dual inline package (DIP)

How to Identify Connectors

Using high-quality connectors will reduce troubleshooting for a project and prevent failures over time. A friend of mine who has been building autonomous robots for 15 years once told me that a robot is actually a careful study in the design and use of connectors. While hacking you will often want to take a signal from one circuit board to another or to provide a different power source.

There are hundreds of connector types in use today. I have outlined two such connectors, which are used in the upcoming chapters.

Insulation displacement connectors

IDC connectors are very common and allow you to quickly connect a multi-conductor ribbon cable to a large number of tiny metal sockets. This type of connector is used in almost every IDE hard-drive cable. The number of supported connections can range from as few as 8 to almost 100. You can see what a small IDC connector looks like by itself in Figure II-7 and connected to a piece of ribbon cable in Figure II-8. These connectors are attached to the cable using a special tool or a pair of pliers.

Figure II-7: IDC connector

Figure II-8: IDC connector on cable

Figure II-9: DB9 connector

Figure II-10: DB25 connector

DB9 and DB25 connectors

These connectors are commonly used to connect to the serial port of a PC. A DB9 connector is shown in Figure II-9; a DB25 is in Figure II-10.

The pins on these connectors can be connected to a cable by soldering the wires to the connector. Some types of these connectors have an IDC connector on the back to allow connection to a cable without soldering.

How to Read a Manufacturer's Data Sheet

In the chapters that follow, you will need to consult the specification for a number of integrated circuits to determine how to properly connect the components according to the given schematics. These specifications are called *data sheets*. The easiest way to learn how to extract the data-sheet information is to walk through one. Each company has its own format, but the information provided is common.

The sample data sheet we will tour is for a voltage regulator. Figure II-11 shows the first page of a data sheet with some of the more important information labeled. Location A is the name of the company that makes the part. Location B is the part number; this is the same part number that appears on your schematic diagrams. A short phrase describing the function of the component is located at C. The text under location D is an overview of what the part does and what it can be used for. (Often, you'll find brief comments on the packages here as well.) Location E describes the top-line features and important technical specifications to keep in mind. Location F shows the pin numbers and the function of all the available packages as well as the codes for each package.

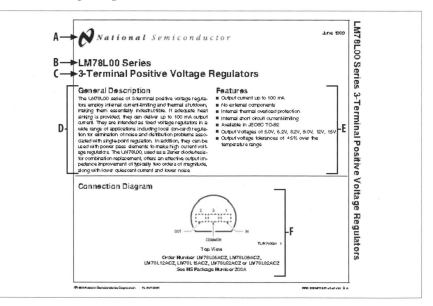

Figure II-11: Example data sheet

As you learn more about electronics, you can use the information in the rest of the data sheet. For now, all you need to know is how to connect the part in the circuit you are building.

How to Use a Plug Board to Create a Simple Circuit

The plug board is a circuit prototyping tool that allows you to quickly build a circuit without soldering parts together. It is a set of plastic blocks with holes in it spaced 0.1 inches apart; you can see what one looks like in Figure II-12. Wires connect each hole horizontally and vertically. Rows 1, 2, 3, and so forth are wired together as per the dashed line in Figure II-13. The two slim outside and center plastic blocks are wired vertically according to the red and blue lines printed on them. Most plug boards on the market follow this convention, but be sure to check the data sheets for the particular model you want to use, or check the plug board manually with a multi-meter.

You can create temporary circuits on a plug board by pushing the metal pins on an integrated circuit into the holes in the plug board, as shown in Figure II-14. You can push resistors, capacitors, and other components into the holes as well. Make electrical connections between parts of the circuit by taking a piece of solid core wire, stripping the insulation off of the ends, and pressing the ends into the appropriate holes in the plug board. Most plug boards will accommodate solid core wire of 24 or 22 gauge. Do not use stranded wire, as it will be very difficult to press the small strands into the holes.

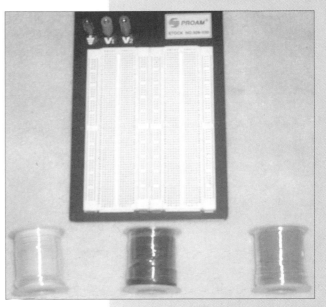

Figure II-12: Plug board and wire

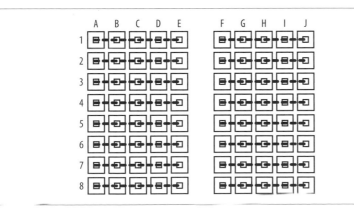

Figure II-13: Horizontal plug board wiring

Figure II-14: Plug board close-up

Plug boards are useful for quick prototyping of digital circuits with signals that run up to about 10 MHz as well as any audio circuit.

Let's have a little fun with a small circuit on a plug board. Gather together the components for the circuit shown in Figure II-15: a small plug board, some 24-gauge solid core wire, and a 9V battery.

Plug each of the integrated circuits into the plug board (make sure that you purchase the parts in a DIP package), and use the 30-gauge wire to make the connections. You don't need to be super-neat in your connections. Inspect your work before you connect the power. Don't forget to connect power and ground on the CD4040 component even though the pins are not shown in the schematic in Figure II-15.

Connect a 9V battery to Vcc and speak into the microphone. You should see the LEDs flash when you speak. Play with the circuit a bit. Change the value of C3 to 1 uF and 0.1 uF to see what happens. Change R3 to 1K Ohms. Move the LEDs to different pins. Experiment with the circuit. This is the beauty of using a plug board: changes can be tried out in a few seconds with no soldering.

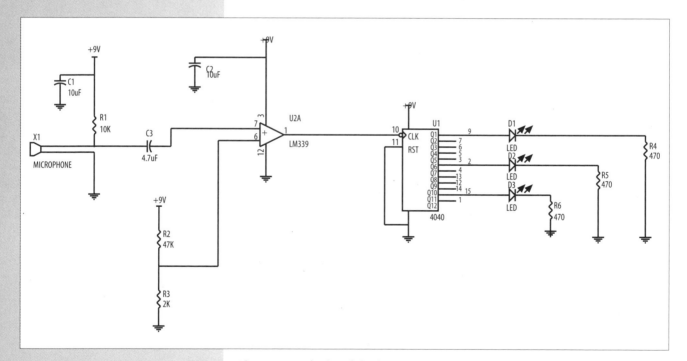

Figure II-15: Plug board circuit

Summary

These skills should allow you to build the advanced projects in the book, such as the one in Chapter 8, How to Hack a Building-Size Display. The parts mentioned here are ones that are commonly used, but the list is by no means exhaustive. To expand your knowledge of what is available, read through an electronics component catalog such as the one from DigiKey (*http://www.digikey.com*). When I have a bit of free time, I like to browse the catalog to see what new chips and connectors are available. Browsing the web sites of the actual component manufacturers is also a good way to learn more. Read through a few data sheets and applications notes for new parts from one of the big semiconductor companies. The application notes are usually good tutorials on how the new parts work and what types of circuits can be made with them, and can often give you ideas for a new hack of your own.

How to Build a Digital Video Recorder

7

Cost

$0–200

Time

a weekend

Difficulty

moderate

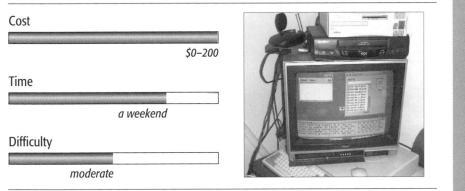

What You Need

- An Intel- or AMD-based PC running at 400+ MHz
- A Brooktree-based video capture card
- An NTSC video output converter
- An optional IR remote
- Other items listed in Exhibit A

In 1998, two companies, ReplayTV and TiVo, began shipping a new type of home video recording device. These new devices, dubbed personal video recorders or PVRs, combined an embedded computer, modem, hard drive, and video compression/decompression hardware. The PVR allowed you to record television programs onto a hard drive and program future recordings using an onscreen program guide. The program guide is downloaded automatically every night from a web site via a built-in modem. Another interesting feature is *live pause,* where a live TV program can be paused and resumed.

Both of these devices use a paid-access program guide. The software that runs them, although based on Linux, is not easy to modify or hack and can cost $300 or more.

I will show you how to build your own quick-and-dirty Linux-based PVR using parts you probably already have around the house. When you are done, the system will not only record and play back programs, but the files produced can be accessed from any other PC on the same network. You can even take these files and burn VCD (video CD) format disks for archival purposes. If you have a PDA that can access your home network, you can use it as a remote control instead of a dedicated IR remote control.

Credits

All photographs and code listings copyright © 2003 Russell Pavlicek.

Project Overview

This project uses a standard PC with video input and output cards to record and play back standard NTSC video signals. We will cover how to build a unit with just the basic time-delay recording functions, but additional features such as live pause and a full GUI program-guide interface can be added later. The costs should be minimal, as you probably already have an old PC that will work well for this hack.

You will put together a PC system, load a recent version of the Linux operating system, and then load several video capture and playback utilities.

I would like to thank Russell Pavlicek for inspiring this hack. You can check out his web site at *http://www.linuxprofessionalsolutions.com/pavlicek/ tv.html*.

Hardware Assembly Instructions

This project requires putting together a standard PC. You do not need to go out and purchase the fastest PC on the market; a machine that runs at 400 MHz or faster should be sufficient for the basic functions. You may want to get one a bit faster to ensure smooth video under all conditions.

Put together an Intel- or AMD-based PC with these components:

- 400+ MHz Celeron/AMD/Pentium processor.
- Brooktree 878-based capture card. The Pixelview PlayTV Pro card should do the trick.
- AGP or on-board VGA video card (16-bit color depth minimum).
- PCI or on-board 10/100 Ethernet.
- A USB mouse.
- Minimum of 128 MB of memory.
- Large hard drive. I recommend at least a 60GB, 7,200rpm hard drive.
- TVator Pro. This box takes a VGA signal and converts it to a regular TV signal. It should run about $45 and is available from *http://www. antec-inc.com/*. If you have a video card that already supports NTSC video output, you can avoid this part.
- Optional X10 video transmitter and receiver.
- Optional IR remote. This should be under $10 and would remove the need for a USB mouse to operate the system.
- USB keyboard and VGA monitor for system build. You will remove them for normal operation.
- Optional TV set to watch the programs.

Video Capture Cards

Almost any cheap, no-name video capture card that says it uses the Brooktree 878 chipset should work. Cards with this chipset are well supported by the Video4Linux project, upon which the software for this system is based. The video capture card market is very dynamic, so you should check *http://www.video4linux. net/* before buying a card.

In general, older cards may work better due to more mature software drivers.

You will probably want a slim case for the parts as well. A complete PC may even be available from eBay or a local computer shop with all of these parts already installed. The HP desktop PC case and system pictured in Figure 7-1 was upgraded with a new hard drive and worked well for this project.

Figure 7-1: Home-built PVR in place

Put the PC together and test it out with a standard VGA monitor before proceeding. You can install any operating system you like for testing because it will be replaced later.

Software Setup Instructions

The first thing you need to do is install a Mandrake Linux Version 8.2 package on your computer. Next, you will install a number of Video4Linux drivers and software packages. Finally, you will test out your system.

1. Install Mandrake Linux Version 8.2

Download or purchase a copy of Mandrake Linux 8.2 and install it on the PC you've constructed. The software should recognize all of the hardware. You will need to use a standard monitor when installing the software because it requires at least 800 by 600 resolution.

Which Version of Linux?

There are a number of Linux packages available today that will probably work with this project. Mandrake 8.2 was used and tested because it included XAWTV (X Athena Widget set for TV) and drivers for most video capture cards. If your Linux package does not include drivers for your video capture card and the XAWTV video record/playback utilities, you will need to obtain and load them yourself.

What Is a VCD?

VCD stands for video CD. VCDs use a file format that can be burned onto a standard compact disc and played back on most DVD players. For details on how to go about this, check out *http://sourceforge.net/projects/vcd-master/*.

Card ID

If you have chosen to use a different capture card, the "card=16" in this code should be changed to the card you are using. Check this web site for card ID details*: http://sdb.suse.de/en/sdb/html/cg_wintv.html*.

2. Configure the system

1. Start by creating a login account. A login of tv with no password will work well.

2. Create a directory to store your recorded programs. A directory called "shows" should work.

3. Add these lines to the */etc/modules.conf* file:

```
pre-install videodev modprobe -k tuner type=2
options bttv gbuffers=2 card=16 radio=1 fieldnr=1
```

4. Create a script that triggers video recording. Below is an example script called *rec* that you can locate in */home/tv*:

```
#!/bin/bash
if test -z "$2"; then echo "usage: channel lengthoftime"; exit; fi
f=shows/'date +%y%m%d-%a-%H_%M'
echo $f >> /tmp/TV_rec.err
echo "  Recording channel $1 ($2) at 'date'" >> /tmp/TV_rec.status
killall -9 xine 2>> /tmp/TV_rec.err
killall -9 mplayer 2>> /tmp/TV_rec.err
killall -9 xawtv 2>> /tmp/TV_rec.err
v4lctl setchannel $1 2>> /tmp/TV_rec.err
v4lctl volume 100 2>> /tmp/TV_rec.err
mencoder -tv  on:driver=v4l:device=/dev/video0:norm=NTSC:
          width=320:height=240 -oac copy -ovc lavc -lavcopts
vcodec=mpeg4:vbitrate=800 -vop pp=lb -endpos $2 -o $f.avi 2> /dev/
          null > /dev/null
echo "        Ended recording channel $1 at 'date'" >> /tmp/TV_
          rec.status
```

If you wish the files to be VCD-compatible, remove the mencoder line and replace it with:

```
streamer -n ntsc -q -t $2 -s 320x240 -r 20 -o $f.avi -f jpeg -j
86 -F stereo 2>> tmp/TV_rec.err
```

The mencoder format allows a very high frame rate (up to 27 fps on the system tested).

To operate the script, pass it the following arguments: the channel number, and a number of minutes and seconds to record. It will then record a file in the format "YYMMDD-day-HH_MM.avi" (e.g., 021008-Tue-19_00.avi) in the *shows* subdirectory.

This script does a lot of things that aren't really crucial. All the output is redirected to a log file for debugging purposes. It also writes to a status file before and after the recording.

If you are running other programs and your Linux PVR is not a dedicated machine, the killall -9 command is a bit harsh. You can replace this with a simple kill command instead or add a series of escalating termination commands to the script.

5. Create a script that triggers file playback. The script called *play* should be located in the home directory of the "tv" user and should look something like this:

```
#!/bin/bash
xine --auto-play=fh $1* > /tmp/TV_xine_play
```

This script accepts the name of the file you wish to play.

6. Create a script that can record programs at a later time. The Linux *cron* utility can be used for this purpose. Here is an example crontab file that triggers regular recording of several programs:

```
SHELL=/bin/bash
# Daily cleanup of anything over a week old
45 04 * * * $HOME/weekly_cleanup >> /tmp/TV_cleanup
# French News
00 19 * * * $HOME/rec 29 29:00
# Red Green
00 23 * * 6 $HOME/rec 3 28:00
```

7. Create a cleanup script that gets rid of old programs and reclaims disk space. The following script called *TV_cleanup* should be located in */tmp*:

```
#!/bin/bash
date
del_it="`find shows/ -mtime +6`"
if test -n "$del_it"; then echo "Deleting " $del_it; rm -f $del_
    it; fi
```

3. Test out the system

Now that you have all the base software loaded, you will want to start playing with time-shifted recording and playback. Follow these steps:

1. Boot up the system and log in as "tv".

2. Plug in an antenna source to the TV capture card.

3. Execute the record and playback scripts to ensure that everything is working correctly.

4. If you have successfully recorded and played back a program using a standard PC monitor, it is time to switch to a TV set where you will be watching your shows.

Hacking TiVo and Replay/SONICBlue Systems

One of the easiest things you can do to extend the current TiVo and ReplayTV boxes is to add additional hard drive space. There are a number of web sites devoted to this that you can check out. Here are a few:

http://rtvpatch.sourceforge.net/
http://tivo.samba.org/
http://www.tivofaq.com/

The procedures generally involve purchasing a new hard drive, connecting it and the original PVR hard drive to a Windows PC, and running some special software.

Raffi Krikorian has written an excellent book on TiVo hacks titled *TiVo Hacks: 100 Industrial-Strength Tips & Tools* (O'Reilly). It has some great enhancements for your TiVo.

Project Demo

Now that you've put together the hardware and loaded the appropriate software components, it is time to set up the system and record some TV shows!

Take your completed PC system and set it up next to the TV set you want to view your programs on. Follow these steps:

1. Power up the Linux box.

2. Ensure that a live cable TV or antenna is plugged into the TV capture card.

3. Connect the TVator Pro to the VGA output of the PC.

4. Connect a TV set to the output of the TVator Pro.

5. Connect the PC to your local area network.

6. Log in remotely and set up the crontab files to record your favorite shows.

7. Play back your favorite shows by executing the *play* script from a remote login.

Your completed system should now look something like the setup in Figure 7-2. You're done. Time to enjoy some TV!

Nifty GUIs

This project describes how to build a system with a simple, text-based user interface. If you are interested in something a bit fancier, check out these web sites. In order to run this software, you may need to have a machine that is a bit faster than 400 MHz.

> http://www.mythtv.org/
> http://freevo.sourceforge.net/
> http://eboxy.sourceforge.net/
> http://www.cadsoft.de/people/kls/vdr/`

Figure 7-2: Home-built PVR in action

Extensions

This system gives you the basic capabilities of video record and playback, but there are a number of other interesting features you could add.

Dedicated IR remote control

The Linux InfraRed Control (LIRC) package allows you to use an inexpensive Packard Bell infrared remote (often available on eBay for under $10). This remote connects to the serial port.

You need to load the LIRC serial port driver instead of the standard Linux driver. Because it's only recently been integrated into Mandrake, LIRC can be difficult to set up.

Note that */etc/lircd.conf* defines a series of codes corresponding to button names. Part of the flexibility of LIRC is that the button names are definable. Use whatever names make sense to you given the remote in question, but be sure to use the exact same button names when you refer to them in */etc/lircmd.conf* and *~/.lircd.conf*. I have configured *.lircd.conf* to use XAWTV by pressing Aux1, and xine by pressing Aux2. By using the mode structures (also not documented exceptionally well), the remote buttons are reprogrammed to provide appropriate input for each program. It's really quite cool.

Add the following autostart script in *.kde/Autostart/*:

```
#!/bin/bash
irexec 2> /tmp/irexec.err > /tmp/irexec.out &
irxevent 2> /tmp/irxevent.err > /tmp/irxevent.out &
```

Add the following line to */etc/modules.conf* to load the LIRC driver for the serial port:

```
alias char-major-61 lirc_serial
```

The files used to configure LIRC for the Packard Bell remote are listed in Exhibit B.

You will need to modify the XFree86 server configuration according to the instructions in the LIRC documentation.

When you start *xine*, load the playlist with all the AVI files in the *shows* directory. Then use the menu within *xine* as the playback menu. It's not perfect, but it's a decent start.

Wireless PDA remote control

If your PDA has an 802.11b wireless card and you have an 802.11b gateway to your home network, you can run a Telnet session from the PDA to the Linux PVR and trigger all record and playback functions. With a little clever hacking, you can set up a simple web server on the Linux PVR and access a simple control page from the wireless PDA.

Noisy Video

After playing with the system for a while, you may notice a series of static vertical noise lines on the TV image. It varies by station and can be adjusted by wiggling the TV capture card. As it turns out, this is a frequent problem on many types of capture cards. If you want to modify the capture card to fix this potential problem, go to: *http://www.avsforum.com* and search for "VERTICAL NOISE BARS".

VCD burning

If your system has a CD burner installed and it is supported by Linux, you can make CDs that contain your video files. These can then be played back on any PC or a home DVD player.

You will need to download a set of VCD file-manipulation tools from *http://sourceforge.net/projects/vcdmaster/* and install them. A large number of software packages can create VCD-compatible images, which can then be burned onto a CDR.

Share files over a network

If you wish to allow other Linux machines to access your recorded programs, you can accomplish this in a number of ways.

- Enable the FTP daemon on the source machine, and use FTP to get the desired files.

- Use the mount command to mount the remote directory for NFS.

- Enable the SSH daemon and use the SCP command to get the files.

If you want Windows-based machines to be able to access the files, enable Samba and configure it appropriately.

Exhibit A: Bill of Materials

You will need all of the parts on this list. If you don't build your own PC, be sure that you have the VGA to NTSC converter, the TV set, the optional remote control, and a compatible video capture card.

Item	Quantity	Notes
PC	1	400+MHz Celeron/AMD/Pentium processor with ATX motherboard (or compact motherboard) capable of supporting the chosen processor with 3 PCI slots, 2 USB ports, CD-ROM drive, floppy drive, case, power supply, and optional AGP graphics slot
Video capture card	1	Brooktree 878-based capture card; the Pixelview PlayTV Pro card works well
Video card	1	AGP or on board VGA video card (16-bit color depth minimum)
Mouse	1	USB or PS/2 based
Keyboard	1	USB or PS/2 based
Memory	1	128 MB minimum
Hard drive	1	60 GB or more, 7200 rpm
Linux operating system	1	Downloaded Mandrake Linux and Video4Linux drivers
TV set	1	To display your recorded programs
Remote control	1	Optional; Packard Bell model BPCS #146541 or other brand
CD read/write drive	1	Optional; allows saving of programs in VDC format
VGA to NTSC converter	1	TVator Pro; available from *http://www.antec-inc.com*

Exhibit B: Dedicated IR Remote Control Support Files

These files can also be found at *http://www.linuxprofessionalsolutions.com/pavlicek/tv.htm.*

/etc/lircd.conf

```
# Copyright (C) 1999 Christoph Bartelmus
#
# You may only use this file if you make it available to others,
# i.e. if you send it to <lirc@bartelmus.de>
#
# this config file was automatically generated
# using lirc-0.6.5(any) on Tue Oct 15 02:57:40 2002
#
# contributed by
#
# brand:                          irr.tmp
# model no. of remote control:
# devices being controlled by this remote:
#

begin remote

  name   PackardBell
  bits          16
  flags SPACE_ENC|CONST_LENGTH
  eps           30
  aeps         100

  header      9007   4528
  one          571   1667
  zero         571    557
  ptrail       541
  repeat      9001   2285
  pre_data_bits 16
  pre_data      0x8F7
  gap         107827
  toggle_bit     0


    begin codes
        Menu                     0x00000000000008F7
        Mute                     0x0000000000008877
        Help                     0x00000000000020DF
        Phone                    0x000000000000609F
        Message                  0x00000000000022DD
        SR5                      0x000000000000629D
        CD                       0x000000000000A05F
        Aux1                     0x000000000000E01F
        Aux2                     0x000000000000A25D
        Aux3                     0x000000000000E21D
        Enter                    0x000000000000708F
        ChannelUp                0x000000000000B04F
        ChannelDown              0x00000000000030CF
        Display                  0x000000000000F00F
```

/etc/lircd.conf (continued)

```
        VolumeUp              0x00000000000048B7
        VolumeDown            0x000000000000C837
        N1                    0x00000000000042BD
        N2                    0x000000000000C23D
        N3                    0x000000000000E817
        N4                    0x00000000000002FD
        N5                    0x000000000000827D
        N6                    0x0000000000006897
        N7                    0x00000000000040BF
        N8                    0x000000000000C03F
        N9                    0x000000000000A857
        Asterisk              0x00000000000000FF
        N0                    0x000000000000807F
        Pound                 0x00000000000028D7
        MB1                   0x000000000000B847
        MB2                   0x00000000000038C7
        ArrowUp               0x000000000000906F
        ArrowDown             0x00000000000050AF
        ArrowLeft             0x00000000000010EF
        ArrowRight            0x000000000000D02F
    end codes

end remote
```

/etc/lircmd.conf

```
#
# lircmd config file
#

PROTOCOL IntelliMouse
#PROTOCOL MouseSystems

# ACCELERATOR start max multiplier

ACCELERATOR 2 30 5

#ACTIVATE * MENU

MOVE_N  * N2
MOVE_NE * N3
MOVE_E  * N6
MOVE_SE * N9
MOVE_S  * N8
MOVE_SW * N7
MOVE_W  * N4
MOVE_NW * N1
#MOVE_N   * ARROW_UP
#MOVE_E   * ARROW_RIGHT
#MOVE_S   * ARROW_DOWN
#MOVE_W   * ARROW_LEFT
#MOVE_IN  * CH_UP
#MOVE_OUT * CH_DOWN
```

/etc/lircmd.conf *(continued)*

```
#BUTTON1_TOGGLE * 5
#BUTTON2_TOGGLE * 0
#BUTTON3_TOGGLE * LIST

#BUTTON1_CLICK * OK
#BUTTON1_CLICK * MUTE
#BUTTON3_CLICK * POWER

# BUTTONx_CLICK, BUTTONx_UP, BUTTONx_DOWN are also possible

MOVE_N * ArrowUp
MOVE_S * ArrowDown
MOVE_W * ArrowLeft
MOVE_E * ArrowRight

BUTTON1_CLICK * MB1
BUTTON2_CLICK * MB2
BUTTON3_CLICK * Help
```

/etc/lircd.conf

```
begin
        button = Enter
        prog   = irxevent
        config = Key Return CurrentWindow
end
begin
        button = SR5
        prog   = irexec
        config = xterm -geometry 50x20+80+40 &
end
begin
        button = Aux1
        prog   = irexec
        config = xawtv -geometry +50+70 &
#     flags  = once
        mode   = tv
end
begin
        button = Aux2
        prog   = irexec
        config = xine -f shows/*avi &
#     flags  = once
        mode   = xine
end

begin tv
        begin
                prog = irxevent
                button = Asterisk
                config = Key f xawtv
        end
        begin
```

/etc/lircd.conf *(continued)*

```
                prog = irxevent
                button = Pound
                config = Key q xawtv
        end
        begin
                prog = irxevent
                button = ChannelUp
                config = Key space xawtv
        end
        begin
                prog = irxevent
                button = ChannelDown
                config = Key Page_Down xawtv
        end
        begin
                prog = irxevent
                button = Menu
                config = Key ctrl-z xawtv
        end
        begin
                prog   = irxevent
                button = Mute
                config = Key KP_Enter xawtv
        end
    begin
            prog   = irxevent
            button = VolumeUp
            config = Key KP_Add xawtv
    end
    begin
            prog   = irxevent
            button = VolumeDown
            config = Key KP_Subtract xawtv
    end
        begin
                prog = irxevent
                button = N0
                config = Key KP_0 xawtv
        end
        begin
                prog = irxevent
                button = N1
                config = Key KP_1 xawtv
        end
        begin
                prog = irxevent
                button = N2
                config = Key KP_2 xawtv
        end
        begin
                prog = irxevent
                button = N3
                config = Key KP_3 xawtv
        end
```

/etc/lircd.conf *(continued)*

```
        begin
                prog = irxevent
                button = N4
                config = Key KP_4 xawtv
        end
        begin
                prog = irxevent
                button = N5
                config = Key KP_5 xawtv
        end
        begin
                prog = irxevent
                button = N6
                config = Key KP_6 xawtv
        end
        begin
                prog = irxevent
                button = N7
                config = Key KP_7 xawtv
        end
        begin
                prog = irxevent
                button = N8
                config = Key KP_8 xawtv
        end
        begin
                prog = irxevent
                button = N9
                config = Key KP_9 xawtv
        end
end tv

begin xine
        begin
                prog = irxevent
                button = Asterisk
                config = Key f xine
        end
        begin
                prog = irxevent
                button = Pound
                config = Key q xine
        end
        begin
                prog = irxevent
                button = Menu
                config = Key g xine
        end
        begin
                prog = irxevent
                button = Display
                config = Key space xine
```

/etc/lircd.conf *(continued)*

```
        end
        begin
                prog = irxevent
                button = N0
                config = Key 0 xine
        end
        begin
                prog = irxevent
                button = N1
                config = Key 1 xine
        end
        begin
                prog = irxevent
                button = N2
                config = Key 2 xine
        end
        begin
                prog = irxevent
                button = N3
                config = Key 3 xine
        end
        begin
                prog = irxevent
                button = N4
                config = Key 4 xine
        end
        begin
                prog = irxevent
                button = N5
                config = Key 5 xine
        end
        begin
                prog = irxevent
                button = N6
                config = Key 6 xine
        end
        begin
                prog = irxevent
                button = N7
                config = Key 7 xine
    end
    begin
                prog = irxevent
                button = N8
                config = Key 8 xine
    end
    begin
                prog = irxevent
                button = N9
                config = Key 9 xine
    end
    begin
```

/etc/lircd.conf *(continued)*

```
            prog   = irxevent
            button = VolumeUp
            config = Key shift-v xine
    end
    begin
            prog   = irxevent
            button = VolumeDown
            config = Key v xine
    end
        begin
                prog = irxevent
                button = ChannelUp
                config = Key Right xine
        end
        begin
                prog = irxevent
                button = ChannelDown
                config = Key Left xine
        end
        begin
                prog = irxevent
                button = Mute
                config = Key ctrl-m xine
                config = Key ctrl-M xine
        end
end xine
```

How to Hack a Building-Size Display

8

Cost

$50–5000

Time

several weekends

Difficulty

very difficult

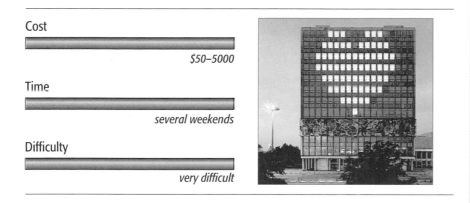

What You Need

- x86-based computer (Intel or AMD) running Windows with a free printer port
- One LED driver board
- 144 ultra-bright LEDs
- 100 meters of CAT5 wire
- 5 amp, 5 volt DC power supply
- 20' x 5' roll of chicken wire
- 10' x 18' white sheet or frosted plastic shower curtain
- Hot-melt glue gun and glue or silicon rubber sealant
- Electrical crimp tool and metal crimps
- Other items listed in Exhibit A

In 2001, a group of determined individuals with a keen eye toward art and technology created a project called "Blinkenlights." This project took a twelve-story building and turned it into a large bitmapped display upon which they put animations, static images, and a working interactive "Pong" game.

The project was completed by the Chaos Computer Club of Germany, which was celebrating its twentieth anniversary. They wanted to mark the occasion and give a gift to the city of Berlin. From September 12, 2001 to February 23, 2002, an office building in Berlin was hacked to become a giant interactive computer.

Behind the building's front windows on the top eight floors they placed 144 lamps. A computer switched each lamp on and off independently to produce a monochrome matrix of 18-by-8 pixels, transforming the building into a huge display. In the evening, an ever-changing array of animations and images could be seen from several miles away. There was even an interactive component: spectators could play the old arcade classic Pong on the building using their mobile phones, and passersby could place their own "love letters" on the screen.

Credits

Photographs copyright © 2003 Chaos Computer Club and Rene Schneider (Figure 8-28).

145

The Berlin Blinkenlights installation was planned and built in four weeks, and ran for 23 weeks and 5 days in total. Even today, the Chaos Computer Club (also known as the CCC) continues to improve the system, and they have released the software for free under the GPL. Linux and PDA-based tools and simulators for creating animations and images for the system can be found at the Blinkenlights web site (*http://www.blinkenlights.de/*).

In this chapter, I will first describe how to build a smaller version that can use the side of your house instead of a twelve-story building for the display area. Next, I will describe how to build the project as it was implemented in Berlin.

If you decide to wire up a large building, I would suggest that you get together a group of friends to help out. There is a lot of wiring required to set up this hack. If you build the smaller "home" version, you can probably wire it yourself.

I would like to thank Björn Barnekow (programming, design), Fiedel (electronics), Packet (programming), Papillon (installation), Prom (programming), Sven Neumann (programming), Tim Pritlove (project coordination), Tobias Engel (programming), and the entire Chaos Computer Club for their support and information. I would also like to thank Rene Schneider for his contribution to the small-scale hardware assembly instructions.

Blinkenlights

The term "blinkenlights" was first coined to describe the diagnostic lights found on many early computers.

Project Overview

There are several configurations for this hack. You can build a display system that will fit on the side of your house, on a small desktop-size system, or on a twelve-story building.

If you wish to build the home-size system or the desktop system, continue with the hardware construction steps here. If you wish to build the large building system, skip ahead to the Large-Scale Hardware Assembly Instructions section.

Small-Scale Hardware Assembly Instructions

In this section, you will assemble a custom LED driver board, construct an LED frame, and load an application onto a PC. Obviously, the small version of the project requires quite a bit less time to build and set up than the building-size version. The most time-consuming task of the mini-Blinkenlights project will probably be the wiring of the LED drivers and the LED frame.

If you don't want a home-size display, you can build a simple desktop system by building only the circuit and using shorter wires to connect smaller LEDs to the outputs of the 4049 ICs. See *http://www.jalcds.de/blinkenleds/* for details.

1. Determine where you will set up the system

Locate a flat vertical surface at least 10 feet tall and 18 feet wide, with easy access. An ideal area is the side of a building with two windows 20 feet apart at the top. A hallway wall of a college dormitory is also an excellent choice.

Measure the area where you want to set up the display. You will need to use this measurement later when you build the holding frame.

2. Assemble the LED driver board

You will now build the circuit board specified by the mini-Blinkenlights schematics in Exhibits E through M. One of the circuit boards has 144 LED driver output pins connected to the LED on the frame, along with a few ground return wires. The Shift Register board can be mounted up to 25 feet away from the PC via a long printer cable. You may be able to get longer distances, but you will have to experiment.

All the components should fit on one or two prototype perforated boards. Look ahead to Figure 8-2 for an example of this.

Install sockets for all integrated circuits

Trim one piece of perf board to a rectangle with the dimensions of 4" x 5", and one to dimensions of 12" x 6". Take the first piece of perf board, install the 18 16-pin IC sockets, and place them in a manner similar to what is shown in Figure 8-1. Solder the pins of each socket to the metal in the holes. The easiest way to do this is to gently bend the two opposite corners of the socket to hold the unsoldered socket in place, flip the circuit board over, and solder these two corners before soldering the rest of the pins. Add a 25-pin printer port connector (P7) and a latching power connector (buy a hard-drive power extender cable and cut off the connector end you will need).

Next, take the second piece of perf board and install 18 20-pin IC sockets. Leave room on the edges of the board for the connectors. The power for the entire circuit board will come from an external PC-style power supply.

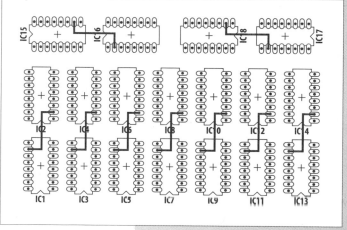

Figure 8-1: Hand-built circuit board

You should install the sockets in the board so that if any IC is incorrectly wired and becomes damaged when you apply power to the circuit, you don't have to resolder the part in place again. Just pop out the bad part, and pop in a replacement.

Connect all integrated circuits

Once all the sockets have been soldered in place for the controller board, you need to connect them according to the schematic diagrams in Exhibits E through H.

This is a good time to check your work to ensure that everything is wired properly. You should also check that the power and ground wire are not shorted together by using a multi-meter to measure the resistance between these two parts of the circuit. The meter should read infinite resistance (or at least over 1 mega-Ohm) when you place the probes on these parts of the circuits. Also spot-check the wires you soldered by setting a multi-meter to measure resistance. The meter should read close to zero resistance when you place the probes at the end of each circuit you wired. Check as many places as possible, since you just completed a lot of wiring, and even one mistake can cause the circuit to fail.

Lay out your circuit according to the diagram in Figure 8-2. Connector P7 connects to a PC parallel port. Connectors J1 through J9 and J11 through J13 are optional. They can be used to connect the Shift Register (Exhibit F) and LED Driver Connectors circuits (Exhibit E) to the LED Buffers circuit if you build them on two separate boards. If you place all of the chips on one board, these connectors are not required. If the circuits are separated, ensure that the ribbon cable used to connect them is no longer than six inches in length.

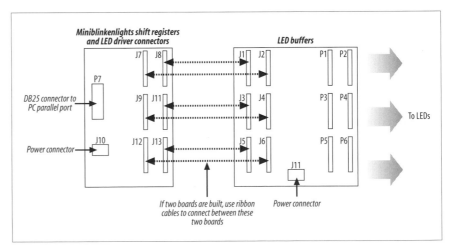

Figure 8-2: Small-scale system board overview

Install all components and test circuit board

After you have soldered all of the sockets in place, wired them, and checked your work, install the integrated circuits. Press each chip into the socket, making sure they are oriented correctly.

Before you connect the power supply, ensure that you have properly connected the terminal. Use a multi-meter to measure the voltage on the pins you intend to connect to the board and ensure that 5 volts is where you expect it. If you connect the power supply backward, you will probably destroy all of the chips you just wired.

Place circuit board in enclosure

This circuit board can be placed up to 50 feet from the controlling PC, so you will need to enclose the circuit board in a plastic or metal box. If done properly, this enclosure will keep the electronics away from the elements and allow it to be placed outside next to the LED frame. A number of electronics distributors, such as DigiKey and Mouser, sell various plastic enclosures. Check their catalogs for models that will fit your circuit board.

After placing and mounting the circuit board inside the enclosure, you will need to cut holes in the box to allow access to the power cable, the printer cable, and the LED connections. If you plan to place the box outdoors, seal the holes after all the cables have been installed with RTV silicon sealant.

3. Assemble and wire the LED frame

This will probably be one of the most time-consuming steps. You now need to decide how far apart to place the LED "pixels." If you want the biggest possible display, simply take the height of the available area measured in Step 1 and divide it by 8 to get the vertical resolution. Take the width and divide it by 18 to get the horizontal resolution. These two numbers will be the vertical and horizontal spacing for the LEDs, respectively.

Gather together all of your LEDs, the wire mesh, some solid copper wire (you can use CAT5 wire), a crimping tool, and 144 open metal crimps. All of these items, with the exception of the LEDs, can be found at your local hardware store. The LEDs can be purchased at DigiKey. Any LED will work, but I suggest that you use a super-bright LED. This particular LED is red. White LEDs are available at substantially higher cost: $0.37 each for the red LEDs and $2.49 each for the white LEDs.

From the measurements in Step 1, roll out and connect together sheets of the wire mesh to make a rectangle of the desired size. Make sure that the metal mesh strips are securely fastened together. The mesh will serve not only to support the LEDs but also as an electrical return path (ground) for the driving current. The dual use of the mesh will greatly simplify the wiring. You can see what this looks like in Figure 8-3.

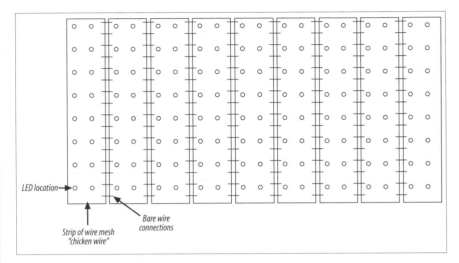

Figure 8-3: Wire mesh setup

One you have connected the strips of wire mesh together, you will need to connect the LEDs to the mesh. The long leg of each LED needs to be electrically and structurally held onto the wire mesh. Begin by bending the leads of the LED as shown in Figure 8-4. Bend the short leg toward the flat side and the long leg toward the other side. You may need to change the height at which you bend the legs of the LED to accommodate your individual setup, but make sure that the longer leg is bent close to the LED body.

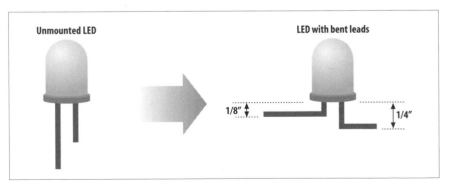

Figure 8-4: LED bends

Now take the LED with the bent legs and attach it to the wire mesh at evenly spaced points, as previously identified. Attach the short LED leg to the metal mesh with an open metal crimp. Each crimped LED should look something like Figure 8-5.

Mount each of the 144 LEDs in this way over the surface of the wire mesh, making sure that they all face outward.

4. Wire the LED frame to the LED drivers

It is now time to connect the LED drivers to each of the LEDs previously mounted on the metal mesh frame. Measure the distance that the LED frame will be from the control PC and LED driver circuit boards. Cut 19 pieces of CAT5 wire to this length, plus 10 feet.

Solder groups of 24 wires to a female DB25 connector according to Exhibit M. This connector will mate with one of the female connectors on the LED driver circuit boards. Solder the ground wire to one wire from the separate CAT5 bundle. Since each bundle has eight wires, this bundle requires three lengths of CAT5 wire. Grab one wire for ground from a shared-ground-only CAT5 wire.

After all the wires have been soldered to DB25 connectors, label each bundle, and lay it out on the floor next to the LEDs and wire mesh. Solder each wire to the long leg of each LED, and seal the LED and wire in hot-melt glue according to the diagram in Figure 8-6. You may also want to place each LED at a location where there is more than one wire of the mesh to secure things and use a small wire tie to ensure that nothing moves.

The hot-melt glue serves two purposes: it insulates the drive wire from the wire mesh (which is ground), and it holds the LED in place. Before the hot-melt glue cools and hardens, make sure that the LED is facing upward and that the solder connection between the long LED leg and the drive wire does not touch the wire mesh.

Figure 8-5: LED connection to mesh

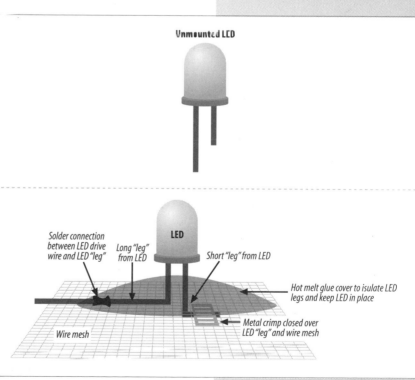

Figure 8-6: LED mounted to mesh

Repeat this for each of the 144 LEDs. After soldering each LED and before sealing it, you may want to test your handiwork. Use a multi-meter to measure either resistance, or set it to the diode test position. Touch the red probe to the wire connected to the long LED leg and the black probe to the wire mesh. If everything is soldered correctly, the LED should light up a little when the meter is set to the diode measurement mode.

5. Install a light diffuser over the LEDs

The LEDs are very strong point light sources. Since the LEDs are spaced out on the wire mesh, it may be hard to see a clear image of the animation being displayed. To overcome this, you may want to install some sort of light diffuser in front of the LEDs.

One way to do this is to place a white cloth sheet or frosted plastic shower curtain in front of the LEDs. The sheet will need to be spaced away from the LEDs if you want to make the light from the LEDs look like large pixels. This can be accomplished by building a frame out of PVC pipe to hold the sheet and wire mesh in place, as shown in Figure 8-7. I will leave it to you to design this simple assembly if you decide you need it.

Alternatively, you can add a small light diffuser on each LED. Low-cost Ping-Pong balls are an option. Cut a small hole in the back of each ball and mount them over each LED.

You can also omit the diffuser altogether and just show the bare LEDs.

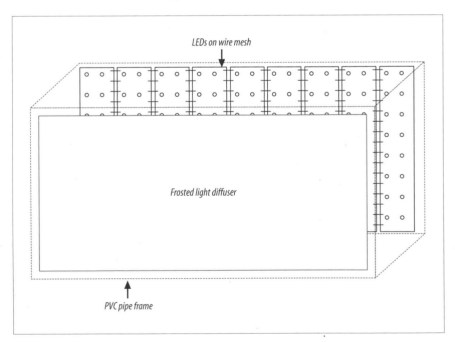

Figure 8-7: LED diffuser

6. Mount the system on your house

After you have tested the LED array on the ground and installed the optional light diffuser, it is time to mount the system on your target building.

It is probably safest to drop hoisting ropes from the windows where the array will be secured and slowly pull it up just under the window height. Secure the ropes that hold everything in place and carefully connect the wires.

Your hardware is now complete! Skip ahead to the Software Setup Instructions.

Large-Scale Hardware Assembly Instructions

The CCC installed the Blinkenlights system on the top 8 floors of a 12-story building. Behind each of the 18 front-facing windows on each floor, there was a single lamp on a handmade tripod. Each lamp was connected to a power source via a relay; if the relay switched on, the windowpane became lit. The building in Berlin had all of the windows painted white to act as a diffuser, which may not be practical for you. Instead, you can place a white cloth or paper sheet in front of each window to keep the light from looking like a point source. All of the lamps should be similar to ensure uniform illumination of all of the "pixels."

In the Berlin project, each relay was connected to the control floor via a cable. All the cables came together in a huge bundle of cables connected to the Blinkenlights Chaos Control Center. An amplifier provided the cables with the necessary power to switch the relay; the control computer was capable of switching each relay independently. More than 5,000 meters of cable was required to wire the building.

In the following steps, you will find an appropriate building for your display, build the relay drivers and boxes, and wire the building.

1. Choose a building for installation

The Blinkenlights system consisted of a matrix 18 pixels wide by 8 pixels tall. You should choose a building in which the number of windows facing outward is close to this number, but it does not have to match exactly since you can create smaller animations and images with the software tools. You could even build the display on an 18-story building with 8 windows across; in this case, you would need to create the images and animations sideways.

The building should have easy access to each of the window "pixels." You will be running a cable from each lamp to a central controlling PC, so make sure that you can access stairwells between floors. Each window should have an electrical outlet near it as well.

While inspecting a prospective building, take some quick measurements for the total length of wire you will need.

2. Install the digital I/O card

Control of the Blinkenlights pixels comes from one or more parallel I/O cards. The software runs on top of the Linux operating system and uses the drivers for cards based on the Intel 8255 parallel I/O integrated circuit. Here are several potential vendors for these cards:

- Webtronics (*http://www.web-tronics.com/*) offers the ACL-7122 144-port ISA card. This card contains all of the necessary ports so you only need one.

- Kontron (*http://www.kontron.com/*) also offers ISA cards based on the 8255 chip.

- A German company called Decision Computer (*http://www.decision-computer.de/*) offers an ISA card with 192 ports (Part #82192V).

The card will most likely come with a flat ribbon cable that plugs into a connector to bring the 144 digital outputs to the outside of the PC. You may need to remove one of the expansion slot covers to allow the cable to escape.

Install the card(s) in an unused ISA slot in the PC that you intend to use as the main controller.

3. Build relay drivers

The digital output board is unable to directly drive the lamp relays by themselves. A relay driver must be built for each lamp. The relay drivers are in turn driven by the digital output board.

The members of the CCC built their own relay drivers and relay boards. The relay drivers were located next to the controlling PC, and actual relays were located next to each lamp. This made the system safer by keeping all high voltages away from the controlling PC.

Construct 18 relay driver boards according to the schematic diagram in Exhibit C. Build your relay drivers in groups of eight transistors to keep the size of the individual circuit boards smaller and make it easier to troubleshoot and fix. When you have completed this step, the boards should look like those in Figure 8-8.

You may instead want to buy the relay drivers with the relays included. WebTronics (*http://www.web-tronics.com/*) carries an 8-port relay board with drivers (Part #Kit-74) for about $33. You will still need to purchase and assemble 18 of these, but it can save time over building drivers from scratch.

Figure 8-8: Relay drivers

You will need to purchase the relays as well. Purchase at least 144 relays whose contacts are rated for 120VAC at 3 amps; the driving coil should be rated at 12V DC. Hold on to these relays; you'll be using them in Step 6.

4. Obtain lamps and build stands

You now need to obtain the lamps that will light up each pixel. Any medium power lamp can be used, but the CCC found that low-cost halogen work lamps were particularly effective. You can see what one of these looks like in Figure 8-9. Small halogen lamps can be found in most home supply stores and on the Web (check *http://www.cornerhardware.com/* for the Regent Quartz Halogen Clip Light model #CL150). The Regent lamp is nice in that it has a clamp to allow easy and flexible mounting.

You can also use the popular torchiere lamps sold in many home supply stores. These lamps already have a stand and the light location can be adjusted. If you choose to use these, you can skip the rest of this step and proceed to Step 5.

A 150-watt lamp should be sufficient. If you want to use a more powerful lamp, you will need to select a relay that can handle a larger amount of power.

The lamps will need to be mounted in the middle of each window so that the maximum amount of light can be seen on the outside of the building. Simple plans for a lamp stand are shown in Figure 8-10. The CCC built a simple tripod stand out of 2" x 2" wood planks, using wood screws or nails to secure the wood together. You may need to experiment with this design to accommodate your exact placement requirements. Build one first, get it right, and then build the remaining 143.

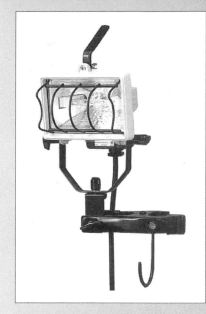

Figure 8-9: Halogen lamp

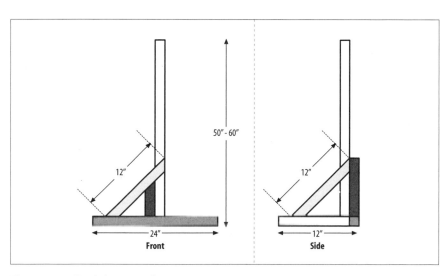

Figure 8-10: Simple lamp stand

Figure 8-11: Forest of lamp stands

When you are done, you should have quite a forest of lamp stands, as shown in Figure 8-11.

5. Connect the relay drivers to the ISA I/O card

The second most time-consuming task will be wiring the digital output board to the relay drivers. The key to getting things right is careful planning and excess labeling of all wires and connectors.

You can see an overview of how all of the outputs from the ACL-7122 ISA card will be connected to the relay drivers in Figure 8-12. Each 50-pin connector on the 7122 board controls three relay driver boards. A 50-pin ribbon cable is required for each connector and group of three relay driver boards. Build six circuit boards according to the schematic in Exhibit D. Each of these boards will connect the PC digital I/O card to three sets of relay drivers.

The most foolproof way to make the connection between the output board in the PC and the relay drivers is by building two connector interface cables per 50-pin connector on the ISA card. This cable pair makes the connections more durable by taking stress off of the delicate ribbon cable from the ISA card, and allows for easy troubleshooting in case something does not work immediately.

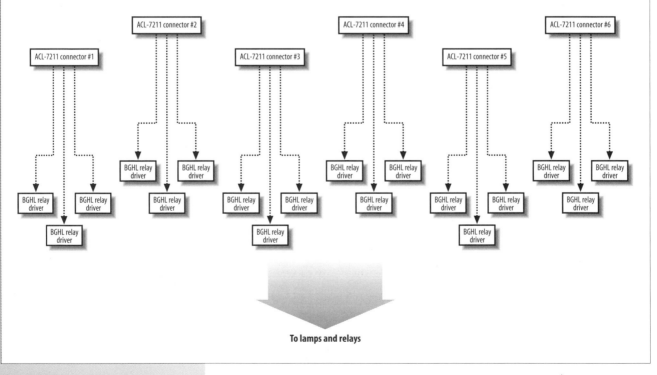

Figure 8-12:
ISA card to relay driver overview

The 50-pin connector labeled J2 in Exhibit D connects to one of the 50-pin connectors on the ISA card. The wires from J2 are in turn connected to P1, a common DB25 connector. This cable from J2 to P1 should be kept short. It is intended to bring the relay drive signals from the connectors inside the PC to just outside the PC. P1 is in turn plugged into P2, which splits the drive signals. All six of these cables are shown in Figure 8-13.

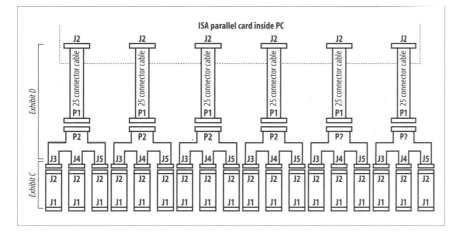

Figure 8-13: Parallel card cabling overview

Solder groups of three relay driver boards together, as shown in Figure 8-14. You will notice that each relay board and individual driver is labeled and that the wire bundle is held firmly in place with hot-melt glue and tie wraps. This makes the wiring easier to manage and incorrect wiring easier to troubleshoot.

After connecting each group of three relay driver boards to the control PC either by using the interface board or by soldering the relay drivers directly to the PC control signals, it should look something like Figure 8-15.

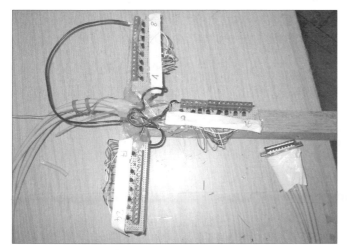

Figure 8-14:
Three relay driver boards

Figure 8-15:
Complete system setup

Figure 8-16: ISA card cable bundles

You can see the wiring going into the back of the control PC in Figure 8-16. Notice again that the cables are labeled and that both hot-melt glue and duct tape are used to keep the bundles together and prevent the delicate solder connections from breaking.

6. Build relay boxes and connect the lamps

Each lamp requires a relay to switch it on and off. You control these relays by the relay driver board constructed in Step 5.

You now need to build a relay box for each lamp according to the illustration in Figure 8-17. If you don't mind cutting up the cord to the light, go with Option #1. Slice open the lamp cord, pull out one of the wires (either black or white), and connect it across the two relay pins. If you want to keep the light cords intact, go with Option #2 and add an outlet that has been wired to the relay.

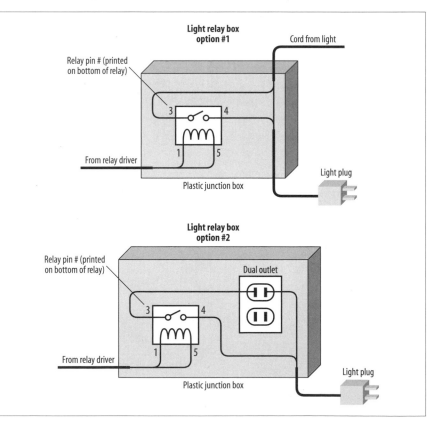

Figure 8-17: Relay box designs

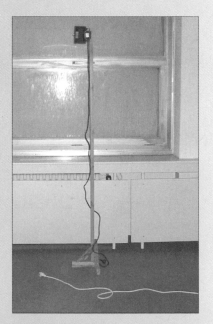

Figure 8-18: Lamp in front of window

When you have completed this step, attach each lamp to its stand and place it in front of a building window (see Figure 8-18). You may want to place a sheet of white paper in front of each window to make the illumination look more uniform from the outside.

You can see what a lamp on its stand looks like from inside the building in Figure 8-19. Place the lamp as close to the center of the window as possible to make the window pixel as bright as possible.

Once all of the of relay drivers are connected to the individual lamps, your setup should look like the setup shown back in Figure 8-15. You can make it look a little more organized by using duct tape to keep each floor wire bundle separate.

Figure 8-19: Inside view

7. Wire the building

Wiring the building is probably the most time-consuming task of the large-scale project. Each lamp must be individually connected back to the relay driver boards through a pair of wires. The goal is to wire the building according to the illustration in Figure 8-20. The notation above each window in the diagram can be decoded as follows: the first letter and number

C0: PCD1	C0: PCD0	C0: PBD7	C0: PBD6	C0: PBD5	C0: PBD4	C0: PBD3	C0: PBD2	C0: PBD1	C0: PBD0	C0: PAD7	C0: PAD6	C0: PAD5	C0: PAD4	C0: PAD3	C0: PAD2	C0: PAD1	C0: PAD0
C1: PBD3	C1: PBD2	C1: PBD1	C1: PBD0	C1: PAD7	C1: PAD6	C1: PAD5	C1: PAD4	C1: PAD3	C1: PAD2	C1: PAD1	C1: PAD0	C0: PCD7	C0: PCD6	C0: PCD5	C0: PCD4	C0: PCD3	C0: PCD2
C2: PAD5	C2: PAD4	C2: PAD3	C2: PAD2	C2: PAD1	C2: PAD0	C1: PCD7	C1: PCD6	C1: PCD5	C1: PCD4	C1: PCD3	C1: PCD2	C1: PCD1	C1: PCD0	C1: PBD7	C1: PBD6	C1: PBD5	C1: PBD4
C2: PCD7	C2: PCD6	C2: PCD5	C2: PCD4	C2: PCD3	C2: PCD2	C2: PCD1	C2: PCD0	C2: PBD7	C2: PBD6	C2: PBD5	C2: PBD4	C2: PBD3	C2: PBD2	C2: PBD1	C2: PBD0	C2: PAD7	C2: PAD6
C3: PCD1	C3: PCD0	C3: PBD7	C3: PBD6	C3: PBD5	C3: PBD4	C3: PBD3	C3: PBD2	C3: PBD1	C3: PBD0	C3: PAD7	C3: PAD6	C3: PAD5	C3: PAD4	C3: PAD3	C3: PAD2	C3: PAD1	C3: PAD0
C4: PBD3	C4: PBD2	C4: PBD1	C4: PBD0	C4: PAD7	C4: PAD6	C4: PAD5	C4: PAD4	C4: PAD3	C4: PAD2	C4: PAD1	C4: PAD0	C3: PCD7	C3: PCD6	C3: PCD5	C3: PCD4	C3: PCD3	C3: PCD2
C5: PAD5	C5: PAD4	C5: PAD3	C5: PAD2	C5: PAD1	C5: PAD0	C4: PCD7	C4: PCD6	C4: PCD5	C4: PCD4	C4: PCD3	C4: PCD2	C4: PCD1	C4: PCD0	C4: PBD7	C4: PBD6	C4: PBD5	C4: PBD4
C5: PCD7	C5: PCD6	C5: PCD5	C5: PCD4	C5: PCD3	C5: PCD2	C5: PCD1	C5: PCD0	C5: PBD7	C5: PBD6	C5: PBD5	C5: PBD4	C5: PBD3	C5: PBD2	C5: PBD1	C5: PBD0	C5: PAD7	C5: PAD6

Lamp relay driver ID# — Window — Lamp and relay

Figure 8-20: Overview of building wiring

Chapter 8, How to Hack a Building-Size Display

Figure 8-21:
Building hallway cabling

indicate each connector pin (the 50-pin connectors) on the ACL-7122 card; the second number indicates each port on that connector (A, B, or C, as indicated in the documentation that comes with each board); and the last letter and number indicate each data bit from that port. The building is wired in a linear fashion starting in the upper right corner (as viewed from the outside of the building). Each light is then wired in order from right to left, wrapping back to the right side after all of the windows on a level have been connected.

Before you begin wiring, estimate how much wire you will need. This amount will obviously vary according to the size of the building you are wiring, but you can use a few techniques to minimize it.

If you use CAT5 Ethernet wire, you will get four wire pairs per cable. To minimize the amount of CAT5 you need, I suggest that you use six of the wires in each cable to drive individual relays and the remaining two as return wires. Because each floor of the building has 18 windows, you will only need to run three CAT5 cables to each floor. Since you will have only two return wires on each cable, you will need to solder these two wires to a set of six wires on each floor. You can see what this looks like in Figure 8-21.

There are many ways to wire the building, but I would suggest that you start on the top floor and wire one floor at a time, testing each one before proceeding to the next. Test the lamps back at the relay drivers by getting a small piece of wire and touching the +12V power to the resistor on the base of each driver transistor momentarily. Have a second person standing at each lamp and telling you whether each lamp lights up. You may need a small two-way radio to be able to hear each other.

The wiring on any one floor should be laid out on the floor with each wire untangled to allow easy trouble-shooting.

When you bring all the wires back to the main control PC, you may need to bundle the wires and push them out of the way. It will look something like Figure 8-22 when you have completed this step.

Figure 8-22: Cable bundles over cubicles

Software Setup Instructions

There are two versions of the software that you can run depending on which size system you have built. If you're building the large building-size system, go to the Large-scale software section. If you're building the home or desktop system, go to the Small-scale software section.

Large-scale software

Three computers are used to control the building-size Blinkenlights system. Although it would have been possible to put it all on one system, the CCC decided to separate the modules (control, playback, telephone interactivity) in order to allow distributed development and operation. Since the modules communicate using standard network protocols, you can run all of the software on a single machine. Control of the system is from either an email interface or from a GSM mobile phone. This flow of data can be seen in Figure 8-23.

Figure 8-23: Software overview

Download the software from *http://www.blinkenlights.de/blinkentools. en.html* and install it according to the included files. The site also includes a software simulator that allows you to design and preview animations without having to first set up the hardware. You may want to play around with the software simulator first to get a feel for how the processes interact.

The software is partitioned into three components:

- Chaos Control Center (the module name is "blccc")
- Matrix Control (the module name is "windowmatrixd")
- Telephone interface (the module name is "blinkenisdn")

These three processes use UDP to communicate.

The Chaos Control Center module reads a playlist and broadcasts frame packets to the Matrix Control module. The "windowmatrixd" process then extracts these frames and writes them to the 8,255 digital output ports.

The telephone interface process sends telephone line state information (ONHOOK, OFFHOOK) and event information (DTMF keys pressed) for each line to the Chaos Control Center. This module was designed for an ISDN interface, and so will require some hacking to support a different interface. Whenever the telephone interface detects an OFFHOOK event (an incoming call is detected and answered), it starts the Pong game. When the telephone interface detects an ONHOOK event (the calling party hangs up the phone), the system returns to the playlist movies.

Since all of the processes will be run on a single machine, you need to change all the target addresses to 127.0.0.1 so that everything runs locally.

Locate one animation and run it. Watch the building display to make sure that everything is wired properly. You may need to correct wiring mistakes at the interconnect boards. Try a few of the animations from the web site and design a few of your own.

The Pong-like game was designed to work with an ISDN phone system, but you may be able to hack the code a bit to make it work with a standard PSTN system.

Small-scale software

If you have built the desktop- or home-size version, download the mini-Blinkenlights software from *http://www.jalcds.de/blinkenleds/software.php*. Install this software according to the included instructions. The software runs under Windows and can utilize all of the original Blinkenlights movie files. This software is all you need to run the smaller version of the system. When running, it will look like Figure 8-24.

After you've wired and connected the LED and wire mesh to the LED drivers, test out the system before you mount it.

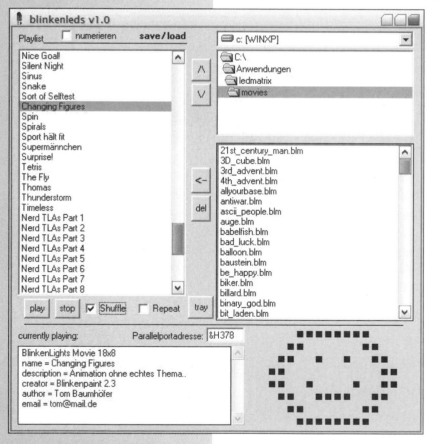

Figure 8-24: Small-scale PC software

Project Demo

After you've set up the system you've decided to build, carefully apply power and load one of the Blinkenlights movies. You can see a desktop system running in Figure 8-25.

And, as Figure 8-26 shows, having a whole building lit up with animated movies can be very impressive.

Wireless Extensions

One of the most time-consuming tasks when setting up a large building is running the wires to each lamp. With some additional hacking, it is possible to use low-cost wireless links to eliminate the thousands of meters of wire.

A single transmitter attached to the control PC can broadcast one frame of data 25 times per second. Each receiver has a unique address and looks for its state (either on or off) for that frame of data. At the end of the transmission, all of the receivers make their state change. Each receiver needs a strong signal from the transmitter connected to the control PC. An easy way to accomplish this is to place the control PC and transmitter in front of the building windows at street level, therefore ensuring line of sight to each receiver. An overview of this idea is shown in Figure 8-27.

Figure 8-25: Desktop system LEDs

Figure 8-26: Large-scale system in action

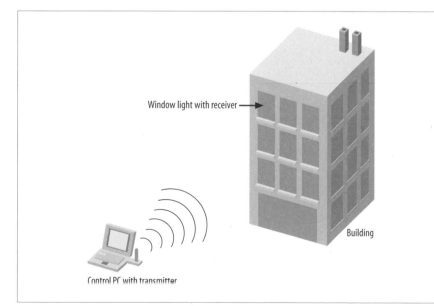
Figure 8-27: Wireless system overview

Channel Coder/Decoder

A company called RadioTronix has a nice application note on channel coding (*http://www.radiotronix.com/an401.pdf*). It outlines a simple and effective method for encoding data for a radio channel.

Error Control Coder

The radio channel will likely have noise on it from time to time. To prevent noise from hindering reliable data reception, an error-correcting code should be applied to all data.

You'll find a good explanation of error correcting codes at *http://www. eccpage.com/.* The web page also includes C source code. For this simple system, I recommend a BCH code.

Each frame should be organized into a packet and a few command codes defined.

Each lamp (or set of lamps) must be outfitted with an addressable radio receiver. Several companies sell low-cost radio receivers that can be used for this purpose. Figure 8-28 shows a block diagram of a wireless lamp controller, and Figure 8-29 shows a block diagram for a simple transmitter.

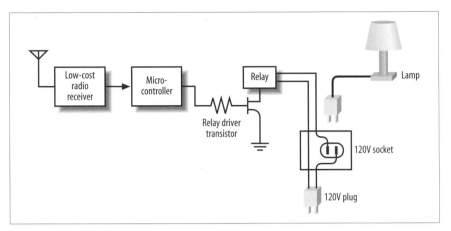

Figure 8-28: Wireless lamp receiver

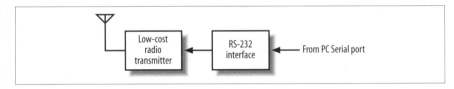

Figure 8-29: Wireless transmitter

The radio link provided by the inexpensive receivers will require additional software to allow for reliable data transmission and reception. Figure 8-30 shows the different operations that the data must undergo in order to be reliably transmitted over a "raw" radio link. There are many other methods available, but this one is simple and reliable.

Figure 8-30: Wireless transmitter software

In order to receive a radio channel coded packet, the inverse of the transmit operations must be performed. This chain of functions is shown in Figure 8-31.

Figure 8-31: Wireless receiver software

Exhibit A: Small-Scale Bill of Materials

Item	Quantity	Notes
Wire	200m	CAT5 wire used to connect LED Buffer board to LEDs on frame
Chicken wire	180 square feet	Hardware store
74ABT244	18	U1-U18; DigiKey Part #296-3967-5-ND
Resistor	144	R1 through R24 x 6; DigiKey Part #150QBK-ND
LED	144	D1 through D24; DigiKey Part #67-1612-ND
74HC4094 (4094)	18	U19-U35; DigiKey Part #296-14290-5-ND
20 pin IC socket	18	U1-U18; DigiKey Part #AE8920--ND
16-pin IC socket	18	U19-U35; DigiKey Part #AE8916-ND
1uF capacitors	6	C1-C6; DigiKey Part #P992-ND
4-pin AT power supply connector	2	J8, J11; Hard drive power splitter cable available from local computer store
50-pin connector	6	CON2; DigiKey Part#CSR50T-ND
DB25 connector, male	6	P7; DigiKey Part #CMP25T-ND
DB25 connector, female	6	P1-P6; DigiKey Part #CFP25T-ND
50-pin ribbon cable	40'	J2; DigiKey Part #R008-50-ND
Standard ATX PC power supply	1	Computer store
Blank prototype board	6	DigiKey Part #V2010-ND
Crimp tool	1	
Open metal crimps	144	

Exhibit B: Large-Scale Bill of Materials

Item	Quantity	Notes
144-port digital output board	1	Kontron PCD 10216B-P, Webtronics ACL-7122, or Decision Computer Part #82192V
Relay	144	DigiKey Part #Z140-NS
Lamp	144	Halogen or incandescent light
Wire	5000m	CAT5 wire
Lumber	144 sets	2 x 2 wood beams
Transistor	144	Q1-Q8; DigiKey Part #2N3904-ND
Resistor	144	R1-R8; DigiKey Part #4.7KQBK-ND
Diode	144	D1-D8; DigiKey Part #1N4001DICT-ND
50-pin connector	6	J2; DigiKey Part #CSR50T-ND
DB25 connector, male	6	P1 x 6; DigiKey Part #CMP25T-ND
DB25 connector, female	6	P2 x 6; DigiKey Part #CFP25T-ND
9-pin terminal block	18	J2; DigiKey Part #277-1280-ND
12-pin terminal block	18	J1; DigiKey Part #277-1283-ND
4-pin terminal block	18	J1; DigiKey Part #277-1275-ND
50-pin ribbon cable	40'	DigiKey Part #R008-50-ND
Plastic junction box	144	Hardware store
Electrical outlet	144	Hardware store
Blank prototype board	6	DigiKey Part #V2010-ND

Exhibit C

Exhibit C: Large-Scale Eight-Port Relay Driver

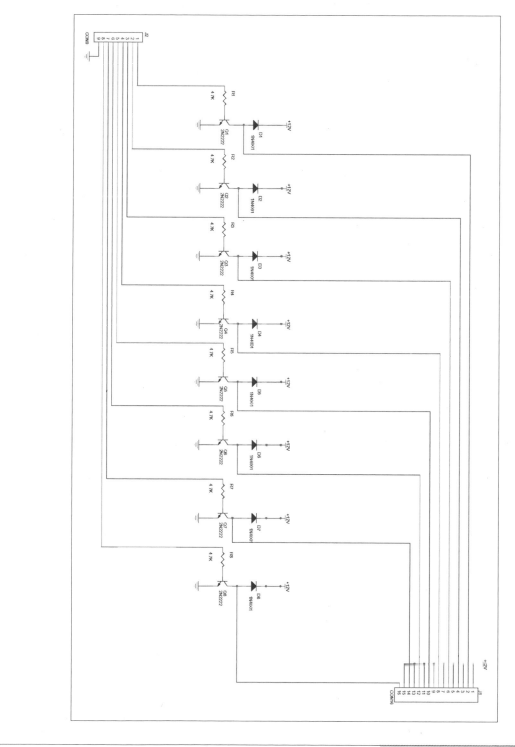

Exhibit D: Large-Scale Digital Interface to Relay Driver

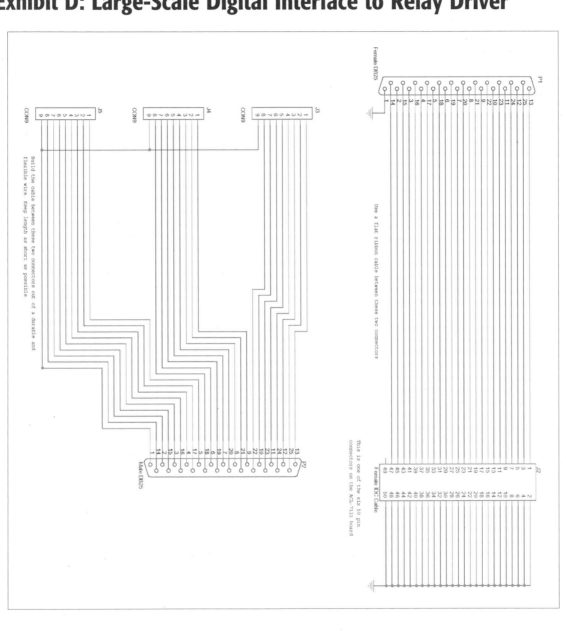

Exhibit E: Small-Scale LED Driver Schematic (page 1)

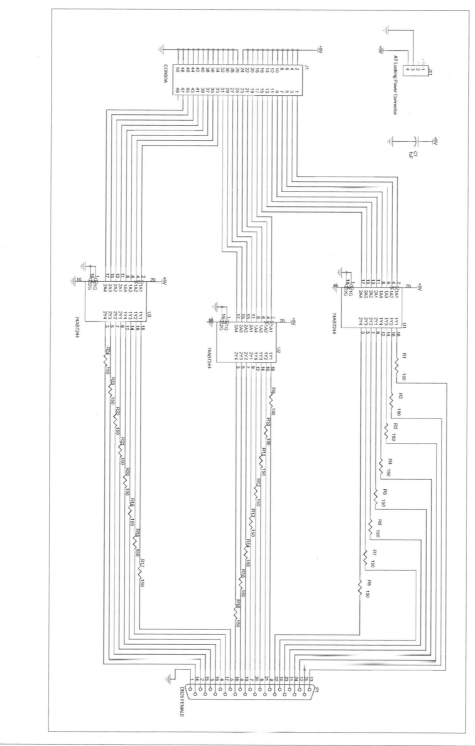

Chapter 8, How to Hack a Building-Size Display

Exhibit E: Small-Scale LED Driver Schematic (page 2)

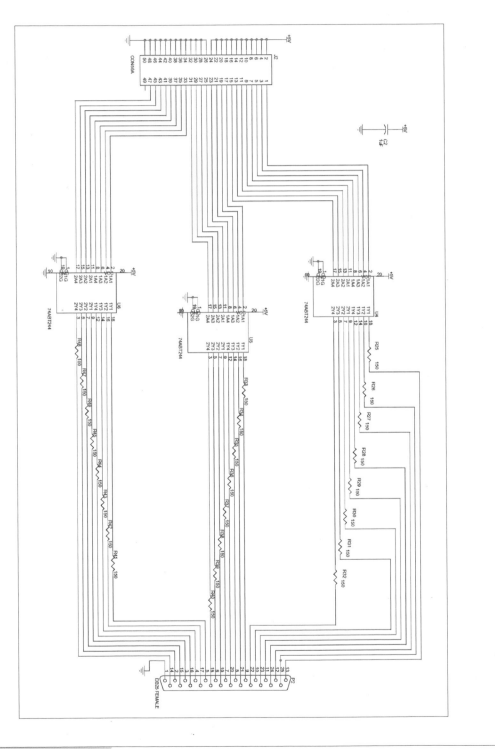

Exhibit E: Small-Scale LED Driver Schematic (page 3)

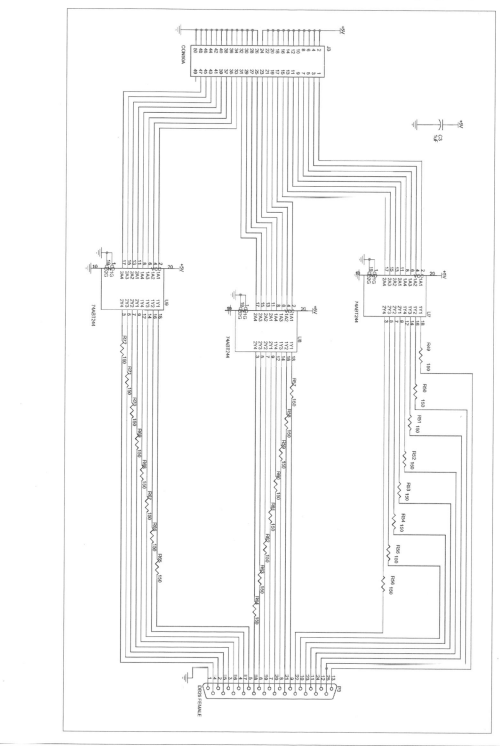

Exhibit E: Small-Scale LED Driver Schematic (page 4)

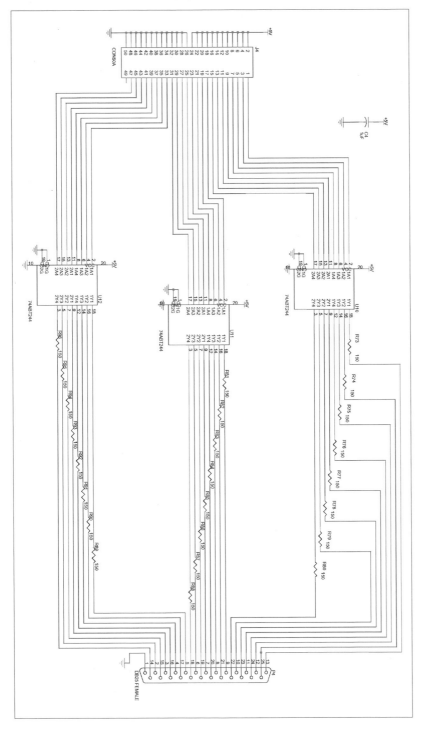

Exhibit E: Small-Scale LED Driver Schematic (page 5)

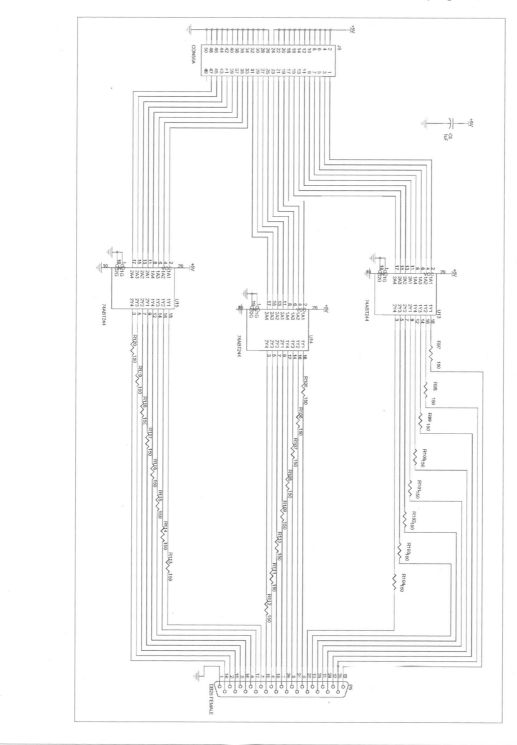

Exhibit E: Small-Scale LED Driver Schematic (page 6)

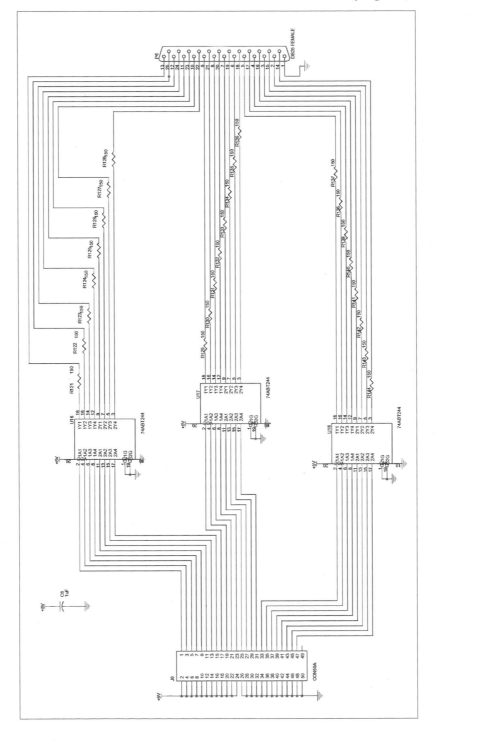

Exhibit F: Small-Scale Shift Register Schematic

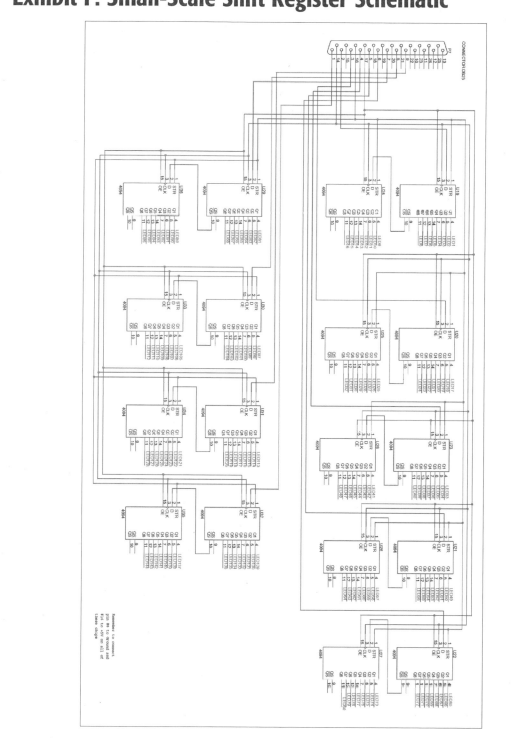

Exhibit G: Small-Scale Connectors

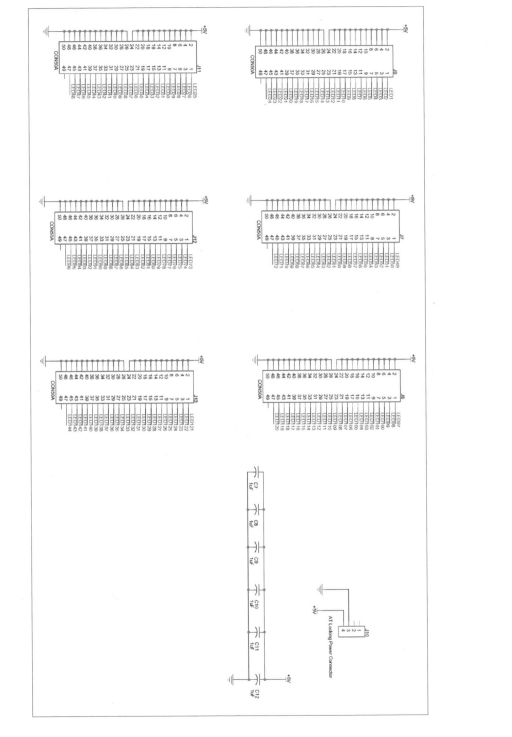

Exhibit H: Small-Scale LED Wiring

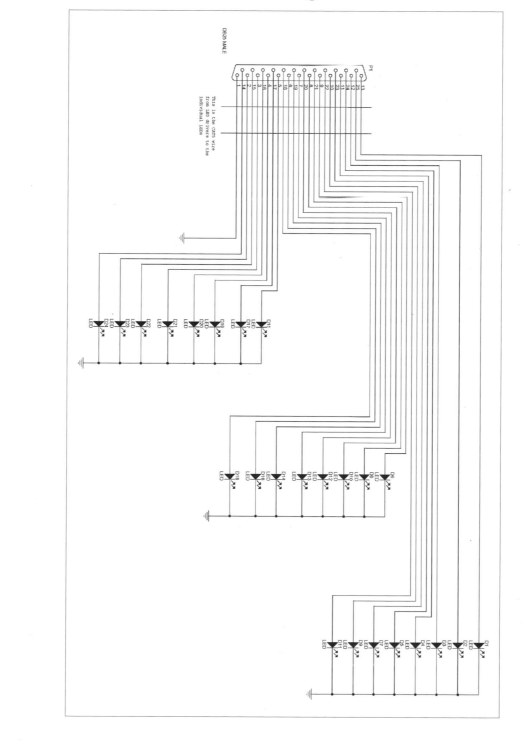

How to Build a Cubicle Intrusion Detection System

Cost

$100

Time

a weekend

Difficulty

difficult

What You Need

- Laser diode module or Radio Shack entry alert
- BasicStamp2 controller
- Empty 35mm, APS film canister, or other small, opaque, drillable container
- Other items listed in Exhibit A or B

One of the first jobs I had out of college was at Apple Computer. My office was on a huge open floor that had been partitioned into cubicles.

The work I did at Apple involved some level of concentration, and the sounds from others in adjacent cubes would often distract me. To combat these distractions, I would wear a set of headphones to block out external noise. Unfortunately, a new problem soon became apparent: I could not tell when someone had come into my cube to ask me a question. The person in the cube next to mine had the endearing habit of sneaking up behind me and either grabbing my shoulders or tossing a ball of paper at me. I would, of course, jump when startled in this way, and it invariably ruined my concentration for several minutes.

I decided to solve this new problem with a quick hardware hack. I built a "cubicle intrusion detector" using a laser pointer, a BasicStamp2 (a complete microcontroller you program using a version of the BASIC language), and a photo-detector. The system worked by shining the light from the laser pointer onto a photo-detector connected to a microcontroller. I directed the laser light across the entrance to my cubicle and, using a small mirror, reflected it back at the photo-detector so that the beam would be broken if anyone walked into the cubicle. When a coworker interrupted the beam of light, a signal sent to a remote indicator warned me that someone was about to sneak up behind me. A diagram of my setup is shown in Figure 9-1. This system can also be built using an infrared beam entry alert, saving you the time of assembling the laser system.

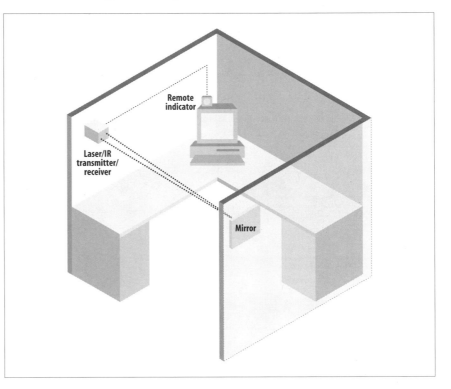

Figure 9-1: Intruder detection system in operation

I also added an LCD to the system to display the number of times my cube had been entered.

Project Overview

You will first build a small circuit board that holds a microcontroller, photo-detector, and laser diode. (Or, if you choose to use an off-the-shelf Radio Shack entry alert system, simply assemble a microcontroller board.) Next, you will program the controller with a small piece of software and set up your system.

For this hack, you will need to know how to solder and how to program a BasicStamp2 controller.

Hardware Assembly Instructions

I recommend using the BasicStamp2 SuperCarrier board, which has space for a BasicStamp2 controller (as well as a prototyping space for additional electronics). I used this board to save some time when I built my cube intrusion system, but you can also build the project on a blank printed circuit board (PCB). The schematic diagrams at the end of this chapter show all the components you'll need.

Radio Shack makes an entry alert product that includes all the optics and infrared light transmission/detection electronics. This product may be substituted for the laser and photo-detector we'll be installing in this hack. The main advantages of using the Radio Shack box are that its optics are prealigned and that you won't have to assemble this part of the system. You will spend a little more money, however; the entry alert costs more than $60.

The laser module I used is a small component you can buy at Radio Shack. If you want to use a pen-style laser pointer, you will need to devise your own mounting system to hold it in place. DigiKey's laser diode module costs about the same as an inexpensive laser pointer pen. I chose the DigiKey module as it is smaller and easier to work with.

The following instructions apply whether you choose to build everything yourself (with or without a SuperCarrier board) or you use an entry alert.

1. Assemble the electronics

For this step you will need to gather the BasicStamp2 controller, the SuperCarrier board, and the electronic components listed in either Exhibit A or B, depending on what kind of system you're building.

Solder components to the circuit board (laser-based)

This step is applicable to those assembling the laser-based system. If you are not using the SuperCarrier board, you will need the small, blank PCB.

Mount the electronic components to the SuperCarrier board prototyping area as specified in Exhibit D. You can see a picture of the completed board in Figure 9-2.

When this task is completed, skip to Step 2.

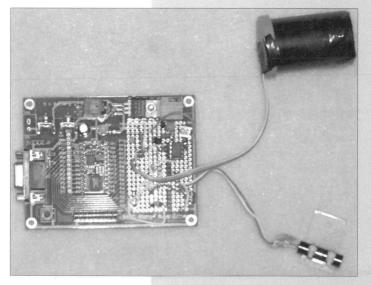

Figure 9-2:
Controller board with components

Figure 9-3: IR photo detector

Solder components to the circuit board (Radio Shack)

The Radio Shack entry alert box contains all of the electronics necessary to detect an interruption in its infrared (IR) light beam. When its beam is broken, it closes a relay. This relay close is read by the circuit described in Exhibit E. You can see what the inside (left) and outside (right) of the entry alert product looks like in Figure 9-3. On the left, you can see the innards of the device; the top ring and lens hold an IR light source, and the bottom ring is the photo-detector.

Build the circuit according to the schematic diagram in Exhibit E on the SuperCarrier board or the blank PCB.

After completing this task, skip to Step 4.

2. Assemble the photo-detector housing

If you're building the laser system, you'll be assembling a photo-detector housing and sensor in this step. Gather the photo-detector, an empty film canister, 12 inches of 28- or 30-gauge stranded wire, 3 to 4 inches of solid core 24-gauge wire, a 2-inch-by-2-inch sheet of red plastic filter (optional), and some black electrical tape to hold the red filter in place.

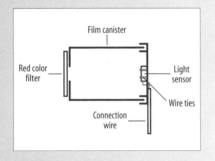

Figure 9-4: Laser detector

The photo-detector outputs a voltage that is proportional to the amount of visible light to which it is exposed. In order to make this sensor directional and detect only the laser, it needs to be placed in a light-tight housing with a small aperture at one end. This prevents regular office lighting from setting off the detector. I used an opaque, empty 35mm film canister; the newer APS film canisters should work equally well.

Begin by drilling a 1cm hole in the bottom of the canister. Next, carefully mount the photo-detector on the inside of the film canister cap. Do this by bending the metal legs of the photo-detector back at a 90 degree angle and poking three holes in the cap to allow them to protrude. Hold the light sensor in place with two wires that wrap over it. A side view of the complete assembly is shown in Figure 9-4. The optional red plastic filter will give you a bit more ambient light isolation, so that office lighting is less likely to produce false signals.

The two pieces of the film canister are shown in Figure 9-5. Note how the cap (left) has been trimmed to allow the canister assembly to sit flat inside the enclosure. A close-up of the back of the cap is shown in Figure 9-6. You can see the three legs from the photo-detector poking through the back as well as the two wire ties that hold the detector in place.

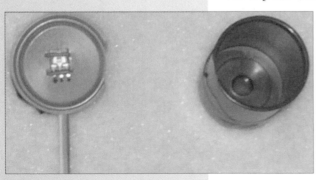

Figure 9-5: Inside of laser detector

After the photo-detector housing has been built, cut off a small portion of the edge of the film canister cap and snap it onto the canister. You see the location of the cut in Figure 9-6. The optional red filter is held in place with some black electrical tape. Place a small piece of electrical tape over the holes in the cap for the photo-detector legs to prevent outside light from leaking in.

Solder three thin pieces of 30-gauge stranded wire, each about 3 to 4 inches in length, to the three leads. I used three wires from a small length of ribbon cable; ribbon cable is preferable because the wires are held together. If you do use individual wires, use three different colors and twist them together when you are done. The twisting will prevent outside electrical noise from producing a false signal from the photo-detector.

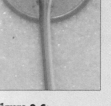

Figure 9-6:
Photo-detector mounting

At the end of the wires, connect three small connectors, which you'll make from the DigiKey single in-line strip sockets. A single order will have 64 individual sockets that can be used to make a number of very small connectors. You can break off a group of three and solder them to either the circuit board or to a wire connector. An example of how these small sockets can work is shown in Figure 9-7. On the left side of the photo is a piece of ribbon cable connected to a single in-line socket, making a male connector at the end of the wires. On the right side is a set of sockets that can be soldered onto a PCB, making a female connector.

Figure 9-7: Small handmade connector

3. Assemble the laser mounting pivot

In this step, you will mount the laser pointer inside the main electronics box (enclosure) on a small pivot. This pivot will allow the laser to be adjusted so that it points directly at the detector after the beam bounces off a mirror.

The pivot can be made from a small piece of scrap plastic. Its exact dimensions are not important, but an example is shown in Figure 9-8. This figure shows the dimensions in inches for the rectangular outline of the part and the diameter and location of the drilled holes. All five holes should be drilled with an approximate diameter of 0.13 inches. It may be easier to drill the holes before cutting out the main rectangular outline. (The mounting location of the laser module is also shown for reference.)

The top hole is used to hold a screw pivot that will allow you to adjust the firing angle of the laser. The other four holes are used to thread tie wraps that hold the laser securely in place.

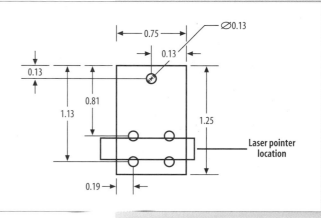

Figure 9-8: Laser pivot design

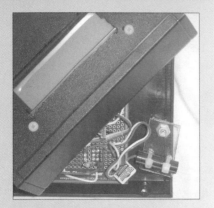

Figure 9-9: Laser pivot

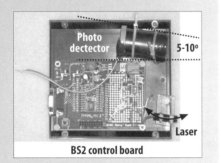

Figure 9-10:
Laser and detector mounting angles

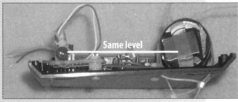

Figure 9-11: Laser and detector

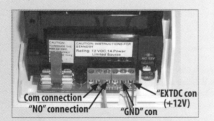

Figure 9-12: Photo-detector wiring

Figure 9-9 shows how the assembly will look when completed. You can see the two tie wraps holding the laser module in place and the pivot screw threaded through the top hole. You may not want to use the tie wraps to attach the laser to this assembly just yet; wait until you've mounted it in the enclosure to allow easy adjustment.

4. Mount SuperCarrier, photo-detector, and laser

In this step you will need the SuperCarrier board plus BasicStamp2 (or the circuit you've assembled onto a blank PCB), the laser diode on a pivot, the photo-detector enclosure, and the plastic enclosure box. I used an electronics enclosure from DigiKey, but other boxes from DigiKey or Radio Shack can also be made to work.

Mount the BasicStamp2 controller board in the plastic enclosure box as shown in Figure 9-10. If you are using the entry alert as the photo-detector, proceed to Step 5, as there will be no laser pointer or photo-detector.

If you are using the laser and photo-detector, mount the photo-detector in place with two sets of plastic tie wraps. The detector should be mounted at an angle of 5 to 10 degrees, as shown in the top right corner of Figure 9-10. The BasicStamp2 controller board is held in place with two 4-40 screws and nuts. You will need to drill holes in this half of the enclosure box for the tie wraps, screws, and laser pivot.

The photo-detector and laser need to be aligned in the same plane, as shown in Figure 9-11. If necessary, use a few extra 4-40 nuts to bring the pivot up to the same level as the photo-detector.

When you are finished with this step, proceed to Step 6.

5. Wire the entry alert

If you are using the Radio Shack entry alert sensor, you will need to connect two sets of wire to it. There are six screw terminals on the entry alert; we will use the five labeled NO, Com, NC, EXTDC, and GND. Connect a pair of wires to the NO and Com screw terminals on the side of the entry alert and another set of wires to the EXTDC and GND screw terminals, as shown in Figure 9-12. Make sure that each of the wire pairs is 30 or so inches long. No wires are connected to the NC terminal.

After securing the wires in place with the screws, use a tie wrap to secure them to the enclosure of the entry alert.

6. Mount the LCD

Now you will mount the two-line LCD on the top of the case. Cut a hole in the top of the case large enough to allow the display to be seen. Drill four small holes in the corners to allow the display to be mounted with two 4-40 and two 2-56 screws and nuts. The instructions that come with the display have the correct dimensions for the front opening and mounting hole locations.

When completed, the top of the case should look like Figure 9-13. The display can be seen in the lower center of the enclosure.

7. Cut holes for power, controls, and laser

You must now cut slots and holes in the front and back panels of the electronics enclosure to allow connections to power, connectors, photo-detector, button, and laser.

The front panel of the case will need notches cut out of it to allow the laser pointer and photo-detector to access the outside. You can make these cuts with a hacksaw and a drill. An accurate cut location is not required. When you have completed this step, the enclosure should look something like Figure 9-14.

Next, you will need to cut three holes in the back panel for the power jack, DB9 serial port connector, and reset button. Again, the hole locations do not need to be very accurate. An example of these cut holes is shown in Figure 9-15.

8. Construct the remote LED cable

Measure the distance from the doorway of your cube (or wherever the intrusion system will be mounted) to where you normally work. Cut a length of shielded cable that is 3 to 5 feet longer than that distance. Connect an LED to one side and a two-pin connector to the other. You may want to place the LED inside a small plastic box to allow it to be easily mounted in front of you on the wall or in the corner of your monitor.

9. Test the system

Before you apply power to the system, you will want to check your work. Make sure that the power supplies are not shorted to the grounds by using a multi-meter to measure resistance. Also, check that the laser and sensor are wired properly, as they are two of the more expensive parts in this project.

Figure 9-13: Enclosure top cutout

Figure 9-14: Enclosure front cutout

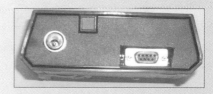

Figure 9-15: Enclosure back cutout

If you are satisfied that your wiring is correct, plug in a 7.5V to 12V DC power supply to the SuperCarrier board or your circuit board. Using a multi-meter to measure voltage, look at the power pins of each integrated circuit to ensure that they read +5V. The laser should light up immediately with a power supply voltage of 3.3 volts.

Quick-and-Dirty Microcontrollers

So you want to control a small circuit, but you don't want the hassle of learning to use an unfamiliar embedded processor.

Fear not. There are a number of tiny microcontroller solutions that are easy to use right out of the box.

I have used the BasicStamp2 controller (*http://www.parallax.com*) for this hack because it is easy to get code running with it, and it is programmed in BASIC. (This is the same language you might have used to program a TSR-80 or a Commodore home computer.)

Other small and simple-to-use solutions include:
- BasicX controller from Netmedia (*http://www.basicx.com*)
- Javlin Java-based controller board from Parallax (*http://www.parallax.com*)
- AtomBasic (*http://www.basicmicro.com*)

10. Program the BasicStamp2 controller

The system still needs "brains" to read the light sensor data and update the LCD. The BasicStamp2 is a small, easy-to-use microcontroller.

Using a Windows PC, you will load the program into the BasicStamp2 controller (see the code listing in Exhibit C at the end of this chapter).

Download the programming software

Begin by downloading the BasicStamp2 editor and programming software for the PC from *http://www.parallaxinc.com/html_files/downloads/downloads_software.htm*. Select the BasicStamp2 editor for Windows V 1.32 (or greater).

The package that you download will be a self-extracting archive. Expand this file by double-clicking on it. Follow the installation instructions.

Connect the cubicle intrusion circuit board to the PC

Using a standard DB9 serial cable, connect the PC serial port to the 9-pin connector on the SuperCarrier or your circuit board.

Program the BasicStamp2

Make sure that you've installed the BasicStamp2 controller on your circuit board and that you've connected the power supply.

Start the BasicStamp Windows editor/programmer. Either type in the program from the code listing in Exhibit C or get a copy from this book's page on the O'Reilly web site (*http://www.oreilly.com/hardwarehacking*).

Select the "Identify" function to ensure that you have the circuit board connected to the PC correctly. Select the "Run" function, and the PC software will download and program the software onto the BasicStamp2.

After loading, reset the CPU using the reset switch on the board. You should see a welcome message on the LCD; if you do not, check the connections to the LCD.

11. Align the system

If you are using the Radio Shack entry alert product, set it up in the doorway of the cube you want "protected." The kit includes a red reflector and instructions on setup.

If you are setting up the laser-based version, mount the main project enclosure so that the laser will fire across the opening of the cube or office you want protected. Mount it with tie wraps, metal coat hangers, or even Velcro. Power it on and look to see where the laser places its dot. Take a small mirror and secure it with double-sided foam tape or other adhesive so that it reflects the dot back at the main enclosure. Use the laser pivot mount to point the laser so that it hits the photo-detector assembly. When properly aligned, the LED on the board will switch off. It will switch on when the beam is interrupted. Multiple mirrors may be used to cover a larger area. The LED laser should be able to project a beam over 50 feet.

Finally, attach the "warning" LED cable assembly to the circuit board and check that it switches on when someone breaks the beam. Place it so that it is inside your field of vision when you are working.

Project Demo

After you have aligned the laser or entry alert box and set the warning LED on your desk so that you can see it, call a few fellow office workers and ask them to step in to your cubicle. Before they arrive, put on a set of headphones and play some of your favorite music. When your colleague enters your cube area, you will see the warning LED switch on. You'll never be surprised again!

Extensions

A number of additional features can be easily added to the system. The laser box currently requires a separate 12V DC power supply. You may want to add a four-conductor RJ-11 connector and pass the power on two of the wires.

If you would like your PC to be able to interface to the cube intrusion system, you will need to add a serial output to the controller via an RS232 level converter such as the MAX233. This chip can be added to any free I/O port on the BasicStamp2. Every time an entry event happens, a byte of data can be sent out and recorded by the PC. You will need to add some code to the BasicStamp2 to enable this feature; I leave this as an exercise for you.

The output transistor, Q1, can trigger other devices such as web cams to grab a series of images each time the sensor is triggered. The Axis web cam (*http://www.axis.com/*) has an input connector that allows external devices to trigger an image capture. This camera can be easily connected to the cubicle intrusion system.

The Q1 output transistor could also be used to trigger a motorized toy or electric water gun to provide a surprise for the unsuspecting intruder. The best way to do this is to replace Q1 with a larger transistor (the TIP112 from Fairchild Semiconductor available, from DigiKey, will work well).

Exhibit A: Bill of Materials for Laser-Based System

Item	Quantity	Notes
1 uF capacitor	3	C1, C2, C4; DigiKey #P11332CT-ND
0.1 uF capacitor	1	C3; DigiKey #P2067-ND
LED	2	D1; Radio Shack #276-1622
Connector	1	JP1; DigiKey #CP-5-ND
Single in-line strip sockets	5	J1, J2, J3, J4, JP2; DigiKey #ED7064-ND
DB9 connector	1	P1; not required if SuperCarrier Board is used; Radio Shack Part #276-1538
Transistor	1	Q1; DigiKey #2N5089-ND
1M-Ohm (1.5 M Ohm ok) resistor	1	R1; Radio Shack #271-312
1K-Ohm resistor	2	R2, R3; Radio Shack #271-312
10K-Ohm resistor	2	R4, R6; Radio Shack #271-312
100-Ohm resistor	2	R7, R8; Radio Shack #271-312
Switch	1	S1; Radio Shack Part #275-1566
3.3V output voltage regulator	1	U1; DigiKey Part #LP2950ACZ-3.3-ND
Laser diode module	1	U2; DigiKey Part #38-1002-ND
5V output voltage regulator	1	U3; optional, included on SuperCarrier; DigiKey Part #LM1117T-5.0-ND
Photo-detector	1	U4; DigiKey #PNA4603H
Operational amplifier	1	U5; LM358, DigiKey Part #296-1395-5-ND
Controller	1	Parallax #BS2-IC
Power supply	1	Radio Shack Part #273-1776
Electronics enclosure	1	DigiKey #SRA31B-ND
SuperCarrier	1	Optional; Parallax #27130
Tie wraps	1 package	Radio Shack Part #278-1656
4-40 size screws	1 package	Radio Shack Part #64-3011
4-40 size nuts	1 package	Radio Shack Part #64-3018
2-56 size screws	1 package	Radio Shack Part #64-3010
2-56 size nuts	1 package	Radio Shack Part #64-3017
Film canister	1	35mm/APS/other opaque canister
LED	1	Radio Shack Part #276-1622
Blank printed circuit board (PCB)	1	Required if SuperCarrier is not used, Radio Shack Part #276-158
Transparent red plastic	2" x 2"	Available from local arts store

Item	Quantity	Notes
Mirrors	At least 1	More for reflecting laser multiple times
Wire	10'-30'	Two-conductor wire (telephone wire will work well); Radio Shack Part #278-870
LCD display	1	BPI-216 LCD display, Scott Edwards Electronics

Exhibit B: Bill of Materials for Entry Alert–Based System

Item	Quantity	Notes
1 uF capacitor	1	C2; DigiKey Part #P11332CT-ND
0.1 uF capacitor	1	C3; DigiKey Part #P2067-ND
Coaxial power jack connector	1	JP1; DigiKey Part #CP-5-ND
Connector	6	J3, J4, J5, J6, J7, J8; DigiKey Part #ED7064-ND
DB9 connector	1	P1; not required if SuperCarrier Board is used; Radio Shack Part #276-1538
Transistor	1	Q1; Digikey Part #2N5089-ND
1K resistor	1	R3; Radio Shack Part #271-312
10K resistor	2	R6, R7; Radio Shack Part #271-312
100K resistor	1	R8; Radio Shack Part #271-312
Switch	1	S1 SW PUSHBUTTON, Radio Shack Part #275-1566
5V output voltage regulator	1	U3; DigiKey Part #LM1117T-5.0-ND
BasicStamp2 controller	1	U6; Part #BS2-IC, Parallax Inc
Power supply	1	Radio Shack Part #273-1776
Entry alert	1	Radio Shack Part #49-312
Electronics enclosure	1	DigiKey Part #SRA31B-ND
SuperCarrier board	1	Optional; Parallax #27130
LCD display	1	U7; BPI-216 LCD display, Scott Edwards Electronics
Tie wraps	1 package	Radio Shack Part #278-1656
4-40 size screws	1 package	Radio Shack Part #64-3011
4-40 size nuts	1 package	Radio Shack Part #64-3018
LED	1	Radio Shack Part #276-1622
Blank printed circuit board (PCB)	1	Required if SuperCarrier is not used; Radio Shack Part #276-158
Wire	10'-30'	Two-conductor wire (telephone wire will work well); Radio Shack Part #278-870

Exhibit C

Exhibit C: BasicStamp2 Software

This software counts the number of times the laser beam has been interrupted, updates the LCD with this information, and looks for reset button events.

```
'{$STAMP BS2}
Button1       VAR     Byte
trip_count    VAR     Byte
N9600 con     $4054
I             con     254
CLR           con     1
LINE2 con     192
L2_C1 con     135
L2_C7 con     199


' cube intrusion system version 1.0
' 5/12/02
' Scott Fullam

Gosub Init_Pins

Gosub Init_LCD

Start:

Gosub Scan_button

if IN1 = 0 then Start
out15 = 1
read 0, trip_count
trip_count = trip_count + 1
write 0, trip_count

serout 0,n9600,[I,LINE2]
serout 0,n9600,["Count:"]
serout 0,n9600,[I,L2_C7]
serout 0,n9600,[DEC trip_count, "    "]
pause 1000
fall_laser:
if in1 = 1 then fall_laser
out15 = 0

Goto Start

Init_Pins:
Input 1
input 2
output 15
output 0
out15 = 0
return
```

Exhibit C

BasicStamp2 Software *(continued)*

```
Init_LCD:
pause 1000
serout 0,n9600,[I,CLR]
pause 1
serout 0,n9600,["Cubemon 1.0"]

return

Scan_button:
' the button used is normall closed and will open up when pressed
if IN2 = 0 then end_state
trip_count = 0
write 0,trip_count
serout 0,n9600,[I,LINE2]
serout 0,n9600,["Count:"]
serout 0,n9600,[I,L2_C7]
serout 0,n9600,[DEC trip_count, "    "]

end_state:

Return
```

Exhibit D: Schematic Diagram for Laser-Based System

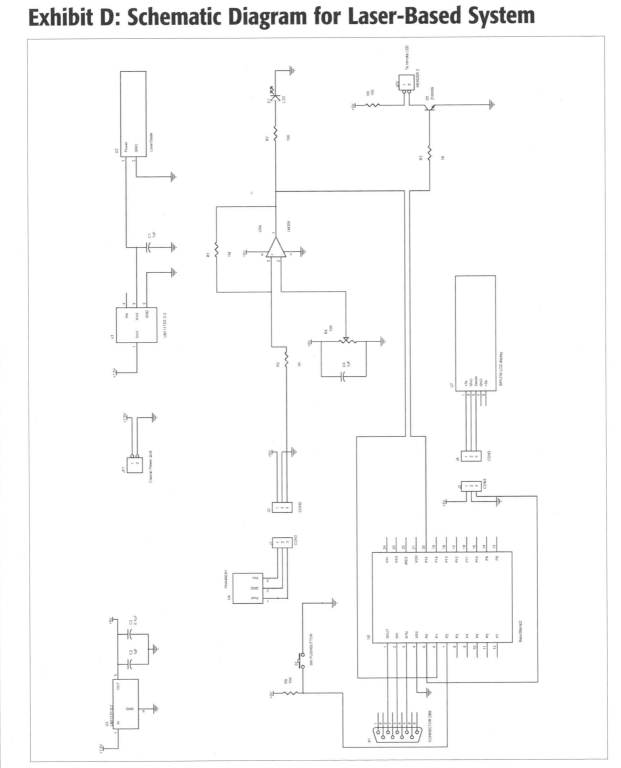

Chapter 9, How to Build a Cubicle Intrusion Detection System

Exhibit E: Schematic Diagram for Entry Alert–Based System

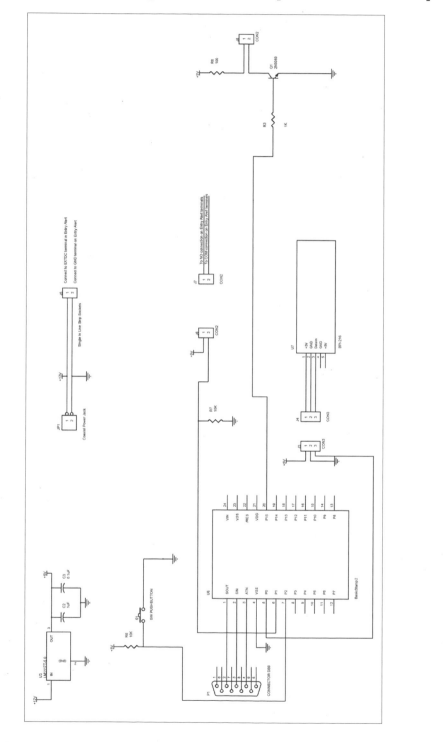

How to Build an Internet Toaster

10

Cost

$50–100

Time

a weekend

Difficulty

difficult

Not too long ago, as I was eating a quick breakfast of toast and orange juice, I was thinking about whether I should bring a coat with me to work. As I crunched on my toast, I recalled the story of a student in the U.K. who had designed and built a toaster that delivered a weather report to his toast. I thought to myself, I have a toaster and I have an extra microcontroller in my parts bin. Why not build my own interactive toaster?

In this chapter, I will show you how you can hack your toaster to toast one of several different patterns onto a piece of bread. You'll be able to display messages and information on a small LCD delivered wirelessly to the toaster from your home PC.

Robin Southgate has documented his Toasty project quite well at *http://news.bbc.co.uk/1/hi/sci/tech/1264205.stm*. His project uses a Java controller and a different mask material from what I use here.

Credits

All photographs copyright © 2003 Scott Fullam.

Toaster Technologies

Nichrome wires are an older heating technology that you see in most toasters. Nichrome is a metal alloy made from nickel and chrome that can heat to several hundred degrees Fahrenheit when a 120-volt current passes through it. It does not melt, is easily bent and shaped, and does not grow brittle with use and time. Nichrome is a common heating element used not just in toasters but also in many industrial heating applications. The wire in a toaster loops over a sheet of mica board, which tolerates very high temperatures without burning or changing properties and does not conduct electricity. It is a very effective base upon which to place the nichrome wire.

The quartz rod heating element I found in a few newer toasters uses a single piece of quartz, which heats when a 120-volt current passes through it. Quartz is not a metal and is not easily bent. This heating rod is mounted in front of a curved reflector to evenly spread its heat to the object being toasted.

Project Overview

This project requires you to open up the toaster and modify the heating coils. Next you will create a "mask" pattern that will cause a pattern to be toasted onto the target bread. Finally, you will build a small microcontroller board that will accept commands via a PC serial port and select a toasting mask pattern.

Before You Start

When I started this hack I had a number of goals in mind:

- I must be able to use a standard toaster
- I should not have to completely gut and rebuild the toaster to make this hack work
- I should be able to toast a variety of patterns onto the bread
- I should be able to create a toaster interface that is simple and easy to modify

I started by opening up an extra toaster I had lying around to see what was inside. I found a lot of breadcrumbs, layers of thin sheetmetal, and mica sheets wound with nichrome wire.

I also spent some time at a local appliance store to see what new toaster technologies were available. I found two types of toasting elements: nichrome wires and quartz heating elements with reflectors (see the sidebar Toaster Technologies).

After this examination, I thought about the various ways of "printing" to a piece of bread. I came up with the following ideas:

- Two-dimensional heating element matrix
- Linear heating element
- Heat shield mask

The two-dimensional heating element matrix would consist of 100 heating points arranged in a 10-by-10 pattern positioned in front of the bread. One hundred transistors or other solid state switches would be needed for control. This could get expensive; a completely new heating array would have to be constructed, and little of the original toaster could be reused.

I next thought about the method by which inkjet printers work: a line of nozzles through which ink is sprayed. Using this model, a line of addressable and controllable heating elements could be constructed. This linear array would be positioned at the top of the toaster, and a motorized platform would slowly raise the toast past this heating array. This seemed rather complicated. Figure 10-1 shows a simple diagram outlining this approach.

Then I thought of the process of toasting patterns as being close to exposing a piece of film to light. Areas of the bread that are covered from the heat would toast much less than areas exposed to the heating wires. I began making a series of aluminum foil masks to be placed between the toast and the heating wires. After experimenting with a number of different sizes and patterns, I determined that a lot of the bread had to be exposed to the heating elements to attain a reasonable toasting time. See Figure 10-2 for a simple diagram outlining this approach.

I then hit upon the idea of using a piece of large diameter copper wire to make letters and shapes. The wire would mask off a relatively small area of the bread from the heating elements, ensuring a reasonable toasting time. The pattern would be a lighter toasted pattern on a darker background. A few experiments with this proved to be successful. I also determined that the wire-formed mask should be placed as close as possible to the item being toasted to ensure that the pattern would be clear. See Figure 10-3 for a simple diagram outlining this approach.

The final matter to address was how to toast more than one pattern onto the bread using the existing nichrome elements. The simplest way was to segment the toasting wire into sections with a wire mask pattern in front of each and switch on different sections, depending upon which pattern was desired. I examined the wiring pattern for one of the sides of the toasting elements and determined how to cut it into sections. I decided to allow only two sections on the first model in order to keep the electronics easy to build and simple to debug. I selected a large relay as the wire switcher because it could easily handle the 120VAC high-current signal for the nichrome wires, with minimal special interface electronics required. In this hack, you'll program your toaster to print only two different patterns.

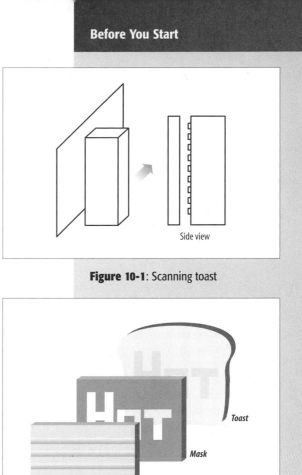

Figure 10-1: Scanning toast

Figure 10-2: Negative toast mask

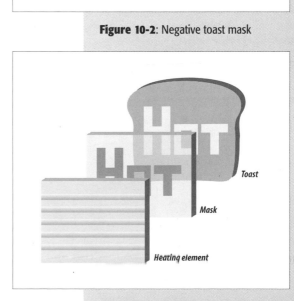

Figure 10-3: Positive toast mask

Hardware Assembly Instructions

In the following instructions, you will first carefully take apart the toaster. You will choose the desired toasting area as well as the toasting pattern. You'll construct a pattern mask using copper wire and secure it inside the toasting area. You'll cut and rewire the nichrome toasting wires and install a relay to switch between the two areas. Finally, you'll add a microprocessor to control the relay, a small LCD (liquid crystal display), and an optional interface to a PC.

1. Disassemble the toaster

You begin to hack the toaster by taking it apart very carefully. If you don't have an extra working one lying around, you can buy one for $20 to $30.

Remove the outer plastic (or metal) covers

The outer plastic covers on most toasters are held in place with a few screws. Carefully remove them and put them aside. Figure 10-4 shows the sides and bottom of my toaster.

Reveal the side toasting elements

After the side panels are removed, you should be able to see one of the mica sheets with nichrome wire around it. You can see a toaster without its sides in Figure 10-5. The mica sheet is held in place by a metal frame. The top piece of this metal frame should be removed. The mica and nichrome wire sheet should now be loose and movable, but will still be held together by several strips of metal that connect the wires to the 120VAC wall power.

Figure 10-4:
Toaster sides and bottom

Figure 10-5:
Toaster insides

2. Modify the nichrome heating element wiring

The wiring for the side heating elements must be modified to allow control of two independent heating zones. For this step you will need three one-foot sections of the high-temperature wire, wire crimps, and a crimping tool. (Go to your local appliance repair store and purchase three feet of appliance wire.)

Cut and modify the heating wires

If you are wiring one side of the toaster, the wiring should look like Figure 10-6. You must cut the wiring into two sections so that the toaster sides can be controlled independently.

Cut the wire at points A and B, as shown in Figure 10-6. The original wiring is shown as dotted lines. The mica sheet is somewhat delicate, so care should be taken when handling it to prevent permanent damage. I accidentally broke a small piece off when cutting the wires. A small break should not cause any problems; if the break is larger, you may be able to repair it with a fire-proof tape called *Kapton tape*.

Follow the diagram in Figure 10-7 to complete the final heating element rewiring. Cut the original wiring at the two cut locations.

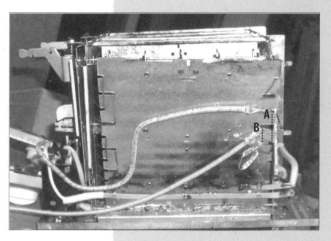

Figure 10-6: Heating element cuts

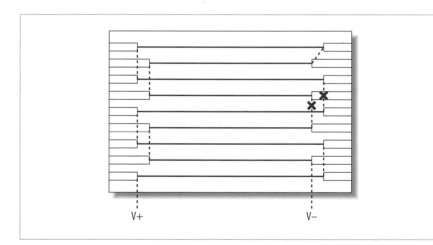

Figure 10-7: Heating element schematic

Add high-temperature wires

You will now add three lengths of high-temperature wire and a small shorting wire to the inside of the toaster. High-temperature wire must be used as insulation because standard wiring will melt and catch on fire when exposed to the heat inside a toaster.

Cut three one-foot lengths of the high-temperature wire. Strip off 1/4 inch of the insulation from the ends of the wires. You will be attaching the wires to the nichrome wire ends made previously using metal crimps. I considered using solder to make the connections, but I was concerned about having a lead-based metal alloy inside the toaster (solder contains about 60 percent lead); also, the solder might melt, since the inside of the toaster can reach up to 500 degrees Fahrenheit.

> The nichrome wire is delicate, so take care when handling it. The high-temperature wire is quite stiff, and may pull and break the nichrome wire when the two are attached together. To prevent this, you may want to pre-bend the high-temperature wire before attaching and installing it. You may also want to use small loops of 24-gauge solid bare wire (strip off the insulation from the wire) to secure the crimps in place.

You will need four metal crimps. If your crimps have a plastic shell on them, take a pair of wire cutters and remove it.

Figure 10-8: Heating element jumpers

At each connection point, insert the stripped end of the high-temperature wire into one end of the metal crimp and the short nichrome wire previously cut into the other. Firmly crimp the two together. Figure 10-8 shows the exact locations that need to be connected for the side wiring. Points A and B will have a wire crimped to them, and points C and D will be shorted together. For two points, C and D, I did not use the high-temperature wire; I took a short length of 22-gauge wire, folded it in on itself until I had a one-inch-long short with 5 lengths of the 22-gauge wire, and crimped it to points C and D. On the left side of Figure 10-8, you will also see where to connect the third piece of wire to an assembly.

Figure 10-9 is a closer look at how the wires are connected to the internal toaster electronics. The locations A, B, C, and D are the same as in the previous photo.

After you make each crimp connection, you will want to add some mechanical strain relief to each connection. The new wires are quite heavy relative to what the nichrome wire can withstand. I took a short piece of stripped 22-gauge solid core wire and made two small holes in the mica sheet next to points A and B in Figure 10-9. I looped the wire through the holes and around the crimp connection, taking care to not let the wire loop touch the nichrome wires on the other side.

You may want to cover over the crimps and new wiring to prevent shorting the line voltage that will soon be flowing through these wires. Normal black electrical tape will melt inside the toaster; instead use Kapton tape, which is capable of resisting high temperatures. Electronics stores, including DigiKey, carry this tape.

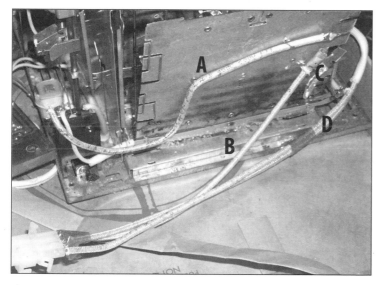

Figure 10-9: Top view of heating elements

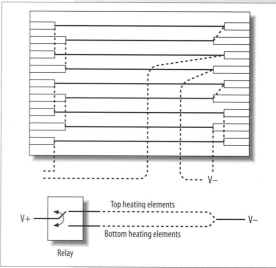

Figure 10-10: Heating element modifications schematic

The organization of the new wiring should look like Figure 10-10 when you've completed these steps. The figure also shows the location of the relay that will switch between the two circuits.

Add a connector to the three new wires

The toaster will now have three new wires on it. A reliable connector should now be added to allow easy testing and final assembly.

Figure 10-11:
Completed heating element modifications

Connect the three wires to a three-pin connector. You may need to pull back a few of the strands of the high-voltage wire to allow them to fit inside the connector. To ensure a reliable connection, I suggest that you solder the wires to the connector pins. The high-temperature wire will not be easy to solder to, so you'll need to use a high-power soldering iron. The completed wiring will look something like Figure 10-11.

3. Add a relay and test your wiring

Before you reassemble your toaster, you need to check to see if there are any wiring problems and confirm that the two-heating element zone can be controlled. You will need to wire in a high-current, high-voltage, single-pole double-throw switch.

Build a SPST switch for testing

A single-pole single-throw (SPST) switch will be used in place of the processor-controlled relay for testing. Use a switch that is rated for at least 10 amps of current at 120VAC. If possible, mount the relay in a project box. You will need to solder three wires to the three leads of the switch. Cut three one-foot lengths of the high-temperature wire and strip off 1/4 inch

Figure 10-12: Test switch

of the insulation from the ends of each. (You do not necessarily need to use the high-temperature wire, though it may be a little safer to do so; any wire that will withstand 120V at 10 amps will do.) You can see a photo of the completed switch assembly in Figure 10-12.

Add the mating connector of the toaster wire to the switch. I used a connector that was shaped to allow it to be plugged in only in one direction to prevent confusion.

Test the wiring

Plug the switch assembly into the toaster connector. Clear an area around the toaster and plug it in. Push the lever down and observe the heating wires: either the top or the bottom should heat up. If this is the case, unplug the toaster, and flip the switch to the other position. Plug it in again, press the plunger down again, and the other set of heating elements should glow red.

If neither or both heat up, check your wiring. Do not proceed until you have fixed the problem.

WARNING
The voltage inside the toaster is dangerous—you can receive a shock that can burn or kill you. When you have the toaster open and plugged in, do not touch any of the heating elements or wiring.

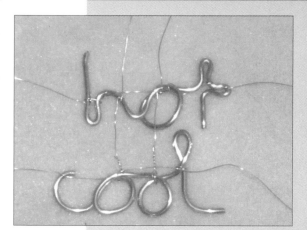

Figure 10-13: Toast mask

4. Build the toast message mask

The toast mask is the mechanism that "prints" the desired message onto the bread in the toaster. After some research, I found that the easiest-to-construct and most effective mask was one made from 8-gauge solid copper wire.

Begin by determining the two messages or patterns you want toasted onto the bread. Try to keep any words short as you will have limited room inside the toaster.

Strip any insulation off a one-foot length of the wire and bend it to the desired shape. You can see an example of my mask pattern in Figure 10-13.

You will probably want to link all of the letters together as I did to make the process of mounting them inside the toaster easier. The 8-gauge wire can be difficult to bend, and you will likely need a pair of pliers. You can also try experimenting with slightly thinner wire; 10- or 12-gauge may work. Do not be tempted to cut out the letters and try to solder them together; solder contains lead, and you do not want any lead near or touching the items to be toasted.

After bending the copper wire into shape, gently wash it with dish soap and dry it thoroughly.

Figure 10-14: Toast mask mounting

5. Install the toast message mask

Before you install the toast mask, you may need to cut some of the metal toast support platform. You can see what should be cut in Figure 10-14.

The toaster mask must be installed as close to the bread toasting area as possible. I used short lengths of 22-gauge wire to hold the mask pattern to the toaster grill inside the toaster. In Figure 10-15 you can see how I installed the mask using the wires inside the toaster. The mica sheet and modified heating wires are attached to the toaster and must be carefully bent forward while you secure the mask. Make sure that the toast mask does not touch any of the heating wires when everything is reassembled. Mount the mask on the bread side of the protective metal grill. It is OK for the mask to touch the toast as long

Figure 10-15:
Toast mask mounting close-up

as you used plain, uncoated copper wire. (Note that in the previous photo, the mask is backward. You should install yours so that the text is readable.)

6. Reassemble the toaster

Replace the top metal bracket holding the mica sheet and heating wires together. Cut a small hole in a corner of one of the plastic side plates to allow the three wires to pull through, as shown in Figure 10-16.

Put the top and side panels back on. The reassembled toaster should now look something like Figure 10-17.

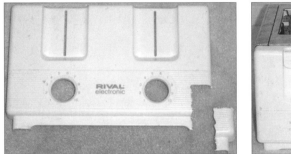

Figure 10-16:
Toaster front panel cut out

Figure 10-17:
Reassembled toaster front panel

7. Build the toast control unit (TCU)

The modified toaster requires a controller that will drive the relay to switch between toasting patterns, read a button, display text on a small LCD, and receive commands from a PC.

Add components to BasicX carrier board

I have chosen to use the BasicX controller and the BasicX carrier for this project. If you don't want to use the carrier board, you can build your own board using perf board and a few IC sockets. The TCU schematic diagram in Exhibit C shows the extra parts to add to the carrier board. Three wires from the relay should be terminated in a connector identical to the one you previously mounted onto the SPDT switch. High-temperature wire is not required for these wires. The board should look like Figure 10-18 after you have soldered these components in place.

Mount the TCU, switches, connectors, and display

After you have assembled the TCU and completed testing, mount the components into a plastic project box as shown in Figure 10-19.

Why the BasicX Controller?

Throughout this book I use a number of different microcontrollers. I do this to let you see how each controller works and give a flavor of the many different solutions available.

Figure 10-18:
Controller board wiring

Figure 10-19:
Completed controller box wiring

Cut a hole in the top half of the plastic box to allow the LCD to be seen when it is mounted in place. Drill four holes in the box that match up to the holes in the corners of the BasicX carrier board. Use four plastic nuts and bolts to hold the board to the case. Do the same to hold the LCD in place on the other half of the case.

8. Connect the TCU to the toaster and test it out

After the TCU has been assembled, connect it to the toaster via the three-pin plug on each side. It should look something like Figure 10-20 when completed.

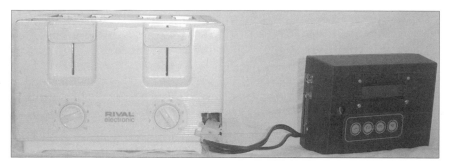

Figure 10-20: Completed toaster and controller box

Without plugging in the toaster, connect power to the TCU. The display will be blank, but the LED on the BasicX controller board should light up. Disconnect the toaster and the TCU, and connect the toaster to the SPDT switch you previously built. Plug the toaster in. Do not touch the switch. Push the toaster lever down and observe the heating coils inside; you should see only the top or the bottom turn red. Unplug the toaster and move the toggle switch to the other position. Plug the toaster in again and press the lever down; you should see the other half of the heating coils turn red.

If the heating coils do not work as they should, you need to unplug the toaster, take it apart, and check your wiring.

WARNING

When working with high voltages, I observe what I call the One-Hand Rule. This means you should keep one hand in your pocket whenever you are handling live, high-voltage circuits. Do not be tempted to use both hands at once; if one hand happens to brush against a high-voltage point and the other is touching a ground point, your body will create a path for electricity to flow across your heart. This high voltage may cause your heart to stop, which is a very bad thing!

Software Setup Instructions

I decided to keep the software running on the TCU simple. It performs the basic functions listed here:

- Controls LCD
- Reads button events from the front panel
- Reads and interprets data from the RS-232 serial port
- Controls heating coil selector relay

The TCU may be operated with or without a host PC gateway. When operated alone, it allows toast pattern selection from the buttons on the front of the TCU. When operated with a host gateway PC, toast pattern selection could be based on data gathered from the Internet by sending a command to the TCU over the gateway serial port.

The software written for the BasicX controller is listed in Exhibit B. The protocol the TCU uses is simple: when it receives the character A, it selects the top heating elements; when it receives the character B, it selects the bottom heating elements. The serial communications port is configured by the software to operate at 19200 bits per second with 8 data bits, no parity bits, and one stop bit. This can be abbreviated as 19200 bps 8N1.

Program the BasicX controller

You'll program the BasicX controller via the serial port of a PC running the BasicX programming software. You will need to type the listing as it appears in Exhibit B into the BasicX editor. You can also download the code from *http://www.oreilly.com/hardwarehacking*.

Start the BasicX software on a PC and open the TCU software file. Connect the BasicX carrier board to the PC serial port and plug in the board. Select the "program" option on the BasicX software; this will transfer the software from the PC to the BasicX controller. You are now ready to test your system.

Project Demo

After assembling the toaster and connecting the TCU, it's time to make some computer-controlled toast! Plug in the TCU and connect it to the toaster via the external three-pin connector. Place a slice of bread into the hacked toaster slot, select the desired toasting pattern either via the buttons on the front of the TCU or via the PC serial port, and press down the toast lever. Voilà!

This version of the hacked toaster can toast the word "hot" or "cool" on one side of a piece of bread. Figure 10-21 shows both selections.

Figure 10-21 Automated toast

Extensions

The TCU relies upon a PC to act. You can just as easily use a SitePlayer (or other embedded web server), as I will use to hack the coffeemaker in Chapter 15. This allows you to control the toaster directly from a web browser instead of having the PC as a proxy.

If you want to toast larger patterns on the bread, you can install a relay that switches the nichrome wires so that either the front or the back is toasted instead of just the top or bottom of one side of the bread. With the additional relay, you could control toasting of both sides independently.

You could also add a high-temperature sensor inside the toaster to determine the temperature during the toasting cycle.

Exhibit A: Bill of Materials

Item	Quantity	Notes
1N4001 diode	1	D1; DigiKey Part #1N4001DICT-ND
HEADER 3 connector	3	JP1, JP2, JP3; 0.100" spaced pins and sockets
HEADER 5 connector	2	JP4, JP5; 0.100" spaced pins and sockets
RELAY DPDT relay	1	K1; DigiKey Part #Z785-ND
Connector	1	P1; DigiKey Part #209F-ND
Transistor	1	Q1; DigiKey Part #2N5088-ND
2K resistor	1	R1; Digikey Part #2.0KQBK-ND
10K resistor	4	R2, R3, R4, R5; DigiKey Part #10KQBK-ND
Switch	4	S1, S2, S3, S4; DigiKey Part #CKN6009-ND
BPI-2162 Line LCD	1	U1; Parallax Part #27923
BasicX controller	1	U2; *http://www.basicx.com*
BasicX carrier circuit board	1	*http://www.basicx.com*
Three-pin connector to toaster	1	DigiKey Part #WM1221-ND
Solder tail style male pins for three-pin toaster connector	3	DigiKey Part #WM1004-ND
Three-pin connector to TCU	1	DigiKey Part #WM1231-ND
Solder tail style female pins for three-pin toaster connector	3	DigiKey Part #WM1005-ND
High-temperature wire	3 feet	10 amps, 120VAC, 300 degreees Fahrenheit
Plastic enclosure	1	Many sources
Voltage regulator	1	U3; DigiKey Part #LM7805CT-ND
Wire crimps and crimping tool		

Exhibit B: TCU Firmware Code

```
Option Explicit

Dim keypad1 as byte
Dim keypad2 as byte
Dim keypad3 as byte
Dim keypad4 as byte

Dim inbuffer1(1 to 20) as byte
Dim outbuffer1(1 to 20) as byte
Dim inbuffer3(1 to 20) as byte
Dim outbuffer3(1 to 20) as byte
Dim ch as byte
dim ch2 as byte
dim lettera as string
Dim letterb as string
dim codea as byte
dim codeb as byte

' Toast Control Unit firmware
' version 1.0
' 5/4/02
' Scott Fullam

Public Sub Main()

Call init_ports()

begin:
Call scan_keys()
Call scan_serialport()
GOTO begin


End Sub

Private Sub init_ports()
Call putpin (5, 3)
Call putpin (6,3)
Call putpin (7,3)
Call putpin (8,3)
Call Putpin (9, 0)
call putpin (10, 0)
call openqueue (inbuffer1, 20)
call openqueue (outbuffer1, 20)
call openqueue (outbuffer3, 20)

' set up com1 for communications to PC
Call OpenCom(1, 19200, Inbuffer1, Outbuffer1)
call Putqueuestr(Outbuffer1, "Toaster 1.0")
```

TCU Firmware Code *(continued)*

```
' set up pin 9 to send data to the LCD
' set to inverted logic, 8 datas bits, no parity
Call definecom3(0, 9, &H88)
Call OpenCom(3, 9600, inbuffer3, outbuffer3)
ch = 254
call putqueue (Outbuffer3, Ch, 1)
ch = 1
call putqueue (Outbuffer3, Ch, 1)
call Putqueuestr(Outbuffer3, " LCD Toast")

lettera = "A"
letterb = "B"
codea = Asc(lettera)
codeb = Asc(letterb)


End Sub

Private Sub Scan_keys()

keypad1 = getpin(5)
keypad2 = getpin(6)
keypad3 = getpin(7)
keypad4 = getpin(8)

' keypad button 1 activates pattern one of the toast
If (keypad1 = 0) then
     call putpin(10, 0)
     ch = 254
     call putqueue (Outbuffer3, Ch, 1)
     ch = 1
     call putqueue (Outbuffer3, Ch, 1)
     call Putqueuestr(Outbuffer3, " Hot Toast")
     call delay(0.5)
' keupad button 2 activates pattern two of the toast
elseif (keypad2 = 0) then
     call putpin(10,1)
     ch = 254
     call putqueue (Outbuffer3, Ch, 1)
     ch = 1
     call putqueue (Outbuffer3, Ch, 1)
     call putqueuestr(Outbuffer3, " Cool Toast")
     call delay(0.5)
elseif (keypad3 = 0) then
     ch = 254
     call putqueue (Outbuffer3, Ch, 1)
     ch = 1
     call putqueue (Outbuffer3, Ch, 1)
     call putqueuestr(Outbuffer3, " button3")
     call delay(0.5)
elseif (keypad4 = 0) then
     ch = 254
```

TCU Firmware Code *(continued)*

```
        call putqueue (Outbuffer3, Ch, 1)
        ch = 1
        call putqueue (Outbuffer3, Ch, 1)
        call putqueuestr(Outbuffer3, " button4")
        call delay(0.5)
else
end if

End Sub

private sub scan_serialport()

If statusqueue(inbuffer1) then
        call getqueue(inbuffer1, Ch, 1)
        if (ch = codea) then
                call putpin(10, 0)
                ch2 = 254
                call putqueue (Outbuffer3, Ch2, 1)
                ch2 = 1
                call putqueue (Outbuffer3, Ch2, 1)
                call Putqueuestr(Outbuffer3, " Hot Toast")
                call delay(0.5)
        elseif (ch = codeb) then
                call putpin(10, 1)
                ch2 = 254
                call putqueue (Outbuffer3, Ch2, 1)
                ch2 = 1
                call putqueue (Outbuffer3, Ch2, 1)
                call Putqueuestr(Outbuffer3, " Cool Toast")
                call delay(0.5)
        else
        end if
end if

end sub
```

Exhibit C

Exhibit C: Schematic Diagram for TCU

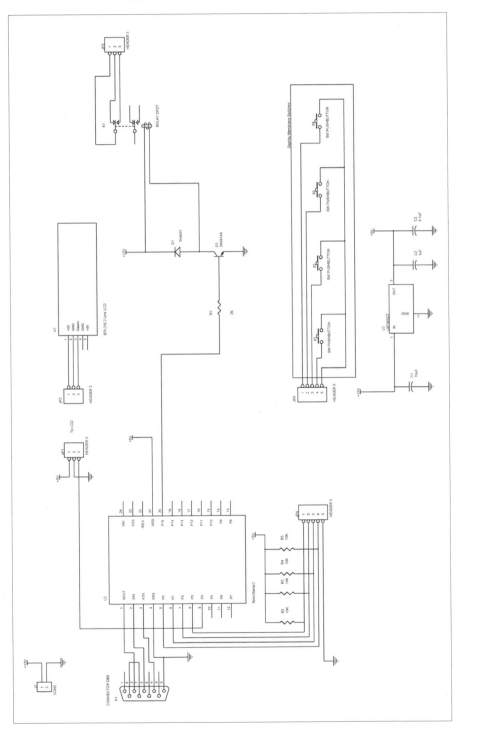

How to Build a Home Arcade Machine

Cost

$500–900

Time

one week

Difficulty

moderate

What You Need

- Basic woodworking tools (jigsaw, electric drill, files, T-square, clamps, Dremel motor tool)
- Medium-density fiberboard (MDF) sheets
- A PC
- Color TV set or PC monitor
- Arcade controls
- Soldering iron and solder
- Other items listed in Exhibit A

Do you have fond memories of spending your entire week's allowance playing Dig Dug, Defender, Pac-Man, Centipede, or any of the other great '80s arcade games? Are you having trouble finding any of these classic games to play? Have you ever wanted a full-size, stand-up arcade machine in your rec room at home?

If you answered "Yes" to any of these questions, read on! This chapter will show you how to hack together a full-size arcade machine that will play just about any arcade game. In fact, you can probably load almost every arcade game into the system. You will need lumber to build the cabinet, a spare PC, a color television set, a TV video board, and a set of arcade controls.

First, I will cover the construction of a full-size, arcade-quality, stand-up cabinet. For many people this will be the hardest part of this hack. Next, you will wire up a set of arcade controls to a front panel and wire them to an interface card. You will then install a TV set and PC inside the cabinet. Finally, you will load a piece of software called MAME on the PC.

The cabinet will give the machine a real arcade feel, but if you find this part of the project a bit much, you can simply build the arcade controls into a box and connect it to the PC. Or, if you want a cabinet but are not feeling particularly handy, you can buy a used arcade cabinet, refurbish it, and install new controls if necessary. Check your local yellow pages for dealers or look on eBay.

You will have several options for the controllers: you can build any combination of joysticks and trackballs. You will want to install at least one joystick and as many as three, depending on which games you want to play. Two-player games and games like BattleZone will require two joysticks, and games like Gauntlet can use three or more. A trackball will make games like Centipede feel like the original. The instructions for this hack allow for a trackball and three joysticks for maximum flexibility. If you don't want to add all of these, just don't drill out the holes for them.

The surface of the control panel will be covered with Formica to give it a clean look and make it a comfortable place to rest your hands when playing.

The basis for these instructions is courtesy of Jeff McClain. Check out his web site at *http://www.webpak.net/~jmcclain/mame/index.html.*

Project Overview

In this project you will build a five-foot-tall cabinet as well as an arcade-quality set of controls for the front. You'll also add an inexpensive PC and a color TV set or monitor inside the cabinet, and then install software called MAME. The MAME software can run under a number of operating systems including Windows, Mac OS, and Linux; choose the one with which you are most comfortable.

Hardware Assembly Instructions

Building the cabinet is by far the most time-consuming part of the project. It will require some carpentry skills and may take a few weekends to complete. It's a lot of work, but when you are done you will have a fantastic-looking video game cabinet. Before you begin, you'll want to familiarize yourself with the plans in Exhibit B.

If you already have an arcade cabinet with a working monitor, you can skip directly to Step 4. If the cabinet needs refinishing, look over "Paint and cover the cabinet" under Step 3.

1. Acquire materials and transfer plans

Purchase the required materials listed in the Cabinet Parts section of Exhibit A from your local lumberyard, hardware store, or plastics supply company. The sheets of wood will be rather large, so you might consider having the materials delivered to you.

Before you start cutting out the various pieces from the large sheets of MDF, you will need to transfer the plans onto the material. Print out a copy of the plans in Exhibit B and transfer the control points to the surface of the wood using a tape measure and a pencil. The cabinet's design is composed of straight lines, which should make the transfer process reasonably simple. The two sides of the cabinet are the same, so you can transfer and cut one side out first and then trace its outline onto the uncut wood.

2. Cut out the medium-density fiberboard

You will need some woodcutting tools to complete this step. Get your hands on a table saw, a skill saw, a small hand jigsaw, a one-yard-long metal ruler, and two sawhorses. (Note that these tools can be rented if needed.)

You'll now cut out the various pieces from the large sheets of MDF according to the pattern in Exhibit B. The biggest problem with 4-foot-by-8-foot MDF sheets is that you can't easily place them onto a table saw. You can make most of the smaller pieces by making gross cuts with a skill saw, and then shape them down to the final dimensions with nice straight lines on the table saw using the fence and T-square. It will be difficult to get the side panels up on a table saw for final trim. Guide the skill saw by hand to make your cuts for these large pieces.

Note that some of the edges and cuts won't match up exactly when you stack them side-by-side. To fix this, lie them back down on the sawhorses, stacked, and trim them back and even, trying to get as close to the original dimensions as possible. Leave a little extra material when you cut out the pieces so that you have something to work with later.

3. Assemble the cabinet

After you've cut out the sides and the supports for the cabinet, it is time to put them together.

Assemble the bottom and sides

In this step, refer to the cabinet plans in Exhibit B. Begin putting the bottom components together with the two side pieces. Use the two parts marked in the plans as "front half of bottom" and "back half of bottom" for the bottom, since it works out better in the 8-foot-by-4-foot sheets to have this section in two parts. Start by screwing the 3-inch-wide "kick plates" (these are the 3-inch-by-2-feet-4-inch strips of MDF from the plans) to the bottom pieces. (This will provide for a 2- to 3-inch elevated floor.) See Figure 11-1 for how this should look.

Figure 11-1: Cabinet sides

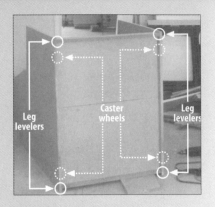

Figure 11-2: Cabinet bottom

If you plan to put caster wheels on the cabinet, you need to cut any slots for these recessed wheels during this step. Do the same for the leg levelers, which will provide an adjustable jack to make the cabinet sit level. It should look like Figure 11-2 when you have completed this task.

Add the top and back panels

Screw the floor to both of the side panels, with the side panels lying on their back edges. Make sure that you counter-sink your screws, meaning that you should drill out a small well so that when you screw two pieces of wood together the head of the screw does not stick out. Figure 11-3 shows a side-view plan of the cabinet. If you are still confused, ask someone in your hardware store.

Next, add the pieces marked "top panel," "back slant cover," and "bottom of marquee" to the locations shown in Figure 11-3, using screws to hold them together.

Screw the L-brackets into the locations indicated in the plans (and circled in Figure 11-4), in addition to the counter-sink screws from the sides. Note that all the cross pieces are recessed roughly one inch from the extreme edge. This makes the cabinet look a little more 3-D, and gives you room to route T-molding slots (more on this later) in the edges for finish work later.

Next, add the front spacer panel above the drawer, and another internal cross support behind it at an angle perpendicular to the front face.

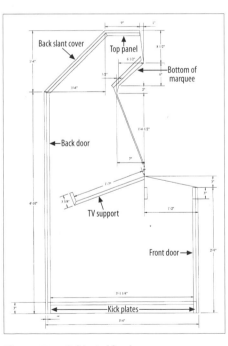

Figure 11-3: Cabinet side plans

Figure 11-4: Cabinet supports

Finally, line up the TV platform and screw in the runner supports. Then put the TV platform on top (for better support). Add a 2-inch-by-4-inch beam for cross support directly behind the TV platform. You can see where these pieces go in Figure 11-4.

Video screen mounting

Install the video monitor shelf, and place a number of small blocks of wood in key places on the TV platform to help support the TV and keep it from sliding back down the platform (details of this are circled in Figure 11-5). You should add metal corner brackets to all four bottom corners for vertical side-to-side stability, since having all of those access doors (front and back) can weaken the cabinet. Cut the holes for the two small fans in the rear slant top, and cut the rear and front doors out of 5/8-inch MDF.

Figure 11-5: Monitor mounts

The cabinet should be looking like a real arcade cabinet now. You can see some of the important details that you will want to incorporate in Figure 11-6. The magnetic latch is an elegant way to keep the front door closed, and the drawer gives you a place to put a keyboard and extra accessories. If you have space, adding additional metal L-brackets in corners will make the structure more sound.

Create a T-molding groove

Later, after the cabinet is assembled and painted, you will want to install the "T-molding," a soft plastic material that will finish off the edges of the wood. Normally, this material has a T-shaped cross section and comes in 25-foot lengths (depending on which vendor you obtain it from). You can see an example of what the T-molding looks like in Figure 11-7. The illustration shows the dimensions in inches for one type of this material.

Before you install it, however, you will need to cut a 1/8- to 1/4-inch groove (depending on which T-molding you purchase) into all of the edges in the front of the cabinet. This can be a very time-consuming process. If you want to take a shortcut, you can remove the portion of the molding that fits into the groove with a sharp knife. You now have a flat strip of molding that can be nailed or stapled to the edge of the wood without having to cut a groove in the edge.

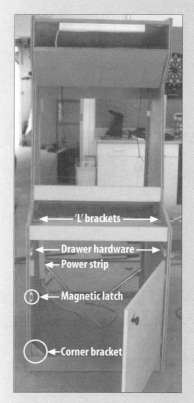

Figure 11-6: Cabinet front door

If you want to cut a groove in the wood, you can try several approaches.

Freehand Dremel tool or router. Purchase the router attachment for a Dremel motor tool and adjust the routing bit to cut a 1/8-inch slot. Carefully run this router bit on all the edges that will need the T-molding. This will likely take four to six hours to complete, and you will need a steady hand. You can also use a real router tool, which should take significantly less time than a Dremel tool.

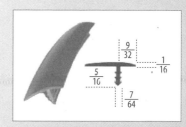

Figure 11-7: T-molding

Monitor Support

The MAME software supports standard PC monitors as well as NTSC video output cards. If you don't want to purchase a color TV set and have an extra monitor available, you can use that instead. You will need to add the appropriate mounting blocks to the monitor shelf.

Figure 11-8:
Cabinet speaker, light, and bezel location

Circular saw with guide. The blade height of most circular saws can be adjusted. If you have one of these saws, experiment a little to see if you can lift it up to a height appropriate for the T-molding groove. You may also want to make a simple wood-block guide to keep the saw blade from wandering when you cut. Also, look for a saw blade with the same thickness and groove as the T-molding you've purchased.

Cut Lexan bezel for monitor

You will now need to line up and cut the front Lexan bezel. Use a piece of 1-inch aluminum angle material and the PVC marquee-mounting plastic for the sides, which you can get from Happ Controls (*http://ww.happcontrols.com*). Place a small line of double-sided insulation weather-stripping tape around the edges to prevent vibration. The bezel should cover most of the background.

Mount speakers and leg levelers

Attach the leg leveler pads and plates with screws. Take the speaker fronts off the satellite boxes and drill two 2.5-inch holes (change this according to the speakers you purchase) in the front slant panel below the marquee. See the diagram in Figure 11-8 for an example. If you like, you can mount the volume control on an L-bracket inside the front door cabinet, which will make it easier to change the volume when playing.

Paint and cover the cabinet

Take everything apart and unscrew all the hinges, drawer slides, knobs, latches, and so on in preparation to paint or cover the whole thing. There are two methods for covering the surface of the MDF: paint or contact paper.

Paint. Use medium-grit sandpaper to sand off the rough edges of the wood, and clean the surface of the MDF with tack cloth (available at your local hardware store). Prime the wood with a gray spray paint and let dry. Paint with two or three coats of your final color paint and let dry thoroughly between coats. Spray paint will likely give the best finish. Paint only in a well-ventilated area and use a paint mask if available.

Contact paper. If you want a patterned look to the outside of the cabinet or you do not want the hassle of painting, you can use colored contact paper. Your local hardware or wall-covering store should carry several types of this paper. Purchase 20 to 30 percent more than you think you need, just in case you make a mistake. Begin by sanding the rough edges of the wood with medium grit sandpaper and clean the surface of the MDF with tack cloth. You may want to lightly spray-paint the areas where the contact paper is hard to fit in order to hide the wood. Apply the contact paper slowly, and make sure to work out the bubbles by rubbing the applied paper with a soft cloth. If you do get a bubble, you can carefully pierce it with a razor blade and smooth it out.

Assemble the marquee

Just above the screen of your arcade cabinet, you will want to have a backlit sign identifying your project. This "marquee" is constructed by printing out a color image onto a wide sheet of paper, sandwiching this paper between two sheets of Plexiglas, and placing it in front of a light source.

You can use an inexpensive fluorescent tube lamp as the light source. Simply mount it behind the marquee. If necessary, add a power cord long enough to reach to the bottom of the cabinet. The plug will be connected to a power outlet in the base.

You can use any image you want for the marquee; to make your own, design an image slightly smaller than 7 inches by 28 inches using your favorite paint program. If you want the classic image, you can get the marquee artwork printed at Kinkos for about $16 from the original TIF file available on the MAME web site (*http://www.mame.net*). Sandwich the print between two Plexiglas sheets of 7 inches by 28 inches each. Before you mount the marquee, install the florescent light fixture by simply screwing the assembly into the cabinet behind the sign. Use some of the marquee PVC stripping from Happ Controls to secure the Plexiglas sandwich to the top marquee location (with the fluorescent light behind it). Step back, flick on the marquee light, dim the lights, and watch as the project begins to look like a true arcade machine. It should look something like Figure 11-9.

Install the T-molding

If you cut a groove for the molding, choose a starting point to install it. Press the material into the groove and add a little hot-melt glue every few inches to keep it in place. If you have a tight fit, use a soft mallet to hammer it into place. If the hot-melt glue does not stick, use a small finishing nail to hold it in place

If you did not cut the groove, you will first need to trim the "leg" off the T-molding. Next, use a small nail every few inches to hold the material in place. You can try long leg staples, but they will not give as clean a finish as the finishing nails.

4. Build the controls

If you don't want to build the entire cabinet, you can build a very nice standalone arcade controller. The enclosure for a standalone controller holds arcade-quality joysticks, buttons, and trackballs as well as interfaces

Figure 11-9: Completed cabinet

to a PC. You will need to build a small box that sits below it to protect the wiring and controllers. If you are interested in other designs for standalone controllers, check out *http://www.arcadecontrols.com/arcade.htm*, which describes a large number of standalone control projects.

The instructions in this section show how to build the controls for the cabinet. This project has the option to install a trackball, control buttons, and up to three joysticks.

I recommend that you build the control panel and test it out with the PC before you mount the PC inside the cabinet. It is easier to troubleshoot problems this way.

There are a number of ways to interface your arcade controls to the PC. You can purchase a commercial key interface board from Happ Controls or other vendors, or you can hack apart a standard 104-key PC keyboard. High-quality key interface boards are available with PCI, ISA, and USB interfaces for your PC and allow you to connect standard arcade buttons and controls to your PC. If you would like to avoid the cost of a commercial board, you can take apart a standard PC keyboard and use its electronics to interface to the arcade buttons and controls. See the later sidebar Hacking a Keyboard.

To create the controller, you will cut out a wood panel, drill rough holes for the buttons and controls, add a nice Formica covering, drill out the final holes, add the buttons and controls, and finish the edges.

For this step you will need a subset of the items in Exhibit A, as shown in Table 11-1.

Table 11-1. List of needed materials for building the controls

Item	Quantity
5' x 2.5' Formica sheet	1
Contact cement	1 tube
#10 1.5" carriage screws	20
#10 nuts	20
#10 flat washers	20
#10 lock washers	20
Crimp wire connectors (0.188")	100
Contact cement	1 tube
Trackball (optional)	1
Joysticks	1–3
20-gauge stranded wire	100'
0.188" diameter crimp connectors	100

Table 11-1. List of needed materials for building the controls (continued)

Item	Quantity
2" x 2" hinges	2
IDE cable	1
Arcade buttons	1–26
Hagstrom Controllers KE72 button interface	1
Happ Controls 3" trackball (optional)	1
Hagstrom Controllers M24 trackball interface (optional)	1
Extra 104-key PC keyboard (if you plan to hack the keyboard electronics to a button interface instead of the Happ Controls boards)	1
Control panel parts cut from MDF	

Build the control panel

Mark all the locations from the template in Exhibit C on the piece of MDF used for the panel. Drill a small pilot hole through the center of each button location to enable you to find the centers after you've glued on the Formica. Also, mark out the area for the trackball (if you want to add it). Since the trackball area is large, you will cut it later with a jigsaw. (I suggest you use a router to clean out and trim the area after you add the Formica.)

Next, cut out a slightly oversized square section of the Formica on the table saw. Make rough marks on it for the control panel size, and add contact cement to both surfaces. Wait a few minutes until it is tacky, then flip the Formica over, line it up, and begin carefully pressing down a small section at a time. This needs to be done pretty quickly before the glue sets. Use a roller to continuously press the two glue surfaces together. After you finish this, let the glue dry completely before proceeding.

Once you've set the Formica top in place, take out the router and install a Formica edge trimmer. Use it to clean up the edges.

WARNING

If you've cut a groove for T-molding, you need to be careful with the Formica edge trimmer; the groove may cause some havoc with the small bearing spinner. The small ball bearings may slip into the groove, causing the edge you are trimming to no longer be straight and clean.

If you are installing a trackball, drill a small pilot hole in the center of the trackball area. Use a jigsaw to cut out the circular area you marked earlier, and use the Formica edge trimmer to clean the rough jigsaw edges. After you are sure everything is dry and set in place, flip the assembly over. Drill each of the button holes from the back side through the small pilot holes, just to punch through the Formica. This will leave a broken edge, but you will drill out 1 1/8-inch holes for the buttons and 1 3/4-inch for the joysticks anyway. Next, carefully drill from the front side with a larger bit. Make sure that the bit has a sharp edge to circumscribe a ring and make a nice edge on the Formica. Once you've completed this step, finish out the final punch through in the wood.

Install joysticks, buttons, and trackball

Place the joysticks and optional trackball on the face of the panel and mark the screw hole locations. Carefully drill down through the Formica, and mount the joysticks and trackball with size 10, 1 1/2-inch carriage-head screws, carefully using both flat and lock washers on the back side to hold them in place. Be careful not to turn the screws too much.

Secure all of the buttons and controls using the hardware included with each.

Interface the controls to the PC

After you have completed the control panel surface and mounted all of the buttons and controls, you will need to get the signals from these controls to interface with your PC. Either purchase a key interface controller or hack a keyboard (see the upcoming sidebar).

Wire the controls

You will now solder the controls to a wiring board. In order to avoid time-consuming troubleshooting of your wiring, try to make everything as neat as possible to help with locating wires later. You can see an example of what this should look like in Figure 11-10. Using lots of little zip ties and some little plastic sticky-backed anchors to zip-tie all the wiring will keep everything neat and routed.

Figure 11-10: Button wiring

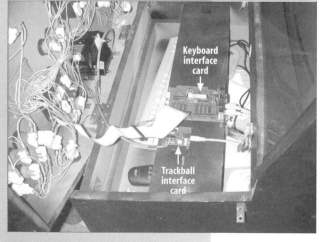

Start out by wiring four separate ground loop paths so that there won't be a catastrophe if one wire breaks. To do this, use the female crimp connectors to wire a loop of daisy-chained connectors, as shown in Figure 11-11. For the switched sides, cut off the end of an IDE cable (40-pin), and solder all 40 leads into a small project proto board, also shown in Figure 11-11. The two leads on each end (1,2 and 39,40) were common or GND lines and went into the two end bus traces, which you should then liberally run twin leads over to the bus bar.

Figure 11-11: Button interface wiring

The Player 1 joystick and buttons can be one loop; the center four-way joystick and buttons and MISC 5 can be another; the Player 2 joystick and buttons can be the third; and the trackball buttons, coin, and player can be the fourth. These all get wired in nice little loops with 20-gauge stranded wire and some small 0.188-inch coupling plugs. The final runs go into a bus bar.

Next, run cut-to-length traces from each control and solder them into each of the IDE cable lines on the project board. Once you've completed this step (it may take a while), mount the project board to the bottom of the control panel near the bottom of one of the hinges; the IDE cable should not stretch when you open the control panel.

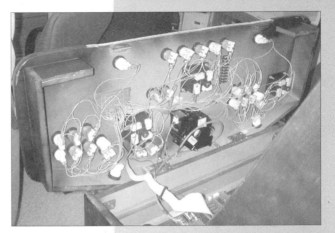

Figure 11-12: Completed button wiring

Mount the KE72 keyboard interface board and M24 trackball interface board with screws and a few small aluminum stand-off tubes on one of the cross braces above the drawer, far below where the control panel stuff (trackball, joysticks, and so forth) will reside when the control panel is in the closed position. These should be pointed toward the rear of the cabinet, so it will be easy to snake keyboard and mouse extensions out the rear and over the top of the drawer unit down to the CPU.

When you are finished, your wiring should look something like Figure 11-12. After you test your wiring, connect the control panel to the cabinet using two hinges, visible along the bottom edge of the control panel here.

A completed control panel should look something like Figure 11-13.

Figure 11-13: Control panel in place

Interface using a key interface controller

Purchase a controller interface card from Hagstrom Controls (*http://www. hagstromelectronics.com/*) and connect each button to one of the key inputs on the control board. These control boards are built for applications such as this, and you will avoid a whole series of problems associated with hacking apart a standard keyboard. There are a number of different interface boards available from Hagstrom, including PCI, USB, serial, and PS/2. Pick the module that has an interface that matches your PC. Figure 11-14 shows a popular encoder, the KE72.

After you have connected the button interface card, you need to figure out which of the 72 ports each button/joystick is hooked up to, so that you can build the keyboard-encoding configuration file.

Figure 11-14: Button interface card

Begin by opening up a sample file, and place a bunch of known characters for each port. Run the *KE72LOAD.EXE* program and open Notepad. Now just start pressing keys, and write down what you see on the screen for all the Player 1 and/or 2 and MISC buttons. Once you've completed this step, it is a simple matter to track down which character you assigned to which port and to begin replacing that character with the MAME characters. If you like, you can trace all the wiring back into the ribbon cable and all the way down, but this can be tedious and error-prone. When you press the keys and observe the results, you're guaranteed to know which port connects to what.

Once you've programmed all the keys, spend some time checking out a few games and playing around with the config file. It's probably a good idea to go into the TAB configuration in MAME and set up all the files (even if you basically use all the same keys) for the General Control. For example, in games that use two joysticks for one player control, like BattleZone and Bezerk, MAME doesn't use the Player 2 joystick as the Player 1's right joy. So go into the General Control and change it so that *all* two-joystick games will be set up this way. Also, MAME doesn't have Player 2 buttons 5 to 10 assigned to any keys. This can be fixed here also. Once you've completed this, all of these games should play well by using the Player 1 joy as the left control and the Player 2 joy as the right.

If you want more of an authentic feel, you can mount a button on the front door for the "Game Start" signal.

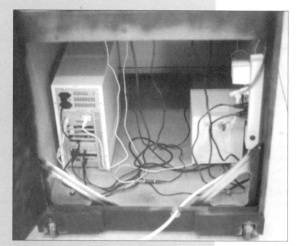

Figure 11-15: Back view of PC

Figure 11-16: Front view of PC

5. Install the monitor and PC

The monitor should slide into the shelf with the holding blocks you built previously. The PC case should fit into the space under the control panel; the door you built will allow easy access to it. See Figure 11-15. The cabinet should have plenty of room for your other video game systems as well.

After you have installed and tested out the PC, close up the doors and you are ready to go. The interior will look something like Figure 11-16.

Troubleshooting

If you find that the keyboard wiring is not working, there are some things to try. Carefully inspect the ground wires. Make sure all of your connections look good. Next, use a multi-meter set to measure resistance. Check that each of the signals from the encoder board goes to the switch you think it does. Inspect each solder and crimp connection.

The best way to avoid problems is to plan your wiring before you start and to label each wire. It may seem a bit cluttered at first, but being able to look at a wire and know where it is connected will save a lot of troubleshooting.

Software Setup Instructions

Now that you've finished your cabinet, it is time to install the software on the PC that will run all of your favorite games. The software you will install is called MAME, or Multiple Arcade Machine Emulator. MAME itself does not have the actual games—it is simply an emulator for all of the old arcade system hardware. You will need to obtain ROM files for the games you want to play.

Installing the MAME software

There are a number of software packages called *emulators* that run all the cool arcade games. MAME is one of the most popular, and it typically runs on top of Windows. Visit the MAME web site *(http://www.mame.net/)* and download the latest version of the software. This site has extensive instructions and help.

PC requirements

Although you can run the software on a minimally configured machine, it is recommended that you use at least a Pentium III with an 800 MHz clock, 256 MB RAM, 15 GB hard disk, and a generic Sound Blaster card. A network card, modem, and CD-ROM are nice to have. Check the MAME web site for the latest info on machine requirements.

Video and sound cards

You will not need the fastest 3-D video card on the market to run 1980s vintage 2-D games under MAME. Most VESA 2.0 or better video cards with at least 2 MB of memory will work well. You may want to choose a card that supports NTSC (standard video) out to allow you to drive a color TV set instead of a computer monitor. A good choice for this is the ATI Radeon board with TV out. If you want NTSC output without having to worry about special cards, you could use the TVator Pro VGA-NTSC converter used in Chapter 7.

A Sound Blaster–compatible card is your best bet for sound support.

Operating system

To check for the current most supported operating system, check the MAME web site. Most versions of Windows that support DirectX can run MAME. There is a version of MAME that runs under DOS as well.

Hacking a Keyboard

A standard PC keyboard can be disassembled, and wire can be connected to where the keys are located. These new wires at each key location can in turn be connected to one of the arcade buttons. This can take a considerable amount of time to complete and if the wrong sets of keys are chosen, things will not work as you expect. If you would like to learn more about this and some ways to avoid problems, take a look at *http://www.arcadecontrols.com/arcade_input.shtml#KeyboardGhosting*.

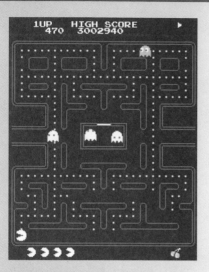

Figure 11-17: Pac-Man (© Atari)

ROM Files

The MAME software creates an actual game processor emulator. This means that it will run the original software that was stored on a Read-Only Memory (ROM) chip. MAME looks for files on your hard drive that contain a copy of these ROM chips. Note that under a strict interpretation of current copyright laws, you must legally purchase an original ROM to be allowed to make a copy of it on your hard disk. A quick search on the MAME site should point you to the appropriate web sites for games.

The ROM files for the arcade games software are rather small compared to today's hard-drive capacities. You should be able to easily store hundreds of games in 1 to 2 GB of hard disk space. A company named StarROMs offers licensed arcade ROMs for a large number of games. Their web site is *http://www.starroms. com*.

MAME software

The MAME software package will expand into a series of directories on your PC. There will be a README file that you should review before proceeding. For example, you can launch the MAME software under Windows by typing:

```
MAME digdug -640x480 -soundcard 1 -depth 8 -sr 11025
```

This causes MAME to run the game "digdug" at 640 by 480 resolution with 8-bit color depth, using a Sound Blaster sound card set with an output sample rate of 11025 samples per second. Note that you must have "digdug" ROM images in the appropriate directory on your PC. To play another game, substitute its filename for "digdug" in the command above.

A number of people have built automated frontends that allow you to avoid using your keyboard and mouse to select from all of the games on your hard drive. See *http://www.mame.net/frontend.html* for details.

Project Demo

Now is the moment you have been waiting for—playing one of those great '80s games on a full-size console. Start MAME with your desired ROM and enjoy! You can now enjoy a vintage game of Pac-Man, as in Figure 11-17.

Extensions

The basic MAME setup requires that each game be started from a Windows or DOS prompt. You may want to make this a little more elegant by eliminating the need to type on a keyboard to start the game. There are a number of automation utilities that show you a list of all games available on your system; you can select these using a joystick on the console.

Resources

These web links are for the parts and board vendors as well as for good MAME software and ROM sources.

> *http://www.mameworld.net/*
> *http://www.hagstromelectronics.com/*
> *http://www.happcontrols.com/*
> *http://www.mameworld.net/*
> *http://www.arcadeathome.com/*
> *http://www.mameworld.net/pc2jamma/*

Exhibit A: Bill of Materials

Item	Quantity	Notes
PC Controller Parts		
27" TV or SVGA monitor	1	27" color TV with SVideo input, remote control, and audio in/out RCA plugs or 17" SVGA monitor
Computer (minimum requirements)	1	PIII-800, 256MB DRAM, Sound Blaster card, 15GB hard drive, VESA 2.0 video card with optional NTSC video output. Optional: 40x Sony CD, 10/100 network card
AT case	1	Baby AT case and power supply
AT keyboard	1	Basic Windows 98 keyboard
KE72	1	Hagstrom Controllers keyboard interface
Trackball	1	Happ Controls professional 3" trackball and black mounting plate
Buttons	Up to 34	Various colors/styles of Happ Controls micro switch horizontal push buttons
Super joystick	1-3	Happ Controls Super Joy (4/8 way configurable)
Misc hardware		Corner brackets, angle brackets, screws, hinges, drawer slide, door magnetic latch, slide latch, bolts, nuts, glue
Paint	15	Primer and textured/chalkboard black paint
ME4	1	Hagstrom Controllers trackball/spinner interface + PS/2 cables
Fan assembly	2	120VAC cooling/ventilation fans with finger guards
Advent speakers	1	Inexpensive bass and satellite powered computer speakers
5' x 2.5' Formica sheet	1	Black marble Formica for controls surface
3.5" floppy	1	3.5" floppy drive
Leg levelers	4	Happ Controls leg levelers and plates
Misc cables	1	PS/2 to AT pigtail adapters, keyboard and PS/2 extensions, IDE cables, mini-plug to RCA cable, mini-plug splitter
Trackball mouse	1	Inexpensive PS/2 3 button trackball mouse
T-molding/PVC	50'	3/4" leather-texture black T-molding from Happ Controls and PVC black marquee sign bracket
6-outlet power strip	1	
Cabinet Parts		
3/4" MDF	2	4' x 8' sheet of 3/4" medium density fiber (MDF) board
5/8" MDF	1	4' x 8' sheet of 5/8" medium density fiber (MDF) board
Panel clamps	4	Clasp/clamps for latching the panel top down
Wire	2 spools	100' of black and red 14-gauge stranded wire for the panel
Wheel assembly	2	Happ Controls low profile wheels

Item	Quantity	Notes
Fluorescent light	1	18" fluorescent lamp for marquee
Crimp wire clips	100	Female wire crimp clips for joysticks/buttons
14-2 type Romex wire	10	Wiring for the AC fans and marquee light
#8 x 2" tapping flat head screw	100	Screws to hold cabinet together
2"x 2" hinge	6	Hardware store
2"x 2" L-bracket	10	Hardware store
3.5" castor wheel	4	Hardware store
Leg leveler	4	Hardware store or pool-table supply company
2" x 2" corner bracket	10	Hardware store
Drawer slide mechanism	1 set	Hardware store
30" x 28" x 3/16" Lexan or Plexiglas sheet	1	Hardware store
Magnetic door latch	2	Hardware store
Contact cement	1 tube	Hardware store
#10 1.5" carriage screws	20	Hardware store
#10 nuts	20	Hardware store
#10 flat washers	20	Hardware store
#10 lock washers	20	Hardware store
Hand tools		Table saw, skill saw, hand jigsaw, two sawhorses, handheld router, formica edge trimmer bit for router, 1/8" router bit, printer's knife
Matte black spray paint	1-2 cans	Hardware store
Optional decorative contact paper for cabinet		Hardware store
Crimp wire connectors (0.188")	100	Hardware store
20-gauge stranded wire	100'	Hardware store
6-outlet power strip	1	Hardware store

Exhibit B: Cabinet Plans

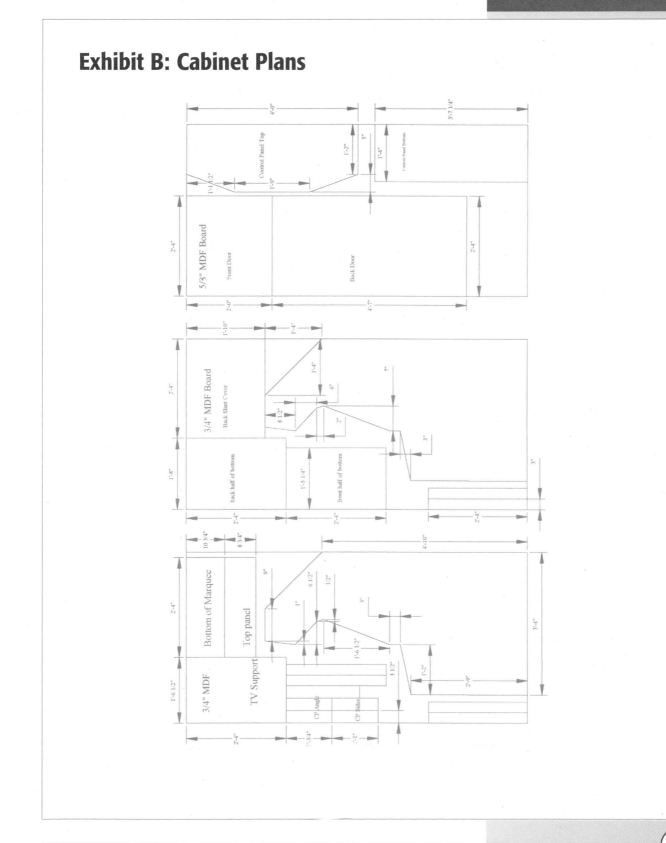

Exhibit C

Exhibit C: Control Panel Plans

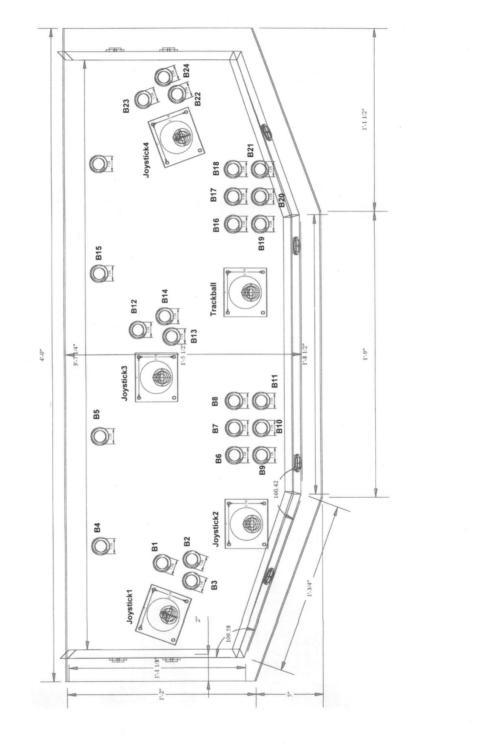

Exhibit D: Controls Schematic Diagram

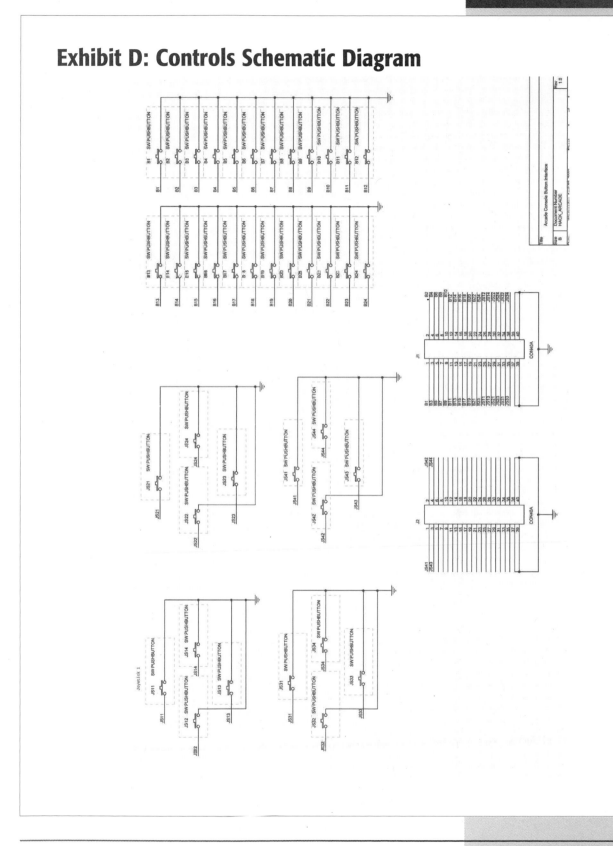

How to Build a Remote Object Tracker

12

Cost
$100–200

Time
a weekend

Difficulty
moderate

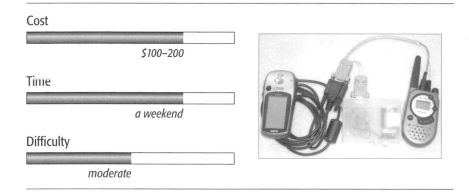

What You Need

- A pair of two-way radios (FRS will do)
- A GPS receiver
- A TinyTrack controller (a kit you will build)
- A Palm OS device or a laptop computer
- A Terminal Network Controller (or a TNC kit)
- Other items listed in Exhibit A

Figure 12-1. PDA map view

Credits
All photographs copyright © 2003 Scott Fullam.

A few years ago I ran across a new offshoot of amateur radio (also called ham radio) that caught my interest. This offshoot combined two technology gadgets that I like: GPS and two-way radios. This new system was called Automatic Packet Reporting System, or APRS. APRS allows you to track the location of a transmitter with GPS accuracy and view this location data on a PDA or a laptop computer. I put together one of these systems and had great fun tracking the location of a friend while hiking. The system also allowed us to send and receive text messages. Normally, APRS uses licensed ham radio transceivers to work, but I decided to use unlicensed Family Radio Service (FRS) radios instead.

In this hack I will show you how to take a couple of these inexpensive, two-way Family Radio Service radios, a GPS receiver, two small off-the-shelf circuit boards, and a PDA, and build a mini-LoJack system for your vehicle, bike, or any other object. Simply install the small black box on a car, a bike, a motorcycle, or even a person, and view its location on a real-time, moving-map display via a PDA or a laptop. You should be able to track objects up to two miles away. The view from the PDA screen will look something like Figure 12-1.

Project Overview

This hack uses the APRS technology developed in the amateur radio community. Depending on the PDA or laptop and operating system you use for this project, you should find a large number of software packages.

You will be putting together a position transmitter package and a data receiver package. The transmitter gathers GPS data and sends it out using an integrated two-way radio. The receiver package listens for the data packets sent by the transmitter using a second integrated two-way radio and then displays the decoded position of the transmitter on its screen. More than one transmitter can be picked up on the receiver. Each position transmitter has its own identification information, so you can easily track hundreds of objects. You can see an overview of how the transmitter and tracker work in the diagram in Figure 12-2.

You will construct the transmitter electronics and receiver electronics, and connect them to the FRS radios and one GPS unit.

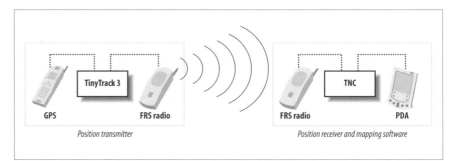

Figure 12-2: Tracking system overview

APRS

In November of 1992, Bob Bruniga (WB4APR) showed a DOS version of an APRS system at the ARRL Digital Communications Conference (DCC) in New Jersey. Bob created the system to report position, weather, and messages between people.

Hardware Assembly Instructions

The following instructions walk you through the construction of the transmitter and the receiver for your remote object tracker.

1. Build a transmitter

You will first assemble the transmitter out of a TinyTrack electronics kit, a low-cost GPS receiver, and a two-way radio. The kit includes all the required electronic components and a circuit board, which means the total assembly time should be only a few hours. The GPS receiver connects to this circuit board via a serial port. Finally, you'll connect the two-way radio to the circuit board through its built-in headset and microphone ports.

Locate a GPS receiver

There are many inexpensive new and used GPS receivers available on the market today. You should choose one that supports NMEA (National Marine Electronics Association) output from an RS-232 interface. Some appropriate models are:

- Any modern Garmin, including the eTrex, GPS12, or GPS V

- Any modern Magellan, including the Meridian and Sportrak series

- DeLorme Tripmate (with a slight modification)

- DeLorme Earthmate (with a data converter)

The modern units from Garmin and Magellan have an RS-232 compatible serial output. A cable from the manufacturer is all that is needed for the external connections.

The DeLorme Tripmate can be used if it is slightly modified. To modify the Tripmate for use with this hack, simply wire up two DB9 male connectors as shown in Exhibit C. The Tripmate operates off of four AA batteries that you install inside the case. If you want to run it from an external power source, add a connector to the DB9 connector on the right side labeled J1. J1 will accept a voltage from 5V to 6V, so you can connect an external battery pack of four AA or larger batteries.

The DeLorme Earthmate cannot be modified in the same way. It sends out data in a format incompatible with NMEA. However, its data output can be converted using the GST-1 NMEA "sentence converter" available from *http://www.byonics.com*. This sentence converter changes the non-NMEA data that the Earthmate sends out into the standard NMEA data required by this project.

I used a Garmin eTrex Vista with PC interface cable, which I bought on eBay, for my system. This eTrex unit requires a special serial port cable, which I also bought on eBay.

Obtain and build a TinyTrack

The TinyTrack is a small GPS position encoder that will transmit GPS data over a radio. A complete kit that includes all the necessary parts as well as a programmed control is available from *http://www.byonics. com*.

Build the kit according to the instructions. It should take an hour or two to solder all of the parts into place. After you put the kit together it should look like Figure 12-3.

Figure 12-3: Assembled TinyTrack

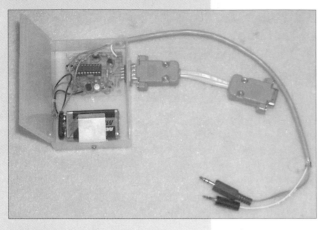

Figure 12-4:
TinyTrack with cables, case, and battery

You will then want to find a small case to hold the circuit board, a power switch, and a 9V battery. Figure 12-4 shows a clear plastic box holding the added radio cable, battery, and power switch. The TinyTrack kit includes instructions on how to connect a battery and the audio cables.

Locate a two-way radio

Two-way Family Radio Service radios have become incredibly popular in the U.S. in the past few years and can be found in almost every electronics and sporting-goods store for less than $40. Look for FRS-type radios, not low-cost walkie talkies. FRS two-way radios transmit and receive at 467 MHz and send out a half-watt signal capable of being received up to two miles away. You will be lucky if the cheap walkie talkies work twenty feet away.

While most moderately priced radios can be made to work with this hack, look for radios that have an external headset jack for both microphone and speaker and that support push to talk (PTT) on the microphone cable.

I used a Cobra MicroTalk model #FRS235 radio for this hack. It has two sockets on the top of the radio. One connects to an earphone and the other to a microphone. The microphone cable plugs directly into these two ports with no modifications to the radio.

I could mention a slew of radio models here, but Cobra, Motorola, Kenwood, ICOM, and Bell should all sell at least one model with a headset jack that supports PTT.

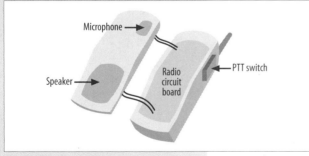

Figure 12-5:
Audio connection inside of a radio

If the radio you want to use does not have a headset jack, it can be hacked to add one. Open up the radio and look for the two wires connected to the speaker, the two wires connected to the microphone, and the transmit switch. Connect the speaker wires to the speaker cable, the microphone wires to the microphone cable, and one of the PTT signals to the transmit signal on the TinyTrack (you will have to experiment to determine which is the correct one).

Figure 12-5 shows a diagram of what the inside of a typical two-way radio might look like.

Connect the TinyTrack, radio, and GPS receiver

Gather together the GPS receiver, the TinyTrack kit, and one of the two-way radios. Inspect the headset jack and determine the size of the plug (or plugs).

If there are two plugs, each should be labeled as either a microphone input or a speaker output. Locate a two-conductor plug from Radio Shack that fits the speaker jack and wire it according to Figure 12-6. The "IN AUD" connection point is marked on the TinyTrack board. The ground connection is next to the battery ground connection. Don't make the two wires too long. You will probably want to use shielded cable to reduce the possible effects of noise, but if you keep the wire pair under six inches, you can probably get away without using shielded cable.

Locate a two-wire plug that fits in the microphone jack in the radio, and wire it according to Figure 12-7. The AUD + and AUD – connection points are to the left of the DB9 connector. Again, use shielded cable and keep the wires as short as possible.

If the radio has a single plug for the headset, you will need to determine which signals are on which wires. To do this, take a headset that plugs into the jack and use a multi-meter, set to resistance, to measure the resistance between pairs of the wires. The two wires that are connected to the speaker (earphone) should measure 16–40 Ohms. It is very likely that the part of the plug closest to the molded plastic will be the ground, the next segment toward the tip will be the Speaker + wire, and the tip will be the Microphone + signal. You can see how a typical three-wire connection might look in Figure 12-8. Your radio may be different, so make adjustments to this diagram based on your measurements.

The DB9 connector on the TinyTrack must be connected to your GPS receiver's serial connector. Depending on the type of connector, you may need to build an adapter. The cable that was included with my eTrex Vista had a female DB9 connector, which I needed to connect to the female connector on the TinyTrack, so I built a small "gender changer" according to the schematic in Exhibit D. This adapter also acted as a null modem, which is simply a set of wires that switch the radio's transmit and receive data lines. You may need to experiment with your specific GPS receiver's cable and adapters to get things to work. The TinyTrack unit has a feature that makes this process a little easier; one of the LEDs will light up green when the GPS receiver has obtained a position fix and the TinyTrack is receiving the data.

Make sure all of the plugs and adapters fit properly before moving on.

A schematic diagram of the cables I used is listed in Exhibit B.

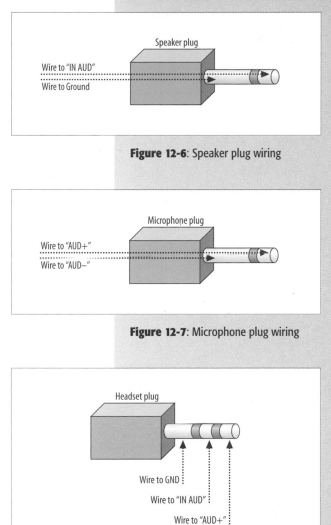

Figure 12-6: Speaker plug wiring

Figure 12-7: Microphone plug wiring

Figure 12-8: Combination plug wiring

Program the TinyTrack

You need to connect the TinyTrack to a Windows PC and program it before it can be used. To begin, simply connect the TinyTrack to the serial port on a PC, apply power to it, and run the TinyTrack Programming utility. The resulting screen should look something like Figure 12-9.

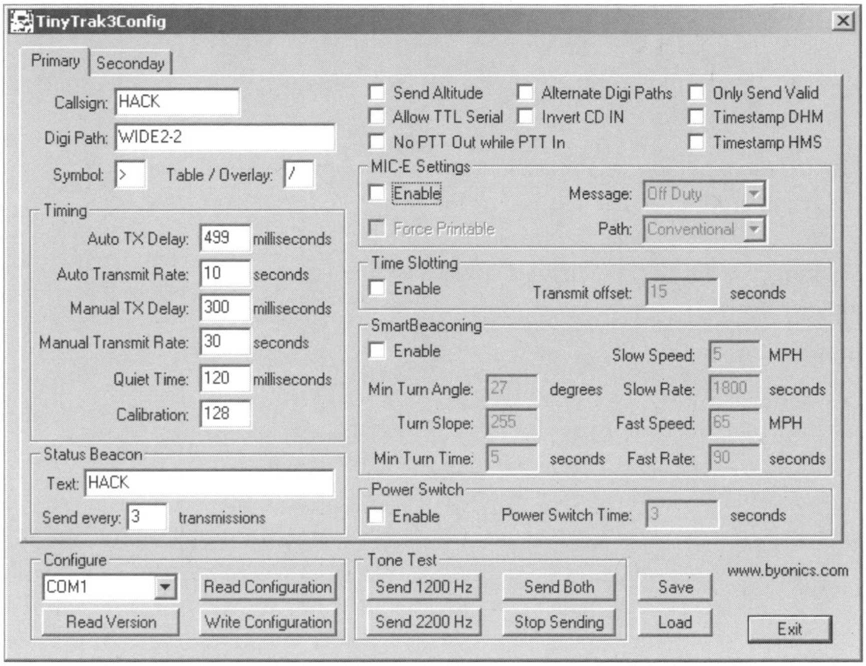

Figure 12-9: TinyTrack configuration software

Each of the following parameters must now be set:

Callsign. If the system were being used with amateur radio equipment, your FCC-assigned call sign would be set here. In this case, enter up to six letters and numbers to uniquely identify this particular transmitter.

Digi Path. Leave this with the default value of WIDE2-2.

Auto TX Delay. Set this to 499. This is the number of milliseconds after you've pressed the transmit key that the TinyTrack begins to broadcast the GPS data. You want this number as large as possible to accommodate the slow response time that some two-way radios have when the PTT is pressed to a generating radio signal.

Auto Transmit Rate. This is the interval in seconds between GPS updates. Set this to whatever interval you want. When you are first troubleshooting the system, set this to a small value, such as 10.

Quiet Time. This is the time that the radio channel must be "quiet" before it will transmit a location packet. If you have many of the position transmitters operating on the same frequency, or if your radio will share a channel with voice uses, set this to a low number, such as 120.

Status Beacon. If you want your transmitter to send out a short text message every few times it sends its location, enter the message here.

Send every _ transmissions. This number controls how often the beacon text message is sent. A setting of 1 will send it every time, a setting of 2 will send it every other time, and so on.

MIC-E Settings. Leave these settings disabled. This is for control of a microphone adapter.

After you have entered all the parameters you want, program them into the TinyTrack by clicking the Write Configuration button. Confirm that you've written everything correctly by clicking the Read Configuration button and verifying that you've saved the values you've just entered.

You can test out the TinyTrack by connecting it to a radio. Use the buttons in the Transmit section of the software to send constant tones. Use a second radio tuned to the same frequency as the first to confirm that everything is working (Figure 12-10).

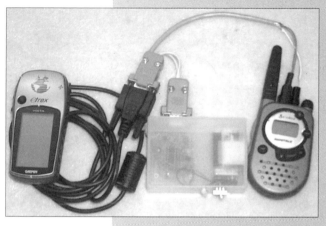

Figure 12-10:
Assembled position transmitter

2. Assemble a receiver

Now that you've assembled the transmitter, it's time to assemble the receiver. You'll construct the receiver using a Palm PDA or a laptop computer, a two-way radio, and either a fully assembled box called a Terminal Network Controller (TNC) or a kit form of the TNC. The Terminal Network Controller listens to the signals the radio picks up and translates them into a data stream that the Palm PDA software then displays. If you choose not to purchase the preassembled version of the Terminal Network Controller kit, you may need to build serial cable adapters.

Select a two-way radio

For simplicity, use the same kind of FRS radio that you chose for the transmitter.

Select and assemble the TNC

A Terminal Network Controller, or TNC, receives signals from the radio and translates them to a data stream that software running on a laptop computer or Palm PDA can interpret. It is a type of radio modem that includes some of the network communications protocol.

Prebuilt TNCs can be purchased from a number of companies. Table 12-1 lists some of the available models and the platforms on which they work.

Table 12-1. TNC models and vendors

Vendor	Model #	Compatibility
Kantronics	KPC3+	PC, Palm, Mac, Linux
MFJ Enterprises	MFJ-1270c	PC, Palm, Mac, Linux
Paccomm	PicoPacket	PC, Palm, Mac, Linux
Paccomm	HandiPacket	PC, Palm, Mac, Linux
Paccomm	Tiny 2 Mk II	PC, Palm, Mac, Linux
Tigertronics	BP-2	PC, Mac, Linux
Tigertronics	BP-2M	PC, Mac, Linux

If you've purchased one of these prebuilt TNCs, it's time to build a set of radio connectors, which you'll do in the same manner as in Step 1. The TNC should include a set of instructions on how to build radio connectors as well. I chose the HandiPacket TNC from Paccomm pictured in Figure 12-11.

If you wish to build a TNC from a kit and save some money (a prebuilt TNC can run $200–$300), purchase the PIC-based KISS mode TNC from *http://john.hansen.net/*. The kit includes a circuit board and all required electronic parts. It should take a few hours to solder the parts together; when you're finished it should look like Figure 12-12.

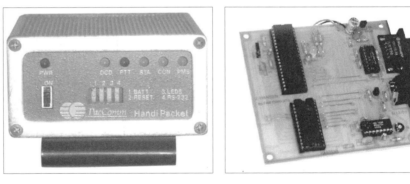

Figure 12-11: Commercial TNC   **Figure 12-12**: TNC kit

The TNC will usually include a cable to connect to your radio or, if not, instructions on how to build one.

Install the software

The radio receiver and the TNC must be connected to a laptop computer or a PDA to display the location of the transmitter on a map. Simply load a software package and run it with the TNC and radio attached.

Palm OS. If you use a Palm OS PDA as your receiver and moving map viewer, download the latest version of PocketAPRS from *http://www. pocketaprs.com/.* The site also has some maps of cities and local areas, which you may want to download to your Palm.

Once you have downloaded the package, you need to set it up. Launch the application. It may take a few seconds to start if there are a lot of maps loaded as well. Tap the "Settings" button and enter a unique six-letter password and numbers for "Callsign." Enter your time zone under "UTC Offset." Select the model of TNC you have under TNC Type. (If it is not listed, enter "KISS Mode".) Uncheck the "Dual Port TNC," "GPS," and "DRjr/microfinder" boxes. Check the "Use Kiss Mode" box if appropriate. Set the "Data rate" box to 1200. Set any "Units" you want. When done, tap "Done." On the next screen, you can enter any data you want. This screen will set up data that can be sent out from your Palm system over the radio. (The Receiver package has the capability to send messages as well.) Tap "Done" to move on to the next screen, and for now, uncheck all boxes.

Laptop PC. If you use a laptop PC as your receiver and map viewer, download a package from *http://aprs.rutgers.edu/.*

If you entered "KISS Mode" in the previous step, you will need to set your TNC to KISS mode. See the instructions that come with your TNC for how to do this.

If you have a HandiPacket, use the PicoPacket setting above.

PocketPC. There is a version of the APRS software available for the PocketPC from the Tucson Amateur Packet Radio group. Go to *http://www.tapr.org/ ~aprsce/* and download the latest version.

Assemble all the receiver components

Connect your Palm device to a serial cable and plug the DB9 connector at the end into a null-modem adapter. If you want to build one instead, follow the schematic diagram in Exhibit D. Connect the two radio plugs into the radio. When you've connected everything, it should look like Figure 12-13.

The various serial port connections may require gender changers and null-modem adapters.

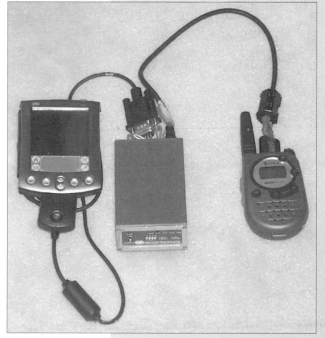

Figure 12-13:
Assembled position receiver

Figure 12-14:
Position reception software

Project Demo

Have a friend carry the transmitter package a few blocks from the receiver system. Make sure both systems are switched on and working on the same radio channel. You should soon see an image like Figure 12-14 on your own APRS screen.

The PDA- or laptop-based receiver can track many location transmitters as long as each has a unique identifier. Once you get one or two working, you may want to extend the range of the system. Read the Extensions section below for some pointers.

Each location transmitter works on a specific frequency or channel, so be sure to set the radios to the same before operation. The software running on the receiver allows you to record and save the received location data for later analysis and enjoyment. Experiment with the settings of the software to see what they do.

The trackers can be a lot of fun in a city, on a road trip, or when hiking in the woods. They can be used to watch the location of runners, bike racers, or the family car. (Just make sure that you tell the person using the car that its location is being watched!)

Extensions

The two-way radio is limited in output power to 500 milliwatts. If you're using well-made radios and operating them in an open environment, you should be able to get several miles of range. If you want a little more range, there are a number of things you can do.

Use a GMRS radio

General Mobile Radio Service (GMRS) radios have a higher power output than two-way radios and are also a little more expensive. Note that if you buy one, you are legally obliged to fill out a simple FCC operating application. There is no test to pass—you just need to fill out the paperwork.

Modify the antenna in your two-way radios

According to the FCC, you are not supposed to modify the antenna on your two-way radio, so what I write here is for information purposes only.

Open up your two-way radio case and locate the antenna and its connection point on the circuit board. Also locate the nearest ground point on the circuit board by using a multi-meter to measure resistance. With one probe touching the minus battery terminal, use the other probe to locate a point with zero or close to zero resistance.

Measure one 6.125" length of 12-gauge copper wire and one 6.125" length of stranded 28-gauge wire (neither diameter need be exact). Disconnect the old antenna and connect one of the lengths to the antenna terminal and the other to the ground point you located. The two pieces of wire should be arranged as in Figure 12-15.

A number of antenna design tools are available on the Web that can help you design other types of antennae. The two-way FRS radios operate at a frequency of approximately 467 MHz. Use this frequency with your web-based tools to calculate antenna component lengths, as their size is dependent on the operating frequency.

If one of your radios will be placed in a fixed location, you can connect the antenna you just built to a piece of low-loss RG-58 50 Ohm coaxial cable and mount the antenna at a tall location. Instead of connecting the antenna to the radio circuit board, connect one end of the coaxial cable.

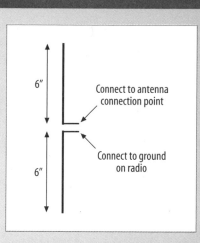

Figure 12-15:
Antenna dimensions

Set up a network of repeaters

If you can mount a radio at a particularly tall location, you can build a *repeater* that picks up data from transmitters and repeats it out. One of these record-and-playback systems is based on a PC sound card and is available from *http://www.synergenics.com/sc/*.

You can also set up TNCs to operate in *digipeater* mode. One small and relatively inexpensive standalone version is the PicoPacket from Paccomm (*http://www.paccomm.com/*). Another inexpensive, PC-based digipeater solution—called the BP-2 and available from Tigertronics (*http://www. tigertronics.com/*)—can be built with a special modem and software for the PC. If you purchase the BP-2, download the appropriate APRS software listed on its web page. The BP-2 connects to the serial port of your PC and uses special software drivers to send and receive radio data. The Tigertronics web page has extensive information on setup and operation.

Enable two-way messaging

The Palm APRS software not only allows you to receive and display transmitter location data; it can also send and receive messages from other Palm-based receivers. If you build two of them, the operators of these two devices could send and receive wireless messages back and forth.

Exhibit A: Bill of Materials

Item	Quantity	Notes
TinyTrack kit	1	TinyTrack3
FRS radio	2	Cobra, Motorola, Kenwood, ICOM, Bell
PDA	1	Any Palm OS 3.01 device with serial port
Palm Serial Port Adapter	1	Varies on Palm Model
TNC	1	HandiPacket from Paccomm, or a TNC kit
GPS Receiver	1	Garmin, Debosme, Magellin
Multi-meter	1	
Soldering iron and solder	1	Low-wattage iron
DB9 connectors	4	2 male, 2 female
22-gauge wire	10'	Used to connect TinyTrack and radio
2-conductor plug	1	
1/8" diameter stereo plug	1	
3/16" diameter stereo plug	1	

Exhibit B: Connection Cable Schematic Diagram

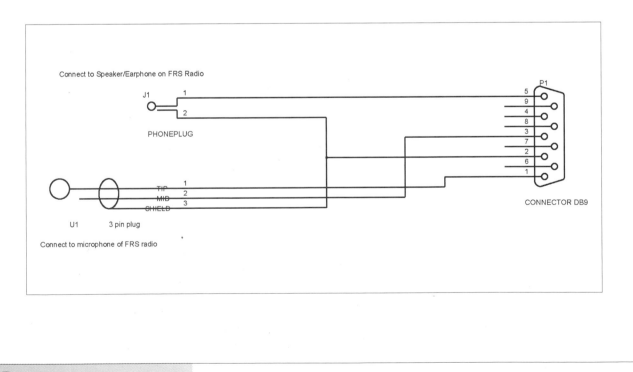

Exhibit C: Tripmate Adapter Schematic Diagram

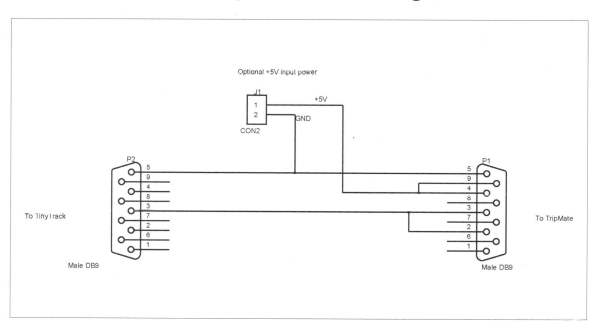

Exhibit D: Gender Changer and Null-Modem Schematic

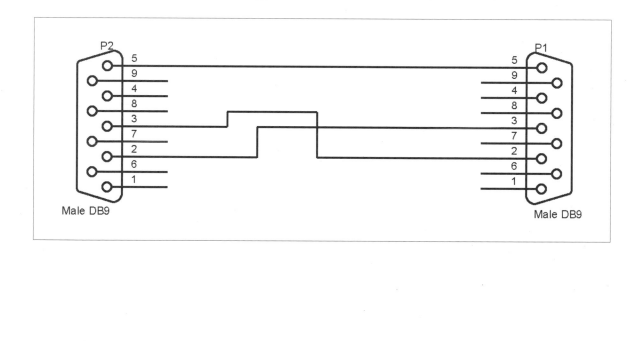

How to Make RC Cars Play Laser Tag

Cost
$50–100

Time
a weekend

Difficulty
difficult

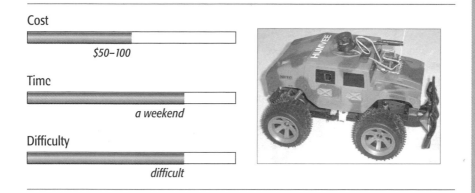

What You Need

- Two radio-controlled vehicles
- PIC chip programmer
- Other items listed in Exhibit A

I used to work at a consulting firm that specialized in toy design. I was the chief engineer and produced 20 to 30 complete prototype (read: hacked) toys per year. One of my favorite projects was hacking radio-controlled (RC) cars.

Radio-controlled cars and trucks are ideal toys for hacking. They're cheap, easily disassembled, and provide a lot of hacking opportunities. For example, you can create a small, autonomous robot; a robot that chases the family cat; a light-following vehicle; or a radio-controlled (RC) car that responds to commands sent from your TV's IR remote control.

In this hack, I'll show you how to hack an RC car to make it play laser tag. Instead of simply racing, the cars can shoot at one another, inflicting and sustaining damage with every hit. To build this hack, you will equip two off-the-shelf RC cars with a microprocessor, a radio link, an IR transmitter, and an IR receiver.

Most radio-controlled vehicles receive power via a DC drive motor that propels the vehicle forward and backward, and another DC motor that turns the steering mechanism to the right and left. Higher-end models use a flammable liquid fuel and move much faster than the all-electric models. In this hack, you need to use the electric-only models.

Credits

All photographs copyright © 2003 Scott Fullam.

Radio-Controlled Vehicle Power Systems

Most RC vehicles you'll find in toy stores are battery-powered. Some higher-end ("hobbyist") vehicles use a chemically powered engine (typically a combination of methanol, nitro methane, and oil). These more powerful engines move the car very fast—over 20 miles per hour in some cases. Electric power is also popular for higher-end as well as lower-end cars. Electric-powered vehicles are cleaner to operate (no messy liquid fuel) and can be operated indoors. This hack can be made to work with either kind of car, but in the instructions I'll assume you're hacking battery-operated vehicles.

Connectors

For projects in which I need small connectors, I use simple 0.100-inch-spaced "break-away" strip connectors. These small sockets can be easily made into either male or female connectors. I usually mount the connector on a circuit board with the female end facing out. I then solder wires into the female end of another connector, leaving the male end untouched, to make a compact and quick connector. You can get these connectors from DigiKey.

Project Overview

The first steps of this hack will be to build and attach an IR transmitter to the front of the vehicle, and then attach an IR receiver to the top. Next, you will build a small microcontroller board with a radio receiver and attach it to the IR transmitter and receiver. Finally, you will attach a radio transmitter to the remote controller. After hacking the hardware, you will load software onto the microprocessor.

Hardware Assembly Instructions

This project is suitable for toy-quality, battery-powered cars as well as gas and battery professional-level vehicles. The circuit board you'll build will borrow power from the vehicle, but can also be powered from its own batteries.

To complete this hack you will first disassemble two battery-powered radio-controlled cars. One you've completed that step, you will add a laser cannon, a hit sensor, and a control circuit board, and finally, you'll modify the remote control.

1. Disassemble the radio-controlled cars

Buy two remote-controlled cars from your local toy store or grab one from your kid's room. I built my car using a Nikko Humvee 1/14th scale 49 MHz model #140001BC.

Be sure to buy one 49 MHz car and one 27 MHz car; if you get both cars at the same frequency, each controller will control both of them.

Take off the top cover of the car chassis. You'll need access to the main circuit board. Next, remove all the screws that are holding the main circuit board in place and carefully pull it away from the body. *Do not cut any wires.*

2. Locate power on main circuit board

Search the main board to see where the battery wires connect. Determine polarity using a multi-meter. Solder a 5- to 6-inch length of wire pair to these points and add a small connector of your choice. You will use these wires to power the circuit.

3. Build the IR cannon and hit-sensor circuit board

You will now need to build a simple circuit board that has a micro-controller, a radio receiver circuit, and an IR receiver decoder circuit. Build this circuit board according to the schematic diagram in Exhibit C.

Figure 13-1:
Controller board close-up

Use sockets wherever possible to allow you to replace a damaged integrated circuit (either from miswiring, static electricity, or a bad chip). Cut a small piece of perforated board and install all of the parts except the integrated circuits (ICs). When you have completed this step it should look something like Figure 13-1.

Before you install the ICs, use a multi-meter to check that power and ground are not shorted together. Measure the resistance between the two parts of the circuit and ensure that it is more than a few kilo-Ohms.

4. Build the hit-sensor optics

Next, you will need to build a small assembly that can detect the infrared cannon signal from your opponent's vehicle. Locate an empty 35mm film canister (the new APS film canisters will probably work, too) and a small piece of reflective paper, which can be obtained at an art store. If you don't have the silver paper, you can try using aluminum foil.

Cut a 1.6-inch diameter circle of the reflective material. Make a cut from the center of the circle to the outside edge so you can make it into a cone.

Take the film canister, cut out three windows along the bottom, and trim the height. Use a small amount of super glue or hot-melt glue to hold the cone you've made inside the canister. When you've completed this step it should look something like Figure 13-2.

Next, take the IR receiver can and solder three wires, each six inches in length, to the three leads. Mount this assembly inside the top of the film canister. Cut a slot in the back to allow the wires to protrude. I used a small length of wire to secure the can to the canister top, as seen in Figure 13-3. You can use glue as well.

A side view of the bottom of the canister with the IR receiver is shown in Figure 13-4. You can see the three leads with wires soldered onto them protruding out the back.

Figure 13-2: IR reflector

Figure 13-3: IR receiver

Figure 13-4:
IR receiver mount side view

Figure 13-5:
Completed IR receiver

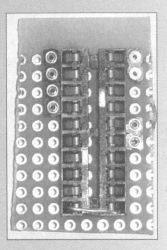

Figure 13-6:
Transmitter circuit board

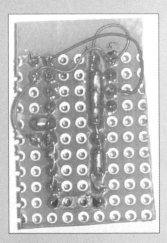

Figure 13-7:
Transmitter circuit board wiring

Finally, tape the cap with the IR receiver to the canister using black electrical tape. You will want to look at the reflective cone from the sides to make sure you can see the small black dot in the center of the receiver. Adjust the cone and cap as appropriate. When you have completed this step, the canister should look like Figure 13-5.

5. Add the IR cannon fire circuit to the remote controller

Now, you will modify the remote controller to add an IR cannon "trigger circuit." You are actually adding a second radio transmitter.

Construct a circuit according to the schematic diagram in Exhibit D. This circuit consists of two chips and a few connectors. I suggest you use sockets already in the board instead of directly soldering to the chips. Using sockets in your board allows you to easily replace damaged parts. Figure 13-6 shows an example of the IR cannon circuit board. Figure 13-7 is a view of the bottom of the board I built, showing my wiring.

When you've completed this step, your board should look something like Figure 13-8. The white wire protruding from the board is the antenna. As the schematic diagram in Exhibit D shows, you should make this wire as close to 17cm in length as you can.

Cut a 6- to 8-inch pair of wires. Solder a small pushbutton switch to one end and a small connector to the other. You can see this switch cable below the completed transmitter board in Figure 13-8.

Open up the remote control and locate the battery terminals. Solder a 4- to 6-inch pair of wires to these terminals. Add a small connector of your choice to the other end. You may want to add a small On/Off switch in line with one of these power wires. If you do not, you will need to remove the battery from the controller when not in use. If your remote controller already has a power switch, you can skip the extra On/Off switch.

Now place the transmitter board in an unused corner of the controller case and mount the switch cable to the case in a position that will make it easy to press. Allow the antenna wire to dangle out of the case. You may need to

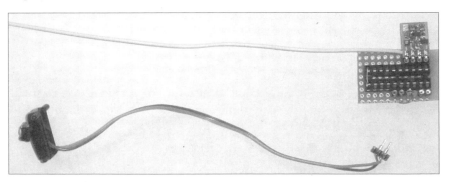

Figure 13-8: Completed transmitter and trigger

drill or cut a small hole for the antenna. Use a small bit of hot-melt glue or black electrical tape to hold the board in place. You can see the location of my transmitter board inside a controller in Figure 13-9.

Before closing things up, use a multi-meter to check that power is getting to the chips correctly. Once closed, you should see only the dangling antenna and extra switch, as shown in Figure 13-10.

Figure 13-9:
Transmitter mounting inside car controller

Figure 13-10:
Completed controller with trigger transmission

6. Mount the IR LED cannon to the RC vehicle

Locate the IR LED and solder a 6-inch pair of wires to the two leads. Solder a small connector to the other end. Make a mark on the wires so that you know the orientation of the LED. Take an old ballpoint pen and cut a 3- to 4-inch length of its tube. Open up both ends and insert the LED into one end; use a little black tape to secure the LED in place. Look for a location on the vehicle to secure this tube and the LED; I used the little plastic machine gun already on the car I purchased. Tape or glue the IR LED cannon in place as shown in Figure 13-11.

7. Mount the hit-sensor optics and IR cannon board to the RC vehicle

Find a point on the vehicle that is not blocked by other plastic parts and mount the hit-sensor optical assembly you built in Step 4. Also find a location for the IR cannon board. Ensure that all of these components have enough wire lengths to reach back to the control board; you may also need to drill a few holes in the vehicle case to feed the power wires through. You can see a good location for placing the hit-sensor optics in Figure 13-12.

Hit Sensor: IR Receiver Chip

The GP1UD26XK IR receiver chip from Sharp contains a number of functions. First, it has an IR phototransistor to receive infrared light energy. Second, it has a signal demodulator, which means that the chip will respond only to a 38 kHz modulated (or pulsed) IR signal. This feature allows the chip to reject light "noise" such as bright sunlight, fluorescent lighting, and random light pulses from shadowing and reflection. The main benefit of using this chip is that it detects only the signals you generate. This 38 kHz signal is commonly used in many remote controllers such as those you might find in your home.

Figure 13-11: IR cannon mounting

Figure 13-12: IR receiver mounting

Software Setup Instructions

After you have verified that power is going to the chips, it is time to program the microcontroller inside the IR cannon and the hit-sensor board. I chose the PIC16F876A controller, which is versatile and reasonably priced. You will need to locate a programmer for this part; I used the ICD2 programmer/emulator from Microchip. A large number of companies offer low-cost (less than $50) programmers on the Web. Do a quick search for "PIC programmer" and ensure that the model you choose can program the PIC16F876A (or whatever controller you use).

I wrote the control software for this hack in C to allow easy debugging. I used the C2C compiler from *http://www.picant.com/* as my C compiler. The very efficient C2C compiler targets the PIC family of processors.

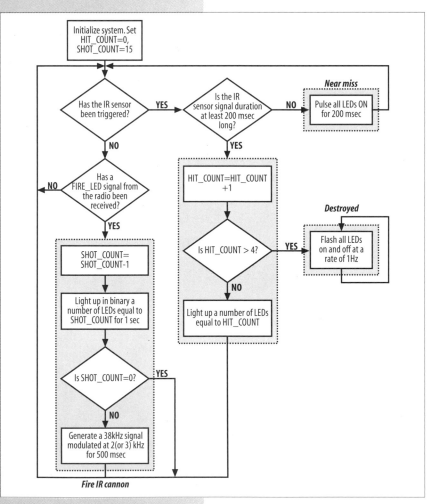

Figure 13-13: System software flowchart

After you purchase a programmer, download an evaluation copy of the C compiler. Compile the code, and then program the processor.

Software operation

The software looks for incoming IR signals and generates outbound IR cannon signals. A simple flowchart illustrating the logic is shown in Figure 13-13.

The IR cannon can be fired only 15 times, and the vehicle can take only four hits before it becomes disabled. Note that the four LEDs are used for three different purposes; the total number of hits will display on the LEDs in binary notation. When a near miss occurs, the LEDs will momentarily flash. After each shot, the total remaining shots flash in binary on the LEDs. When all hits are exhausted, all of the LEDs flash on and off. I've provided all the source code for the project in Exhibit B so you can make your own modifications.

Compile the code

Download a copy of the C compiler and install it on your PC. You will be able to run the demo version for a few weeks before you need to enter a validation key, which you can purchase if you like the product.

Start by creating a New Project, named whatever you like. You can see the New Project menu item in the upper left of Figure 13-14.

Next, create a new file and either type in or download (from *http://www. oreilly.com*) the C code into the compiler editor. The New File menu item is shown in the upper right.

Save the file using a name with the extension ".c". Add the file to the project, as shown in the lower left.

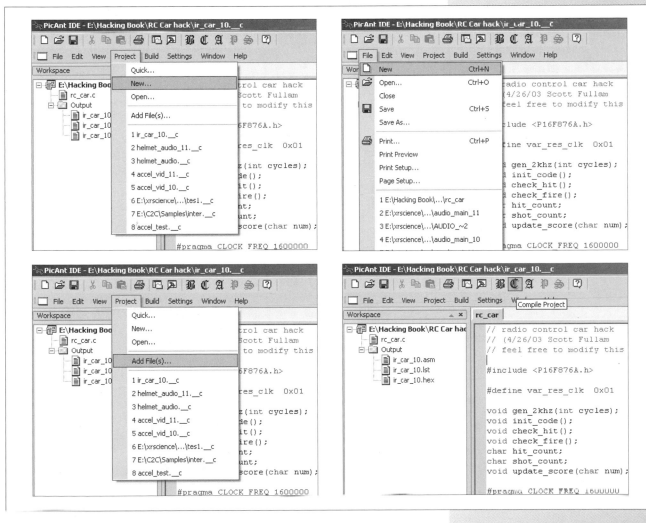

Figure 13-14: Software compiler operation

Chapter 13, How to Make RC Cars Play Laser Tag

IR Cannon Signals

The IR cannon sends out a 38 kHz signal, which is again modulated by a 2 kHz or 3 kHz signal. What this means is that we switch the 38 kHz pulses going to the IR LED on and off at a rate of 2,000 times per second. This is so we can later differentiate between two different IR cannons. The 2 kHz signal, which comes out of the IR receiver part, is decoded by another chip—the LM567 Tone Decoder. In the base software for the system, all vehicles send out the same 2 kHz-pulsed 38 kHz signal. A vehicle will not see its own signal even though its receiver is tuned to do so because the software ignores the hit sensor while the IR cannon is firing. I've left the tone decoders in place so you can more easily make this and other changes yourself.

Since our processor is quite flexible, we use software only on the chip to generate both the 38 kHz "carrier" and the 2 kHz or 3 kHz "modulated" signals.

Now compile the project, as shown in the lower right. The window at the bottom of the screen should show any compiler errors. The compiler will produce a file with the extension *.asm*, which will be used by an assembler. The C2C compiler tool has an assembler or you can use the free one from Microchip.

Program the PIC chip

You'll find a large number of programmers available for the PIC chip; I used the ICD2 tool from Microchip. To program the PIC chip using this tool, start the ICD2 software on your PC with the ICD2 pod connected to a free USB port. Plug the programming cable into the circuit board that holds the PIC chip. I had to build a small adapter to convert the 6-pin modular connector—which the ICD2 expects—to a small mini-connector on my board.

Start the ICD2 software. Open up the *.asm* file produced by the C2C compiler, as shown in Figure 13-15.

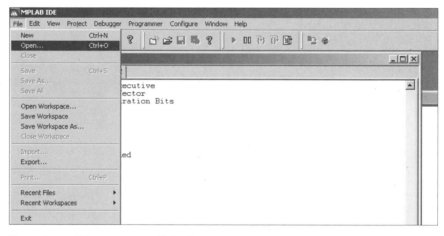

Figure 13-15: Chip programmer file load

Choose the PIC16F876A part from the Select Device menu, as shown in Figure 13-16.

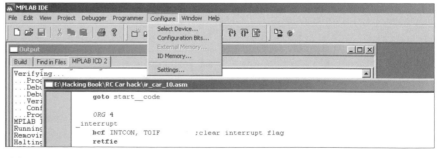

Figure 13-16: Select chip

Run the assembler using the Quickbuild option, as shown in Figure 13-17.

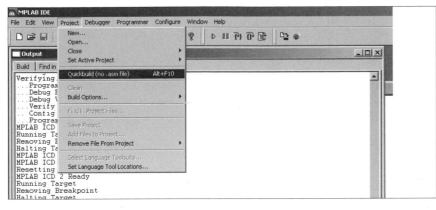

Figure 13-17: Software assembler

If you are using a programmer other than the ICD2, follow the instructions that came with that particular programmer. If you are using the ICD2, make sure that the configuration bits are set correctly, as in Figure 13-18.

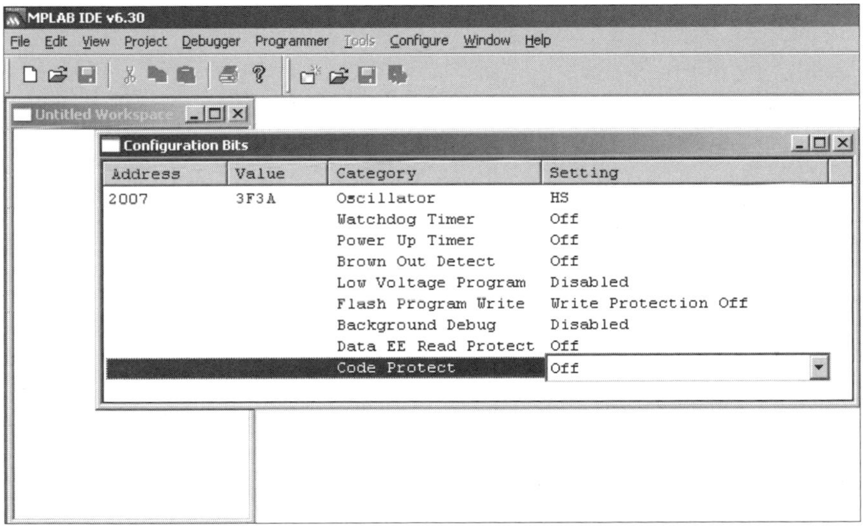

Figure 13-18: Chip configuration

Finally, program the chip as seen in Figure 13-19.

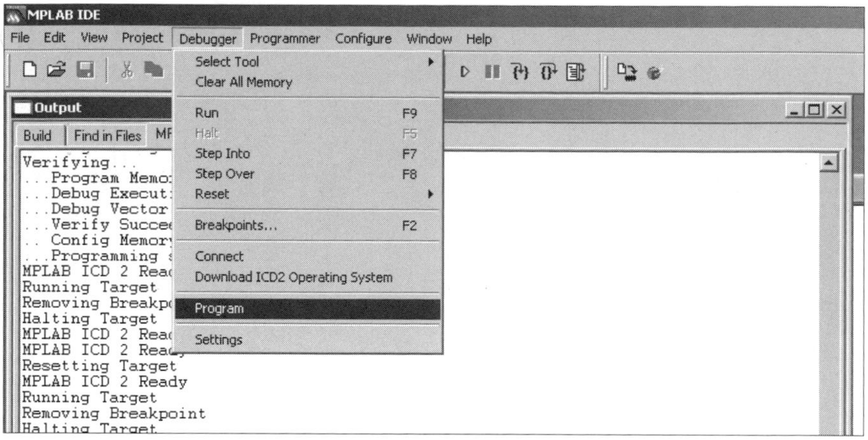

Figure 13-19: Program the chip

Project Demo

Now it's time to plug everything in and have some fun!

1. Plug the controller board into the RC vehicle power supply.

2. Connect the IR cannon and the IR sensor to the control board.

3. Switch on the board.

4. Drive towards your other, similarly equipped vehicle and let the dueling begin!

Extensions

There are many additional ways to hack a radio-controlled car. Among the more fun hacks are modifying the microprocessor software, or adding a small wireless camera, a sound effects chip, another power supply to power your own hardware from the car's battery, or additional sensors.

Software

The version of the software included with this chapter has a few limitations. For example, when you fire your IR LED at the other car, the software does not scan the sensors at the same time, which keeps your car from being hit when firing. This can, of course, be changed. I will leave it to you to discover this and other optimizations and make your own enhancements.

As mentioned previously, you can change how the cars behave when they're hit by modifying this hack's hardware and software yourself. For example, you could make one car less susceptible to damage than the other, which is ideal for rivalries between an older and younger sibling, or between child and parent.

Wireless video camera

An inexpensive wireless camera can be mounted on the car to allow you to sit "in the driver's seat" as you control the vehicle.

You will need two items for this extension: an inexpensive X-10 wireless camera kit and a small LCD television set.

The X-10 camera and 2.4 GHz wireless transmitter can be used as is, but you may find that the camera does not provide very good image quality and is sensitive to light-level changes. You may want to add a higher-quality camera, such as the one used in Chapter 6.

Buy the Xcam2 system from *http://www.x10.com*. You'll have to make modifications to its transmitter, including adding an omnidirectional antenna and a power supply converter.

The antenna that comes with the camera is highly directional, and should be replaced with an omnidirectional one. A simple 2.4 GHz antenna can be built from a short length of RG-174 coaxial cable. Take an 8-inch length of cable and strip away 2 inches of the outer coating, being careful not to cut the metal shield. Roll it back onto the cable so that a 2-inch length of the center conductor is exposed. Add solder to the exposed shield. Now, trim the length of shield and exposed center conductor to 1.17 inches. Cover the peeled-back shield and exposed center conductor with a length of heat shrink to protect everything. Remove the directional antenna from the X-10 transmitter and attach the new antenna so that the 1.17-inch center conductor section is pointing up. You may need to attach a small plastic or wooden stick to keep it upright. Do not use metal; it will interfere with the new antenna.

The X-10 camera expects a 12V power input. Check the voltage output from your radio-controlled car; it will likely be either 4.8V or 9.6V. If your battery supplies 4.8V, you will need to connect a 5V to 12V DC/DC converter. This part can be purchased at *http://www.mouser.com*. If your battery supplies 9.6V, you will need a step-up switching regulator. The MAX 771 can be used to convert the battery voltage to the required 12V for the camera transmitter. Look on the Maxim web site (*http://www.maxim-ic.com*) for details. They even offer an evaluation kit to make construction easy.

The X-10 receiver can be used almost as is. You will need to locate a small LCD TV set with a video-in jack to connect to the X-10 receiver. Simply plug the video cable from the X-10 receiver into the video input on the portable TV set. You may need an adapter, depending on the model display you have. (Small LCD TV sets can be found on most Internet auction sites for less than $100.)

Sound effects

The same audio recording and playback chip used in Chapter 5, How to Hack a Furby (and Other Talking Toys), can be connected to the IR gun trigger to give realistic machine-gun sound effects. The Microchip controller can be connected to the sound chip to allow triggering of explosion sound effects when the vehicle gets hit. Tweak the software to achieve this.

Power supply

The battery pack that most radio-controlled cars use is either a sealed rechargeable pack or a standard AA or AAA dry cell. The voltage they provide may or may not be compatible with your processor and the other components you add. In order to use the existing battery pack to power your circuits, you will need to add a voltage converter. There are two types of voltage converters (or "regulators"): switching regulators and linear regulators.

You will need to check the voltage supply requirements for the processor and sensors. In this project, the PIC chip, IR receiver, and transmitter all use a +5V supply.

Linear voltage regulators. If you're using a radio-controlled car with a sealed battery pack, check the voltage. If it is greater than 5V (typically 7.2V, 8.4V, or 9.6V), use a linear regulator.

If the car operates via AA or AAA batteries, the voltage you'll need depends on how many batteries the car uses. If the car uses four AA or AAA batteries, for example, use a linear regulator to provide power to the PIC microcontroller and sensors.

The venerable LM7805 is the easiest linear regulator to find and use. This part has been around for years, and many different companies make it. Radio Shack carries the LM7805 in its catalog and stores.

Figure 13-20 illustrates a common LM7805 circuit.

Switching voltage regulators. When the source voltage is lower than the desired output voltage, a switching regulator is needed. There are many types available from Maxim Integrated Products (*http://www.maxim-ic.com*), National Semiconductor (*http://www.nsc.com*), or Linear Technology (*http://www.linear-tech.com*).

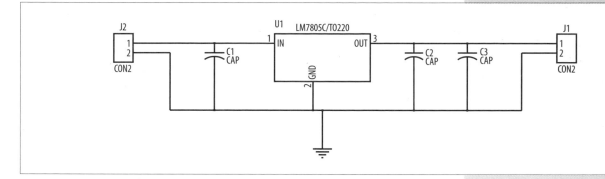

Figure 13-20: Linear voltage regulator

Touch sensors

As a simple alternative to using the IR receivers, you can put small touch sensors on the sides of your RC cars. On the front of the vehicles, you would place a "jousting" lance, and the cars would then battle by striking the touch sensors on the sides of the cars with their lances. The same damage logic used with the IR version would apply here.

Light sensors

A simple, visible light sensor, such as the cadmium sulfide cell, can also be added to the vehicle. This part is available from Radio Shack or DigiKey. Light sensors could be used to make your RC car seek dark or light areas on its own.

Exhibit A: Bill of Materials

Item	Quantity	Notes
0.1 uF capacitor	2	C9, C1; DigiKey Part #P2053-ND
0.2 uF capacitor	1	C2; DigiKey Part #P2053-ND (put two in parallel for each 0.2 uF part)
10uF capacitor	5	C3, C4, C5, C6, C7; DigiKey Part #P2049-ND
1 uF capacitor	1	C8; DigiKey Part # P2059-ND
IR LED	1	D1; DigiKey Part #QED233-ND
Red LED	4	D2, D3, D4, D5; DigiKey Part # 350-1025-ND
CON2 connector	5	J1, J2, J3, J6, J7
CON3 connector	2	J4, J5
CON6 connector	1	J8
2N3904 transistor	1	Q1; DigiKey Part #2N3904D26ZCT-ND
400 Ohm resistor	1	R1; DigiKey Part #400EBK-ND
330 Ohm resistor	4	R2, R3, R4, R5; DigiKey Part #330EBK-ND
2.2K Ohm resistor	1	R6; DigiKey Part #2.2KEBK-ND
10K Ohm resistor	2	R11, R7; DigiKey Part #10KEBK-ND
51K Ohm resistor	1	R8; DigiKey Part #51KEBK-ND
1.1M Ohm resistor	1	R9; DigiKey Part #1.1MEBK-ND
4.7K Ohm resistor	1	R10; DigiKey Part #4.7KEBK-ND
On/Off switch	2	SW2, SW1; SW SPST; DigiKey Part #360-1026-ND
Pushbutton	1	S2; SW PUSHBUTTON
IR receiver	1	U2; IR Rec, Digikey Part #425-1116-ND (or PNA4602-ND with a slight wiring change)
IC, tone decoder	1	U3; LM567C, DigiKey Part #LM567CN-ND
Radio encoder	1	U4; HT12D, purchase from *http://www.abacom-tech.com*
Radio receiver	1	U5; RLP434, purchase from *http://www.laipac.com*
Radio transmitter	1	U6; TLP434A, purchase from *http://www.laipac.com*
Radio decoder	1	U7; HT12E, purchase from *http://www.abacom-tech.com*
Microcontroller	1	U8; PIC16F876A controller, Digikey Part #PIC16F876A-I/SP-ND
Voltage regulator	1	U9; LM7805, Digikey Part #LM7805CT-ND
Crystal	1	Y1; 16MHz, Digikey Part #PX1600MC-ND
PCB	1	Perf board, Digikey Part # 438-1022-ND

Exhibit B: RC Car Hack Software Code

```
// radio control car hack
// (4/26/03 Scott Fullam
// feel free to modify this code

#include <P16F876A.h>

#define var_res_clk   0x01

void gen_2khz(int cycles);
void init_code();
void check_hit();
void check_fire();
char hit_count;
char shot_count;
void update_score(char num);

#pragma CLOCK_FREQ 1600000
// #pragma RESERVE_ADDR_0 // add this line back in if you are using the ICD2 and debugging code
void main()
{
    init_code();
    while(1)
    {
            check_fire();
            check_hit();
    }
 }

void init_code()
{
// set pr2 divider to 25. this plus the prescaler value of 4 will generate
// a 38461 kHz out from CPP1 using a system crystal of 16 MHz
pr2 = 25;
ccpr1l = 0x0D;
// set the diver bits but do not set PWM mode yet
ccp1con = 0x00;
// set up portc 2 as an output, 0,1 as inputs
trisc = 0x03;

// set prescaler to 4 and switch timer 2 on
t2con = 0x05;

// porta 2-5 as outputs. the others as inputs
// set adcon1 so that all pins are digital I/O
adcon1 = 0x07;
trisa = 0x00;


// set up timer1 for 2 kHz (or 3 kHz) modulation generation
t1con = 0x20;
hit_count = 0;
```

RC Car Hack Software Code *(continued)*

```
shot_count = 15;
porta = 0x00;


}


void gen_2khz(int cycles)
{
    int i;
    char temp1;
    for (i = 0; i < cycles; i++)
            {
            tmr1h = 0xff;
            tmr1l = 0x06;
            t1con = 0x21; // start the timer
            ccp1con = 0x0f; // enable the 38 khz output
            temp1 = 1;
            while(!(temp1 == 0))
                    {
                    temp1 = tmr1h;
                    }
            t1con = 0x30; // stop the timer

            ccp1con = 0; // stop the 38khz output
            temp1 = 0;
            tmr1h = 0xff;
            tmr1l = 0x06;
            t1con = 0x21; // start the timer
            temp1 = 1;
            while(!(temp1 == 00))
                    {
                    temp1 = tmr1h;
                    }
            t1con = 0x20; // stop the timer
            }
}

void check_hit()
{
    char hit;
    int i;
    char hit_time;
    hit_time = 0;
    hit = portc & 0x02;
    if (hit == 0)
            {
            for (i = 0; i < 200; i++)
                    {
                    hit = portc & 0x02;
                    if (hit == 0)
                            {
                            hit_time++;
                            }
```

RC Car Hack Software Code *(continued)*

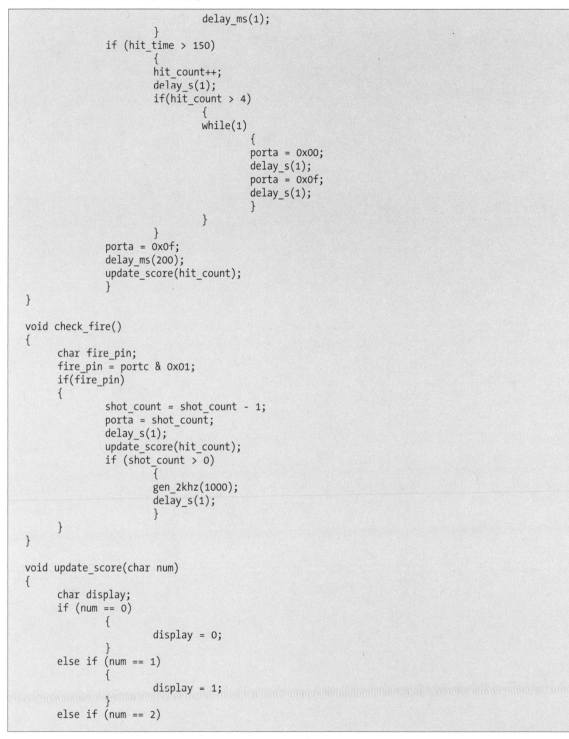

```
                          delay_ms(1);
                  }
         if (hit_time > 150)
                  {
                  hit_count++;
                  delay_s(1);
                  if(hit_count > 4)
                          {
                          while(1)
                                  {
                                  porta = 0x00;
                                  delay_s(1);
                                  porta = 0x0f;
                                  delay_s(1);
                                  }
                          }
                  }
         porta = 0x0f;
         delay_ms(200);
         update_score(hit_count);
         }
}

void check_fire()
{
     char fire_pin;
     fire_pin = portc & 0x01;
     if(fire_pin)
     {
             shot_count = shot_count - 1;
             porta = shot_count;
             delay_s(1);
             update_score(hit_count);
             if (shot_count > 0)
                     {
                     gen_2khz(1000);
                     delay_s(1);
                     }
     }
}

void update_score(char num)
{
     char display;
     if (num == 0)
             {
                     display = 0;
             }
     else if (num == 1)
             {
                     display = 1;
             }
     else if (num == 2)
```

RC Car Hack Software Code *(continued)*

```
            {
                    display = 0x03;
            }
    else if (num == 3)
            {
                    display = 0x07;
            }
    else display = 0x0f;
    porta = display;
}
```

Exhibit C

Exhibit C: RC Car Controller Schematic Diagram

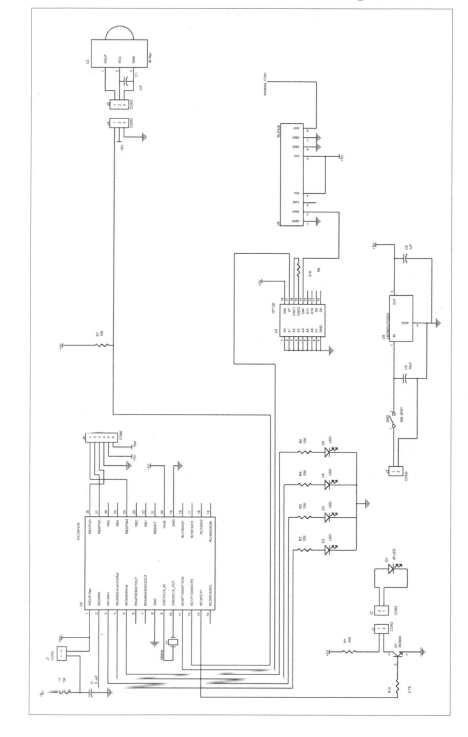

Exhibit D: RC Car Radio Transmitter Schematic Diagram

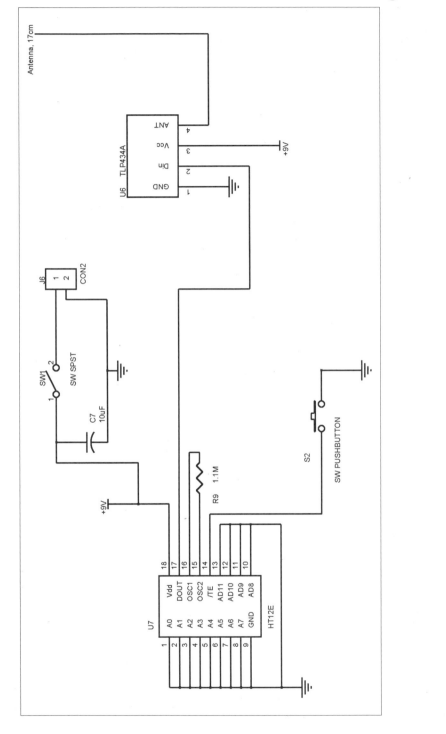

How to Build a Wearable Computer

## 14

Cost
$100–2000

Time
several weeks

Difficulty
very difficult

The prescience of Moore's Law continues as we see the delivery of more and more computer power in smaller and smaller packages. What does this mean? For one thing, building a computer that you can wear has become very feasible.

In this chapter I will outline the components and subsystems you need to build your own wearable PC, and then describe a typical system that you might build. There are a number of companies that make commercial wearable PC systems, but these can cost many thousands of dollars. You'll be able to build your own wearable computer for much less.

This project can take anywhere from a few weekends to many months to complete, depending on the parts you choose and the overall complexity of the system.

I'd like to thank Cliff Leong (*http://www.zerospin.com*) for inspiring parts of this chapter.

Credits

Figure 14-0 copyright © 2003 Cliff Leong. Figure 14-2a, 14-2b copyright © 2002 Io Display Systems. Figure 14-3a, 14-3b copyright © 2003 MicroOptical Corp. Figure 14-4 copyright © 2003 TekGear Inc. Figure 14-11 copyright © 2003 Cliff Leong. Figure 14-13, 14-14 copyright © 2003 Matias Corporation. Figure 14-15 copyright © 2003 Belkin Corporation. Figure 14-20 copyright © 2003 Biocontrol Systems.

Project Overview

A basic wearable system will likely have a central processor unit, a display (usually mounted over one eye), a user input device, a mass storage device, and some sort of power source. This is by no means an exhaustive list, just a general guideline.

You can see several typical components and how they might be connected in Figure 14-1. This particular setup is not the only way to connect the components. You will construct your system based on the components you choose and connect them to suit your needs.

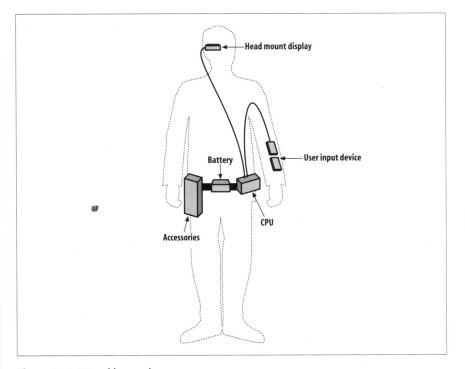

Figure 14-1: Wearable overview

Before you build your wearable system, you might want to take a look at what others have done already. A number of wearable projects are listed at the end of this chapter.

Hardware Assembly Instructions

You can choose from a large number of available components to add to your wearable system. However, the basic components you will need to complete this hack include:

- A display
- A CPU and motherboard
- A power system
- Human input and control devices
- Communications interfaces
- Data and program storage devices
- Sensors and I/O devices

The following sections cover each component system and describe how they can be assembled.

Display

When people think about a wearable computer, often the first thing that comes to mind is some sort of eyepiece display. This type of display allows hands-free operation and keeps whatever you are looking at private. An eyepiece display is often called a head-mount display or HMD. This display will probably be the most expensive part of your system.

If the "Borg" look doesn't appeal to you, you can just as easily choose a small LCD display that is strapped to your arm or held inside a pouch or bag. This small display can then be brought out when needed and stored away when not in use.

Many of the lower-cost displays available are low resolution, at least compared to desktop or laptop monitors. This means you will need to carefully arrange your desktop icons (if you are using a Windows-based frontend to your operating system) or carefully partition your interface to fit in your most used programs.

Today, a number of companies make HMDs that can be useful for building your own wearable computer. The following list describes three that seem quite interesting and are not outrageously expensive. But note that the HMD market changes quite a bit, and there may be other companies out there with new products.

I-Glasses. The I-Glasses product line offers a reasonably priced HMD that accepts and displays either SVGA or NTSC video signals, depending on the model you choose.

These displays cover both eyes when worn, so obviously they aren't suitable for use while walking or engaging in any activity other than using your wearable. You can see both models in Figures 14-2a and 14-2b. They can be purchased for less than $1,000 from *http://www.i-glasses. com/.*

Head-Mount Displays

A number of companies have attempted to produce consumer-level, head-mount displays, but most have stopped manufacturing due to lack of consumer demand. One of the first companies to produce a relatively inexpensive HMD was the Phoenix Group with its Private Eye. This device, though no longer available, worked by moving a column of 240 LEDs back and forth across your field of vision 30 times per second, providing a display area of 720 horizontal pixels. The display allowed only a single color, red, but was relatively inexpensive (less than $1,000) and was built for wearable applications.

Figure 14-2a: iGlasses NTSC

Figure 14-2b: iGlasses SVGA

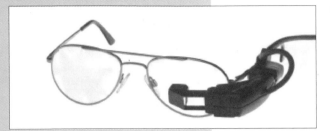

Figure 14-3a:
MicroOptical glasses mount

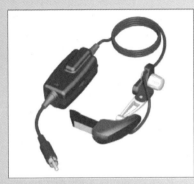

Figure 14-3b:
MicroOptical components

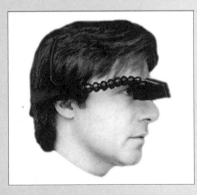

Figure 14-4: M-1 Display

MicroOptical. If you want to be able to see what is in front of you as well as view your wearable display, then the MicroOptical display may be for you. This company offers both monochrome and color displays. You can see the display mounted on a pair of glasses and by itself in Figures 14-3a and 14-3b.

For more information, see *http://www.microopticalcorp. com/HomePage.html.*

M1 Display. The M1 Display also sits in front of one eye. It offers a medium-resolution display built for wearable computers. It is quite lightweight and does not consume a lot of power. The display requires an NTSC video signal to drive it, so you will probably require a VGA-to-NTSC converter.

A side view of the display attached to a simple headband mount can be seen in Figure 14-4. This display can be purchased from *http:// www.tekgear.ca/index.html.*

Hack a camcorder viewfinder

If you'd like to save some money on the display and have the time to hack an old camcorder, you can remove the viewfinder and use it as your display. This process can take some time, but will yield an inexpensive head-mount display.

You will first need to locate a surplus camcorder that has a viewfinder. Carefully open up the camcorder and remove the entire eyepiece. The eyepiece assembly will probably have several wires connecting it to the rest of the camcorder. Keep these wires intact. One of them will be a small piece of shielded coaxial wire, which is where the video signal is fed to the display. There will also be a power and ground wire pair and probably a backlight power pair.

The best way to determine which wire is which is to locate a repair manual for that particular camcorder or search the Web. A good web site for this type of information is *http://wearables.blu.org/hardwear.html.*

Once you have taken apart the viewfinder, you will need to attach a VGA-to-NTSC video converter (available from most computer supply catalogs) to allow your wearable computer display controller to drive the display. The older CRT-based viewfinders can usually display close to 640 by 480 pixels. The newer LCD-based viewfinders will have lower resolution.

You will also have to determine a method for mounting the viewfinder in front of your field of view. Some people have used baseball caps as the mounting platform. The bill of the hat is usually stiff and therefore is a convenient place to mount the hardware. Other people have used the hardware from head-mounted magnifiers (*http://www.mageyes.com/*) to hold the display. You'll have to do some experimentation to get everything working and balanced.

Use a PDA as a display

An old PDA can be used as a "heads-down" display for text and possible graphics. The PDA can be attached to your wrist or arm with a few Velcro straps, and a simple terminal program can be used to display data from the main CPU. A serial or USB cable connects the PDA to the main system. If you desire a graphical interface on the PDA, you can run a web server on the main system and use a web browser on the PDA for control. The web server on the main system would need a set of web-triggered scripts. The PDA could also run a version of the Virtual Network Computer software to allow full access to the main system using a "keyhole" view of the primary desktop display. The VNC software can be found at *http://www. uk.research.att.com/vnc/.*

Simple devices

If you need only simple event notification, you can connect a few LEDs to one of the digital output ports from the main board (use the signal from the parallel port).

Single LEDs can also be used to send out a Morse code stream to allow a text interface. You will have to learn Morse code to use this style interface, but there are a few Linux-based packages that translate text from a terminal into Morse code. You can also use the LED to pulse out simpler codes, such as "blink once when new email arrives." You will want to experiment with this.

Old pagers usually contain a small vibrating motor that can also be used as a notification device.

CPU and motherboard

Many different processors can work well in a portable wearable computer. One of the most popular standards to recently emerge for small computer systems is the PC104 platform. A large number of vendors make different parts for this standard, which makes it even easier to put together a wearable system.

PC104 platform

PC104 standard boards are 3.6" by 3.8" by 0.6". The boards are designed to be stacked on top of each other to save space.

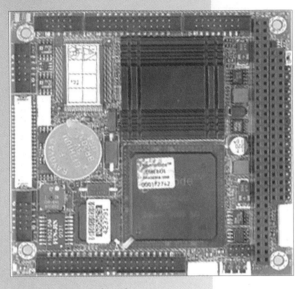

Figure 14-5: PC104 board

The connectors on all PC104 boards are standard as well. Take a look at *http://www.pc104.com/* for links and details. The PC104 board in Figure 14-5 is from *http://www.aaeon. com/*.

A wide variety of expansion boards are also available for the PC104 CPU cards, such as analog and digital I/O, wireless networking, Ethernet, and power supplies.

In order to keep the system as small and low-power as possible, you may want to choose a main CPU board that already has all of your required peripherals. A list of useful ports includes:

RS-232 serial ports. These are useful for older input devices and data modems.

USB port. Many newer peripherals including mice, keyboards, and cameras connect via USB.

Parallel port. This port was often used by older PCs to connect to a printer. It can still be useful today, as it is essentially eight bidirectional I/O pins.

VGA output. The port should support 640-by-480 output. This signal can easily be converted to an NTSC signal for viewing on the various head-mount displays using a VGA-to-NTSC converter.

Compact flash slots. These allow you to plug in a number of off-the-shelf devices such as 802.11b, Bluetooth, and infrared interfaces. These slots are the "little brother" to the larger PC-card slots.

PC-card slots. These allow you to plug in a large number of interface and storage cards used by laptop computers.

Non-PC104 platforms

If you are not interested in using a standard such as the PC104, and you'd instead like to put together a slightly smaller system, several vendors offer single-board computers with standard interfaces. These CPU boards run PowerPC chips, StrongARMs, MIP-based cores, and even x86-compatible processors.

Here is a list of links to find non-PC104 miniature CPU boards:

http://www.zfmicro.com/
http://www.tiqit.com/
http://www.brightstareng.com/index.html
http://www.pfusystems.com/index.html
http://www.compulab.co.il/index.htm
http://www.jumptecadastra.com/

These boards require a special interface cable to bring out all of the interface signals. Such connectors often can be as large as the CPU board itself.

PC-card-size 486 computer

In the late 1990s, the SMOS company offered a PC-card-size 486 board called the Cardio PC. SMOS is no longer around and the Cardio PC is no longer made, but you can still find them on eBay and at surplus computer parts stores.

Palmtop computer

The Compaq iPaq runs a fast ARM processor, has PC-card slots (depending on the model), IR, and wireless I/O, runs for quite a while on its internal batteries, and has a Linux distribution available for it.

Power system

Your wearable computer system will require a power source. You can carry a battery to store energy and recharge it from a wall outlet, or you can look at alternative sources of energy, including harnessing power from the person who is wearing the system. If you are interested in learning more about the limits and possibilities of generating power from the wearer's body to power the system, take a look at *http://testarne.www.media.mit.edu/people/ testarne/TR328/main-tr328.html*.

Batteries

If you are interested in a system that carries a battery and can be charged from a wall outlet or other conventional source, you will need a battery and a power converter. The converter changes the battery voltage to a voltage compatible with the computer system components. The diagram in Figure 14-6 shows how the charge travels from the outlet to your wearable.

Some people have used Lithium camcorder battery packs to good effect. These packs usually supply +7.2V, which must be converted to the required system voltages. The Sony InfoLithium NP-F960 or NP-F950 packs can be made to work, for example. Two of these cells should be connected in

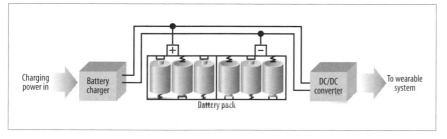

Figure 14-6: Power system

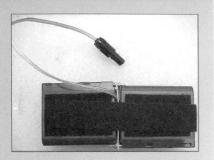

Figure 14-7: Battery pack

Figure 14-8: Bike power generator

series, as seen in Figure 14-7, before being connected to the DC/DC converter. Lithium batteries require their own special chargers; check with the manufacturer for details.

Generators and solar panels

If you expect to be away from a power outlet for long periods of time, you may want to consider a generator to charge your batteries. Small generators will not be able to provide more than a watt or so of power, and may therefore be useful only for running very low-power systems or charging batteries.

Bike generator

If you wear your computer exclusively while you are on your bike, you may want to consider generating power from the rotating bicycle wheels using a small generator. Depending on the model, you can get anywhere from three to ten watts from one of these.

Most of the bike generators output an AC voltage that will need to be converted to DC to be used by your computer.

You can purchase reasonably priced bike generators such as the one in Figure 14-8 from *http://www.oegproducts.com/.*

A simple circuit that will convert the output of this generator to a usable DC voltage can be found in the upcoming section Hand-crank generator.

Shoe generator

In the past few years, some interesting work has been done on generating energy from walking by placing electrical-energy generating objects in the walker's shoes. You can read a thesis that reviews the pros and cons at *http://www.media.mit.edu/resenv/pubs/theses/Jake-Thesis.pdf.* In the thesis, the author attached a hand-crank flashlight generator to one shoe and generated about a quarter of a watt of power from walking. The setup is a bit obtrusive, as you have a large plastic box attached to each foot, but it will provide a reasonable amount of power for your wearable computer.

Solar panels

If you expect that you will be operating your wearable system in areas where there is a reasonable amount of sunlight, you may want to consider a set of solar electric power panels.

Solar panels convert light energy directly into electrical energy. Since your wearable system will probably not be constantly exposed to bright sunlight, it is advisable that you install a set of batteries that can be recharged by the solar panels. In this way, the system will still operate when it is in the shade.

Many companies make and sell small- to medium-sized solar panels. Radio Shack carries a number of small solar panels that regulate voltage, packaged in a plastic housing with connectors. iSun makes another solar product that can be useful; see *http://www.isunpower.com/html/index.html*.

When using solar panels, you will need a voltage converter to regulate the voltage presented to your system and batteries.

Hand-crank generator

A hand-powered flashlight like the one in Figure 14-9 can be easily converted into a general-purpose power generator for either charging a battery or partially powering a wearable computer. This particular model is available from *http://www.lonezone.com*. A search for "hand crank flashlight" on the Web should yield other sources.

This particular hand-crank flashlight will produce just under 2 volts (AC) output and will generate about 250 milliwatts. The output from where the bulb is normally connected must be rectified and converted into a usable voltage.

The circuit in Figure 14-10 shows how this might be done. You can purchase the MP-55 DC/DC converter from Jameco (*http://www.jameco.com*, Part #194925). You can use almost any low forward drop diode in the circuit, such as the 1N5817. Any brand or type of capacitors will also do.

This circuit will provide power only when the generator is running (i.e., when you are squeezing the generator handle) so it might be best to have a battery or a super capacitor in your circuit to allow things to run when you are not doing anything.

The arrangement of four diodes on the left side of Figure 14-10 is called a *bridge rectifier*. It is a common circuit that takes an alternating current power source and makes it into a direct current source. The circuit usually includes a capacitor to smooth out the DC signal on the output.

Figure 14-9: Hand-crank generator

Super Capacitors

Super capacitors can store more energy than regular capacitors. They are almost miniature rechargeable batteries, but with a very short (a few seconds) charge-up time. Try DigiKey Part #P6963-ND, which is a 1F capacitor. You will need to be careful using these caps, as they usually can be charged only to 2-5V.

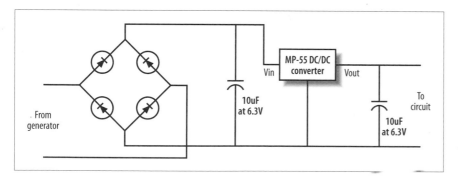

Figure 14-10: AC to DC power converter

DC/DC converters

Your wearable system will need a device to convert the battery voltage to the voltage your components use. PC104 systems can normally run on just a +5V power supply. Some of your boards may require +12V, so you will need the appropriate converters to generate this voltage. Many vendors sell PC104 boards with the required electronics, or you can build one yourself using a DC/DC converter module and a blank PC104 board.

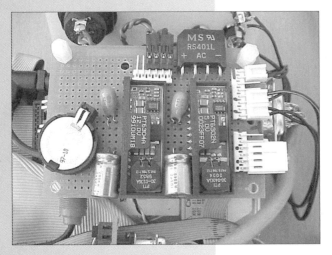

Choose a DC/DC converter that can supply more power than you think you will need. This will allow you to add additional components and boards without having to replace your DC/DC power supply. If battery life is important to you, look carefully at the efficiency rating of the converter: the higher the better.

Several companies make complete DC/DC converters that can easily be used with a PC104 or other wearable computer system. Check out Power One (*http://www.power-one.com/*) and PowerTrends (*http://www.powertrends.com*). You will have to assemble these modules into a system yourself depending on your exact needs, as seen in Figure 14-11.

Figure 14-11: DC/DC power converter

Battery chargers

The battery that powers your wearable will require recharging after it has been drained. If you do not want to remove the battery pack each time it needs recharging, consider adding a charging circuit and connector to the wearable system. In this way you can simply plug a small cable from a wall outlet into the wearable to recharge the battery.

You will need to decide how quickly you want the battery to recharge. You can choose to trickle-charge the battery over ten or more hours, or fast-charge in as little as one hour. Trickle-charging for most battery types is simple and requires only one or two components.

Input devices

Along with a display and a CPU, you will probably want some sort of keyboard and pointing device for your wearable.

Chorded keyboards

Over the years many people have experimented with home-built, single-handed keyboards. There are also a few commercial versions that you can buy, such as the Twiddler input device from *http://www.handykey.com/* (shown in Figure 14-12). The Twiddler has a strap that holds the keypad in the palm of your hand, ready for data entry by your fingers and thumb.

Figure 14-12: Twiddler chorded keyboard

The Twiddler keyboard allows you to enter all of the keys from a standard 104-key keyboard with one hand. This is accomplished by using "chorded" keys, which means that you have to press multiple buttons on the device at once to get a desired key. This typing system can take some getting used to, but will allow one-handed typing without having to look at the keys.

Wearable keyboards

If one-handed keyboards with new entry systems are not your speed, there are several more standard alternatives.

Wrist keyboard

A miniaturized version of a standard keyboard is available from *http://www.l3sys.com/keybd/keybd.html* and shown in Figure 14-13. This keyboard allows only one-handed typing, but you do not need to learn a new way to type.

Half-size keyboard

If a full-size keyboard worn on your arm is a bit too big, you can try a half-size keyboard from *http://www.halfkeyboard.com/*. Each key on this keyboard, shown in Figure 14-14, activates two or more characters. This keyboard does not require leaning a new way to type and is quite compact.

Nostromo SpeedPad

Belkin has recently released a new type of game controller called the Nostromo n50 SpeedPad. It is meant for gaming applications, but it shows promise as a possible one-handed keyboard and directional input controller. The product is designed for use on a flat surface, but with a simple wrist and hand strap, it could easily be used as a wearable input device (see Figure 14-15). The Nostromo is available on eBay or at *http://www.belkin.com*.

Flexible keyboard

If you do not need to enter text when you are moving, then you may simply need a portable keyboard. Recently, a number of "roll-up" keyboards have appeared. These keyboards are made of a soft rubber-like material and are waterproof.

Figure 14-13: Wrist keyboard

Figure 14-14: Half-size keyboard

Figure 14-15: Nostromo SpeedPad

The keyboard shown in Figure 14-16 is made by *http://www.flexis.co.kr/products/epd.htm* and can be purchased in the U.S. at *http://www.man-machine.com/fx100.htm*.

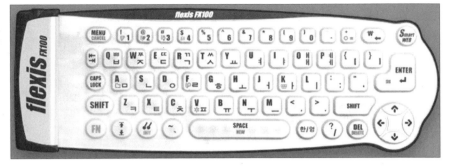

Figure 14-16: Flexible keyboard

Finger mouse

Figure 14-17: Finger mouse

A number of companies now offer a "finger" mouse. This mouse, shown in Figure 14-17, is a small trackball housed in a hand-size package. If you do a search for "finger mouse", you should be able to locate a number of vendors selling them. Since this device is portable and does not require any surface upon which to operate, it makes a good choice for a wearable project.

Speech recognition

If you want your system to be truly hands-free, you may want to consider using speech recognition.

The Windows XP operating system includes speech recognition as part of the base package. There are also third-party packages that perform this function. Several companies also produce speech recognition for use with other operating systems. Here are a few of the more popular packages:

Dragon Speech (*http://www.scansoft.com/*)
IBM Via Voice (*http://www.ibm.com*)
Voiceware (*http://www.voiceware.co.kr/english/index.html*)

These systems usually require a clean voice signal to work well. This means that you will need a boom microphone (with wind screen) mounted in front of your mouth. You can also experiment with other microphone placement schemes.

Voice output

If you do not want to constantly look into a tiny display to see what your wearable system is doing, having your system "tell" you what you want to know may be preferable.

A number of text-to-speech systems are available for most of the popular operating systems. Windows XP includes a text-to-speech engine. Other software packages include:

Fonix (*http://www.acuvoice.com/*)
Flexvoice (*http://www.flexvoice.com/*)
ReadPlease (*http://readplease.com/*)
Emacspeak (*http://sourceforge.net/projects/emacspeak*)
Festival (*http://www.cstr.ed.ac.uk/projects/festival/download.html*)

All you need is a sound card and a small earphone, and you can have your wearable system whisper its status in your ear.

Cameras

Many different USB-based video cameras are available on the market (see Figure 14-18 for an example). These cameras tend to be small and easy to hack apart. Logitech offers several models including the QuickCam Express; see *http://www.logitech.com*.

You can also use a camera to record still and video clips, as well as for image recognition software. Intel has released the Open Source Computer Vision Library available for both Linux and Windows from SourceForge at *http://sourceforge.net/projects/opencvlibrary*.

Figure 14-18: Logitech camera

GPS

If location information is an important component of your wearable computer system, you may want to add a GPS receiver (see Figure 14-19). There are many kinds of GPS receivers, both standalone products and modules you can integrate.

The older DeLorme Tripmate is a low-cost GPS receiver with an RS-232 serial interface. Most of the older models require an RS-232 serial interface, so if you want to add one of these devices to your system, make sure that you have an extra serial port on your motherboard. The newer models offer a USB interface.

Figure 14-19: Earthmate GPS receiver

Wireless communications

John Donne once said, "No man is an island." Your wearable computer system should not be an island either, so you will probably want to add some sort of wireless connection to the Internet or to a specific location.

Bluetooth

A few years ago, a new wireless data transfer standard emerged called "Bluetooth," which promised to replace the large number of serial cables that sprout from most laptop PCs. This standard operates in the 2.4 GHz unlicensed band and is able to send and receive data at just under 1 Mbit per second for up to ten meters.

Adapters that allow connection via this standard can be useful in a wearable computer system. Many mobile phones offer a built-in Bluetooth adapter. If your wearable has an adapter, you can connect your system to the Internet by dialing up through the mobile phone on your belt. Your wearable system could even make phone calls!

You can find Bluetooth interface cards for your system available as PC cards, compact flash cards, USB devices, and RS-232 devices. Choose the PC interface that best suits your needs.

802.11b

802.11b is another wireless data transfer standard that operates in the 2.4 GHz band. It is a popular method for wirelessly connecting computing devices in office and home environments. Several companies now offer access points in restaurants, cafes, and other businesses.

802.11b devices are available with a number of PC interfaces, including Ethernet, PC card, compact flash, and USB.

900 MHz

If you are more interested in a point-to-point connection where you set up and control all nodes on the network, a number of companies mentioned in Chapter 12 offer 900 MHz band data radios. You will need to purchase and set up at least two nodes, a base station, and your wearable to make things work.

Cellular

Many digital cellular phone companies offer connection kits that allow connection to the handset via an RS-232 or USB cable. Currently, most digital phone services allow a low speed (9600 to 14400 bps) dial-up connection. Recently, several carriers have begun to offer packet-switched services that allow a much higher-speed connection that is "on demand," where you pay a flat fee for access.

Storage devices

Your wearable system will need a mass storage device to hold the system and application software. The solution you choose for your wearable computer will need to be smaller and lower power than what you would choose for a desktop computer.

Laptop hard drives

Laptop computers have very similar power and size requirements as wearable computers. A notebook 2.5" hard drive is therefore a good choice, and is available from most PC suppliers. Most of the PC104-based CPU boards have a built-in IDE interface for these drives.

Compact flash–based storage

If your system has a PC card or a compact flash slot, you can install a small mass storage device based on this standard. Hitachi offers a "micro drive" with 1 GB and more of storage. This product is a 1-inch diameter rotating disk drive. Check *http://www.hgst.com* for details.

SanDisk (*http://www.sandisk.com*) offers a number of solid-state Compact Flash storage cards. These cards have no moving parts and draw less power than rotating storage systems, but they are also more expensive.

Disk on chip

M-Systems (*http://www.m-sys.com/*) offers IDE-compatible FLASH memory products. They are low-power and very rugged.

I/O devices and sensors

Many different types of sensors and data-gathering devices can be added to your system. These external devices will typically be connected via RS-232 serial or USB. Devices that you may want to consider include bar-code scanners, extra digital I/O ports for switching things on and off, temperature sensors, humidity sensors, digital compasses, or barometric pressure sensors.

If you want your wearable system to be able to sense the movement of all of your limbs, check out *http://www.troikaranch.org/mididancer.html*. This company produces a body suit that generates MIDI control signals.

If you are interested in using "brain waves" to control your system, BioControl Systems has products that are very cool; see *http://www.biocontrol.com/*. Simply put the head-mounted sensor seen in Figure 14-20 around your forehead and "think" commands to your system.

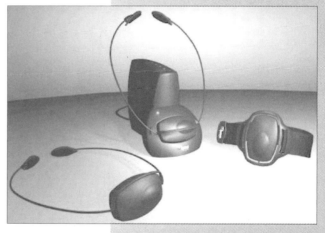

Figure 14-20: BioControl sensor

Putting it all together

Once you have gathered the basic components, it is time to connect them.

Carrying the wearable

First, decide how you plan to carry the system around. Are you building a system to take the place of your laptop so you can sit in a library staring off into your head-mount display and typing term papers? Will the system take the place of your PDA and manage your schedules? Do you want to build a system to explore with some of the new "mediated reality" experiments being performed? Are you interested in building a system to gather data in the field?

Figure 14-21: Carrying pack

Depending on what use you have in mind for your wearable, your carrying case can anything from a simple "belt pack" (shown in Figure 14-21) to a completely wired electronic vest. If you are just starting out, I suggest using a small belt pack that is easy to take on and off. As you build and use the system, it will evolve—you will think of new ways of using it, as well as more convenient methods for putting it together and carrying it around.

Many companies make camera-accessory belt packs that work well. Eagle Creek has a nice line of packs. A fishing vest can also serve as a great platform for holding all of the various parts.

Before you completely pack the system into a small belt pack, you will want to test that everything works well outside of the carrying case so that you can troubleshoot the system beforehand.

Connecting the pieces

The CPU board will be the heart of the system. All the other system components and boards will connect to it. An example system based on a PC104 board is shown in Figure 14-22.

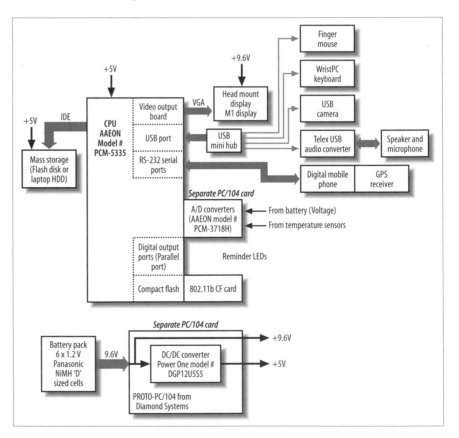

Figure 14-22: Wearable system block diagram

WARNING

As you connect the components together, be very careful to cover exposed power supply cables and connectors. If these are accidentally shorted together, the power supply and/or battery may heat up and cause a fire.

Your keyboard and pointer input devices will likely interface to the main computer via a serial, PS/2, or USB connection.

Your head-mount display will connect to a video output card or port. Depending on which display you have chosen, your output signal will be either VGA or NTSC. If it is NTSC, the display device will probably require a standard NTSC video output from the main CPU board. If your system has only a VGA port, you can purchase a VGA-to-NTSC converter from various sources (do a search for "VGA-to-NTSC converter" on the Web). You can also use the TVator product introduced in Chapter 7.

Software Setup Instructions

Depending on your goals, the software can be the most challenging part of this project. Standard operating systems assume that you have a large, high-resolution display and a large power source. Wearable systems often do not have particularly high-resolution displays and operate off of limited battery displays. Many times the display cannot easily be used, and other forms of human interface must be used instead.

You should first decide what you want your wearable system to do. It may simply be built for the fun of building it, or you may want to solve a particular problem. You will also have to consider which operating system will support the hardware you have on hand.

Operating system software

Several popular operating systems can be used on wearable computers, including Linux, Windows, Windows CE, QNX, Mac OS X, and others. Due to the large number of operating systems available, I will limit my discussion to the most popular three as well as QNX, a small, free OS.

Your OS choice will depend on what you want your wearable system to do. If you want to edit MS Word, Excel, and PowerPoint documents, you should probably use Windows. If you want to experiment with smaller memory footprint systems and are willing to play with the software a bit, Linux might be the better choice.

Linux

Since Linux is an open source licensed software package, it is easy to modify and operate on many CPU platforms. A number of interest groups have put together software packages for wearable computers. Linux will also allow you to put together your own packages.

On most CPUs, Linux supports a wide variety of device drivers. This is important, since some of the components in a wearable system are not always obtainable.

Other open source and freeware Linux-like operating systems, such as FreeBSD, can also be used with success.

Application software available for Linux under the x86 platform is quite large. You are very likely to find everything from productivity applications to real-time image processing software.

You can learn more about using Linux on a small embedded or wearable system at *http://linuxembedded.com/*.

Most PC104 boards are identical to full-size PC boards from a hardware standpoint, so they should run standard Linux distributions with no changes.

Windows

Microsoft Windows (98, 2000, NT, XP) can successfully be used on an x86-based wearable computer. The large number of drivers included and the many vendors that support Windows can allow a system to be built easily.

Windows also allows you to use all popular applications available for the desktop system.

DOS

Many versions of DOS are available that can be used to develop a wearable computing system. DOS can actually be a decent environment in which to develop and run applications for wearable computers. You can even do development of your applications on a standard PC, make an *.exe* file, transfer it to the wearable system, and run it. If you make sure that the desktop PC has the same ports and hardware, the wearable system should behave exactly like the PC-based development version.

You will need a copy of DOS in order to develop and run your applications. One option is to make a bootable floppy under Windows and then use the floppy for your development and runtime environment. If you do this, you will need to add a floppy drive to the wearable system or make the wearable system's mass storage device behave as a floppy. An alternative is to use FreeDOS from *http://www.freedos.org/*. This web site has a great deal of information on using the free version of DOS for development and as a runtime environment.

DOS IDE

If you would like a decent, free, Integrated Development Environment (also called an IDE) for DOS take a look at: *http://www.rhide.com/*.

If you are interested in an alternative pay version of DOS, take a look at *http://www.drdos.com/*. This version has its roots in Digital Research and has been owned by many companies over the years.

Borland has recently offered its older compilers and development tools for free download. Check out *http://www.borland.com/* for details.

QNX

Currently, QNX (*http://www.qnx.com/*) offers a free version of its real-time operating system for noncommercial use. This operating system is small; you can put together a usable image with basic drivers for under two megabytes of ROM.

Application software

After loading the operating system, you may want your system to do something other than drain the batteries and show a system prompt.

Interface applications

A few people have been working on suites of applications that make using a wearable system easy, without having to write your own software. One example is the Sulawesi project from *http://wearables.essex.ac.uk/sulawesi/*. This package is available for both Linux and Windows. It enables interfaces suitable for wearable systems and provides simple software agents to accomplish tasks.

Under Linux, scripts that run at a command-line interface can be very effective when combined with a speech recognition system or a portable keyboard. Single keystrokes can trigger complex scripts that accomplish the tasks you require.

The operating experience of your wearable system will be significantly different from your experiences with desktops and laptops. Since the wearable is always with you and always on, you can look at electronic documents at any time and, if you have you have a wireless device attached, can access full-size web sites from anywhere.

Power management software

You will want to play around with the power management setting of your operating system to allow maximum operating time for your particular needs. The CPU boards recommended in this chapter are lower power than those in standard laptop and desktop computers, but careful power management is still a must. If you add solar panels or a hand generator to help charge the batteries, you may be able to greatly extend battery life.

Simple Input Methods for Low-Resolution Displays

If you are using Linux, there is a utility called *gpm* that allows control of the system with a mouse in text mode. Another utility called *mc* (Midnight Commander) can also be used to control the system under text mode.

If you are using Microsoft Windows, you can try running from a DOS prompt or rearrange the desktop icons under Windows.

Project Demo

You've put together all of the hardware and loaded your favorite operating system with a few applications. Now it is time to test things out.

Begin by making sure that everything works outside of your carrying case. Ensure that any wires that carry battery power are covered. Charge the batteries and power on the system in this open configuration. Run it until the batteries are dead to ensure that everything works. Check the DC/DC converter and the CPU to see how warm they get. You may need to provide ventilation for these items, and they are likely to draw the most power in the system.

After you've tested out the system in the open configuration, carefully pack it into the carrying case and run it for one full battery charge. If you plan to use the system in a damp or rainy environment, be especially careful with how you package it. You may need to encase the boards in a waterproof bag.

Your system should now be ready to use wherever you go!

Wearable System Examples

You may want to look at other wearable systems built at various universities and by individuals. Check out the projects listed below.

http://www.cs.uoregon.edu/research/wearables/
http://hwr.nici.kun.nl/pen-computing/wearables.html
http://wearables.essex.ac.uk/
http://www.eyetap.org/
http://www.xybernaut.com/newxybernaut/home.htm
http://www.media.mit.edu/wearables/
http://wearables.net/wc/
http://www.tekgear.ca/
http://www.electronsoup.com/
http://www.man-machine.com/
http://wearables.blu.org/
http://www.charmed.com/
http://www.tiqit.com/
http://www.via-pc.com/
http://www.handsfreemobile.com/
http://www.wearcomp.org/

Text-Based WWW Interface

If you want to stay in a strictly text-based interface and access the Web, you may want to use a text-based browser called Lynx. The site *http://www.trill-home.com/lynx.html* has information on where to get a copy. There are executables and source code for most computer operating systems. The Lynx browser can also be a basis for an audio-based interface.

Exhibit A: Bill of Materials

Item	Quantity	Notes
Main processor	1	AAEON Model PCM-5335 PC104 platform
Head-mount display	1	I-glasses, Micro-Optical, M1 Display
Power supply	1	PowerOne Model DGP12U5S5 plus PROTO-PC104 from Diamond Systems
Batteries	6	D-sized NiMH cells from Panasonic
Mass storage system	1	IBM 1GB Microdrive
Text input device	1	Wrist keyboard from L3Systems
Pointing device	1	Finger mouse
Wireless network connection	1	802.11b Compact Flash Card
Carrying case	1	Eagle Creek belt pack
Audio interface	1	Optional; Telex USB Audio I/O system
Digital mobile phone interface	1	Optional
Serial or USB cable	1	Connect to mobile phone, GPS unit, camera, or audio system
Camera	1	Optional; any USB Camera
GPS receiver	1	Optional; Garmin Gecko
USB mini hub	1	Optional

How to Build an Internet Coffeemaker

## 15

Cost

$50–100

Time

a weekend

Difficulty

moderate

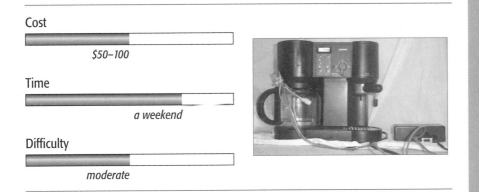

What You Need

- A coffeemaker
- SitePlayer embedded web server
- Temperature sensor
- AD converter
- Wire
- Food-safe plastic tubing
- Silicone sealant
- Five conductor-shielded wires
- Other items listed in Exhibit A

Back in the late 1980s when the Internet was a "new" phenomenon, various groups of people began to connect all sorts of appliances and objects to it. One of the more famous appliances connected to the Internet was a coffeemaker at Cambridge University. The students in the computer science department pointed a camera at the department coffee machine and made the resulting images available via a web page. In this way, sleepy students in need of a caffeine fix could simply open up a web page on their browser and see if there was any coffee to be had.

The Cambridge setup allowed you to see if there was any coffee, but it did not provide any other information about the coffee. It also required its own PC to play host for the camera hardware and the web server.

I will show you how to build your own Internet-connected coffeemaker that does not require a PC host, and which will report not only the existence of coffee but also its temperature. You are therefore assured that you will not walk across the office only to find an empty coffee pot or cold coffee.

Credits

All photographs copyright © 2003 Scott Fullam.

Project Overview

This project uses the SitePlayer embedded web server, which has a special serial port that can be easily connected to an analog-to-digital converter (ADC). I chose the LTC1098 ADC because it was easy to interface to SitePlayer and it had two channels, enough to capture the coffee level and the temperature.

You will construct the electronics, modify a coffeemaker, and program a tiny standalone web server that will monitor your coffee.

A simple block diagram of the system is shown in Figure 15-1. The SitePlayer board has built-in web server software (which saves you from having to write it yourself) and an interface port to the ADC circuit board. The ADC circuit board performs the actual temperature and liquid measurements. The SitePlayer has its own IP address and responds to HTTP requests.

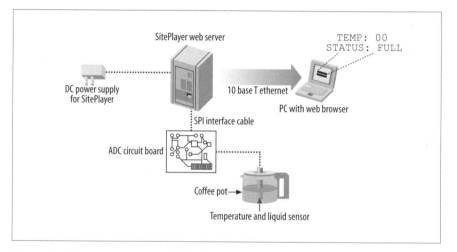

Figure 15-1: Internet coffeemaker block diagram

Hardware Assembly Instructions

This project requires you to build a simple circuit board and then attach it to the mini web server. You will build a heat sensor and glue it into place at the end of the plastic tubing. Finally, you will modify a regular coffee pot so that you can insert the probe.

1. Construct and attach the ADC circuit board

First, you'll build a small circuit card to hold the analog-to-digital converter and the interface connectors. Then you will connect that circuit to the mini web server.

Getting Free Parts

Most semiconductor companies offer free samples of their parts. Check their web sites for details on the parts as well as on sample policies. Usually you need to answer a few questions about your application and potential order volume.

I was able to get two samples of the National Semiconductor temperature sensor and the Linear Technology A/D converter for free simply by visiting their web sites and filling out a simple request form.

Build the ADC circuit board

Construct the circuit according to Exhibit B. A bill of materials for this circuit board is listed in Exhibit A. This low-power circuit board can "steal" power from the SitePlayer, although this external circuit normally requires its own power source.

On the left side of the board shown in Figure 15-2, note the row of five connectors for the temperature and liquid sensors. On the right side you can see the SPI connector to the SitePlayer board.

SPI stands for Serial Peripheral Interface. It is a standard that many microprocessors use to communicate with external integrated circuits.

Figure 15-2: ADC board close-up

Attach the ADC board to the SitePlayer board

Figure 15-3: ADC to main board connection

Attach the circuit to the mini web server board. When you are finished, the two connector circuit boards should look something like Figure 15-3.

For this board, I used crimp-on connectors from DigiKey. You can use just about any dual-row crimp style connector you want.

The SitePlayer board is available with an optional evaluation board that contains all of the connectors you need to make it work with no extra soldering. For this hack, I will assume that you are using the SitePlayer evaluation board. Connect the ADC circuit board you just constructed to the evaluation board, as in Figure 15-4.

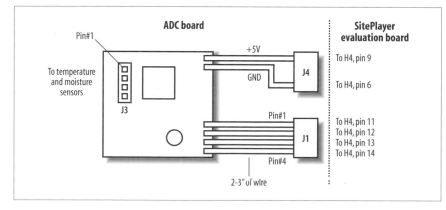

Figure 15-4: ADC board connection details

What Is an Analog-to-Digital Converter?

An analog-to-digital converter, also called an A/D converter or ADC, measures a voltage or a current and changes it to a binary numeric value. Let's say you have an ADC that is powered from a 5V supply, and the input is connected to a 2.5V source. Let's also say that the converter has 8 bits of resolution. Eight bits of data can represent 256 different values. The digital output of the ADC would read half of the digital range (2.5V is half of 5V) or 128. This value of 128 could then be used by software for display or for other functions. Think of it as being similar to a digital bathroom scale. You step on the scale and it shows a number representing your weight.

ADCs come in many different input voltage ranges, resolutions (how many bits of measurement accuracy they provide), and speed (how quickly they convert the voltage or current to a numeric value).

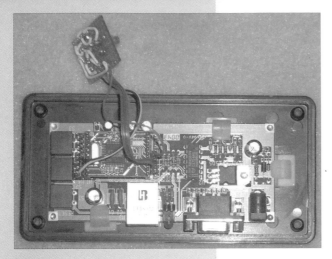

Figure 15-5:
Coffee controller board mounted in case

Figure 15-6: Case side cutouts

2. Mount the SitePlayer evaluation board and ADC circuit board inside a protective housing

Locate a plastic enclosure that is large enough to hold the evaluation board and the ADC board. (I used a plastic box from Radio Shack.) Drill a set of holes in the box that match up to the holes in the corners of the SitePlayer board. Use small screws with nuts to hold the evaluation board in place, as seen in Figure 15-5.

You will probably need to cut three sets of holes in the side of the plastic enclosure to allow connection to power, Ethernet, and the sensor assembly. I cut a rough rectangle in the side of my enclosure, as shown in Figure 15-6.

3. Construct the temperature and liquid sensor probe

The ADC board will convert signals from a temperature and liquid sensor probe. The temperature sensor is a self-contained integrated circuit from National Semiconductor. It is a three-pin device that puts out a voltage proportional to the temperature in Fahrenheit. This voltage is captured by one of the channels of the ADC.

The liquid sensor is built from a single transistor amplifier. The sensor operation is based on the fact that coffee is slightly acidic and therefore will conduct a small amount of electricity. A limited-current voltage source is placed on one side of the sensor, and the base of the transistor on the other. When some slightly conductive liquid is present between these two probes, it generates a signal that is amplified by the transistor. The remaining channel of the ADC captures this signal.

Temperature sensor

Measure out a length of shielded cable to go from the coffee pot to the SitePlayer and ADC board. Three or four feet of cable should work well.

Connect the temperature sensor IC to three of the wires as shown in Figure 15-7. Solder one end of the wire to two of the conductors in the shielded cable before the cable enters the plastic tube (see Figure 15-8).

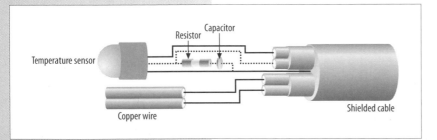

Figure 15-7: Temperature sensor

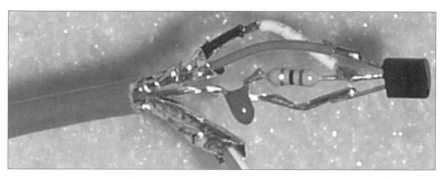

Figure 15-8: Temperature sensor wiring

Liquid sensor

The liquid sensor is constructed from a short piece of plastic-coated speaker wire. These wires will be mounted on the outside of the plastic tube.

Nick the shielded cable and locate the two wires you will use for the liquid sensor. Clip them, solder the speaker wires to them, and seal them up with a piece of electrical tape.

You can see how the speaker wires are connected to the shielded cable in the diagram in Figure 15-9.

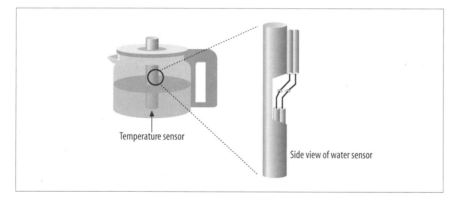

Figure 15-9: Water sensor

4. Seal the probe head

After assembling the temperature and liquid probe, you will need to make the probe tip waterproof so it can be submerged in a pot of hot coffee. I used two methods to seal the sensors: a plastic tube and some silicone sealant.

The plastic tube and sealant must be food-safe and able to withstand temperatures of up to 212 Fahrenheit. The plastic tubing can be easily found in a local plastics supply house or a store that carries home brewing equipment. The sealant I used was Dow Corning 748 RTV sealant, which

Embedded Web Servers

There are a number of small, self-contained web servers on the market today. I chose the SitePlayer for several reasons: it had a built-in Ethernet port so that I could connect it directly to my network; it had a built-in SPI serial port (a special serial port that can communicate with many different types of hardware peripherals) that directly connects to the temperature sensor and A/D converter; and it was simple to program. Once the three SPI signals are connected from the SitePlayer board to the A/D converter, a simple embedded HTML command allows the data to be transferred to the requesting web browser.

If you want to experiment with other tiny embedded web servers that include an Ethernet interface, take a look at the PicoWeb Server (*http://www.picoweb.net/*) or the TINI Web Server (*http://www.ibutton.com/TINI/*).

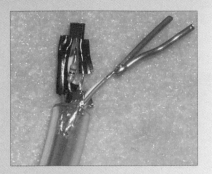

Figure 15-10:
Water temperature and sensor sleeve

Other Ways to Detect Liquid and Temperature

The contact temperature and liquid sensors were chosen because they were inexpensive and simple. The downside to using them is that they require contact with the liquid being sensed. Recently, a number of non-contact temperature sensors have become available on the market for a reasonable cost. With a little bit of hacking, it should be possible to modify a remote temperature probe so that the embedded web server can capture temperature data.

Remote moisture sensing is a little more difficult. Non-contact humidity sensors are available today. One of these sensors could be mounted on the coffee machine just above the coffee pot. The steam from the hot coffee should provide enough 'signal' for the sensor to pick up.

Once you have completed this hack with the contact sensors, you may want to play with these non-contact sensors yourself.

is rated as safe for food contact and will survive temperatures from −67 to 350 Fahrenheit.

Be sure that you select tubing that allows the probe head and cable to easily slide inside the coffee pot. Cut a length of plastic tubing that is one to two feet in length, and feed the cable and probe into the tube so that the temperature sensor sticks out an inch or so, as shown in Figure 15-10. Cover the exposed wire with small bits of insulating tape. This will keep the wires from shorting together when the probe is moved and compressed.

Slide the temperature sensor into the plastic tube so that the top of the sensor is flush with the opening in the plastic tube.

Inject the silicone sealant into the tube so that it fills in the entire area around the taped-over wires. Allow the sealant to flow about an inch down into the tube so that everything is well covered. Make sure to leave the top of the temperature sensor exposed, as seen in Figure 15-11. This will allow accurate and fast temperature sensing. If the sensor is covered, the silicone sealant will act as an insulator, and you will not get accurate temperature readings.

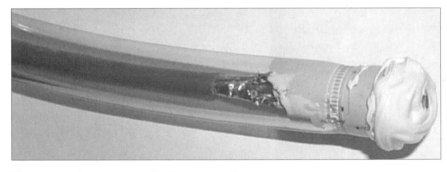

Figure 15-11: Temperature and water sensor sealing

WARNING
Make sure you are in a well-ventilated and dry area when using the RTV sealant.

Allow the sealant to cure overnight. Be sure the temperature sensor and the silicone sealant have dried before continuing.

Now, place the speaker wire with the ends stripped off onto the probe tube using a rubber band. You can see what this looks like in Figure 15-12. Make sure that the two exposed wires are no more than 0.25 inches apart and are secured tightly. Use a few plastic tie wraps to hold the speaker wire next to the tube.

Figure 15-12: Temperature and water sensor final sealing

The rubber band not only serves to hold the water probe wires in place, it also makes the seal at the end of the tube tighter. Remember that this probe will spend a lot of time immersed in hot (or at least warm) coffee.

5. Modify the coffee pot

The coffee pot you intend to use may require some modification to allow it to hold the probe in place. The probe should be positioned so that the tip is close to the bottom of the pot. This allows the water sensor wires to be at the proper level to report when the pot is empty.

Cut a small hole in the lid of the coffee pot to allow the probe to enter, as shown in Figure 15-13. Notice that the hole is cut next to the handle so that the probe does not get in the way when pouring coffee.

Figure 15-13:
Coffee pot cover cutout

Next you will need to configure the probe cable so that it will stay in the pot and be out of the way. Put a kink in the tube with a cable tie, as shown in Figure 15-14. The folded probe tube should now fit easily into the slot cut into the top of the coffee pot.

You may need to adjust the tube fold size and location to get the best fit for your coffee machine. Experiment a little and make sure that the probe and coffee pot fit into your coffee machine when you are finished (see Figure 15-15).

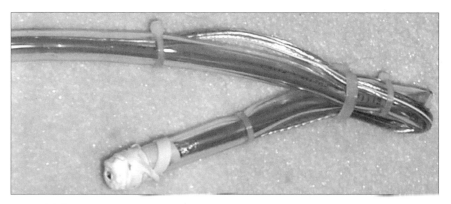

Figure 15-14:
Sensor tubing bend

Figure 15-15:
Sensor to coffee pot mounting

6. Test out the hardware

Plug the probe assembly into the ADC circuit board, plug a live Ethernet cable into the SitePlayer board, and connect the SitePlayer power supply. You should see a power LED light up on the SitePlayer board. If you have a multi-meter handy, check the voltage across the power and ground pins of the ADC chip. It should read +5V; if it does not, check your wiring. Follow each wire from the SitePlayer board over to the ADC board to ensure that each one is connected according to the schematic diagram. Disconnect the ADC board and use a multi-meter to measure the voltage between the ground and +5V pins.

If you are connecting the SitePlayer's Ethernet port to a hub, use a straight-through cable. If you are connecting the SitePlayer directly to your PC, use a crossover cable.

Software Setup Instructions

The SitePlayer is a single-board computer that includes a complete TCP/IP network protocol stack and a 10BaseT Ethernet port. It needs only a small amount of code to fetch the data from the ADC and display it on a web page.

The basic software that runs on the SitePlayer mini web server is a set of special configuration files and a set of HTML web pages that are served up when an external browser makes a request. The web pages provide a simple user interface and contain embedded commands that read the temperature and water levels from the ADC circuit board you just constructed.

First, you'll download and test the pages and configuration files to the SitePlayer using the tools provided with the SitePlayer board. Next, test out the complete system.

The user interface HTML provided in Exhibit C that runs on the SitePlayer is functional but simple. Feel free to hack up the code yourself to add desired features.

1. Program the mini web server

The web pages and configuration files for the SitePlayer are loaded using an RS-232 serial port. Make sure you have a spare cable if you did not purchase the evaluation board. Connect the serial cable from one PC Com port to the SitePlayer serial port.

For the PC you've connected to the SitePlayer, load all of the SitePlayer tools according to the instructions included with it (or download them from the SitePlayer web site).

Determine if your network runs a DHCP server. The SitePlayer is configured to work by default in this environment. If your network uses static IP addresses, you will need to set the SitePlayer for this mode. Connect a serial cable between the SitePlayer and the PC, then start the SitePlayer Serial Tester program. Set the new static address in the IP/Status window and press Set IP Address.

Run the Serial Port Tester tool (included with the SitePlayer tools) and set the IP address manually.

Place these files on your PC in a single directory:

- Listing 1: coffee.spd
- Listing 2: Index.htm
- Listing 3: SitePlayer index.spi
- Listing 4: refresh_index.htm
- Listing 5: refresh_index.spi
- Listing 6: water.htm
- Listing 7: water.spi
- Listing 8: pcadef.inc
- Listing 9: UDPsend_def.inc

These files can be found in Exhibit C of this chapter and on this book's web site at *http://www.oreilly.com/hardwarehacking.*

coffee.spd is the file used by the SitePlayer tools to build the data for the web server. *refresh_index.htm* is the page that the server provides when you first connect to it. *refresh_index.spi* forces a page refresh when the button triggering the ADC read is selected. *water.htm* is a web page that shows the water temperature. *water.spi* also forces a page refresh. *pcadef.inc* is required by the SitePlayer to define the temperature/water sensor interface. *UDPsend_def.inc* is used to define UDP functions on the board.

Launch the SiteLinker tool and the open the *coffee.spd* file. Next, under Download, select "Make Download File." If no errors are generated and the SitePlayer board is connected to the PC and powered on, select the "Download SitePlayer" option under the Download menu.

2. Test out the complete system

When the programming is complete, test out the server to make sure that it responds with a web page. To do this, open a web browser on the machine connected to it, and open the IP address you specified for the SitePlayer board. You should see a web page that looks like Figure 15-16.

Figure 15-16:
Internet coffeemaker web page

Project Demo

You should now have a coffee pot whose coffee status can be queried from any local web browser. Figure 15-17 is a picture of my coffeemaker with the web server connected. The machine is in my kitchen and is connected to the home 10BaseT network.

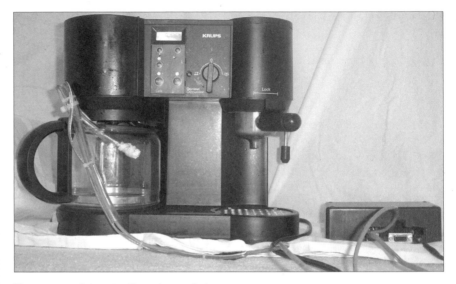

Figure 15-17: Internet coffeemaker ready to go

Next to my bed, I have a PC connected to my home LAN. My Internet coffee machine has a local IP address. When that address is opened up, a web page pops up. It looks like there is hot coffee waiting for me downstairs!

Extensions

Although this hack was built for sensing the temperature and the existence of coffee in a coffee pot, this system could be used in many other places as well. For example, the temperature probe could be placed inside a refrigerator or a freezer, and the moisture probe could be used to detect if the door is open or not. Or, the temperature sensor could be placed inside a PC to measure system temperature.

The SPI port on the SitePlayer board can be connected to other sensors and output ports as well. If you wanted to control a light or a motor from your web server, an SPI-based I/O port chip could be connected to a relay. A web camera could be mounted on a two-axis pan-tilt head with its motors controlled by the SitePlayer.

Exhibit A: Bill of Materials

Item	Quantity	Notes
Web server board	1	SitePlayer development kit available from *http://www.siteplayer.com*
1uF capacitor	2	C2, C1; DigiKey Part #P11332CT-ND1uF
0.15uF capacitor	1	C3; DigiKey Part #399-1424-ND
Connector	1	J1; 0.100" spaced pins, DigiKey Part #929710-10-36-ND
Connector	2	J3, J2; 0.100" spaced pins, DigiKey Part #929710-10-36-ND
Connector	1	J4; 0.100" spaced pins, DigiKey Part #929710-10-36-ND
NPN, 2N2222 Transistor	1	Q1; DigiKey Part #2N5088-ND
100K Ohm, 5% tolerance resistor	1	R1; DigiKey Part #100KQBK-ND
1K Ohm, 5% tolerance resistor	2	R4, R2; DigiKey Part #1.0KQBK-ND
75 Ohm, 5% tolerance resistor	1	R3; DigiKey Part #75QBK-ND
A/D converter	1	U1; Linear Technology, LTC1098CN8
1" x 1" blank PCB	1	Radio Shack
Temperature sensor	1	U2; National Semiconductor LM34
Shielded cable	3'	Any 4-conductor shielded cable or DigiKey Part #C1352-100-ND
Plastic tubing	1'	Hardware store
Silicone sealant	1 tube	Hardware store
Tie wraps	5	Hardware store
Plastic enclosure	1	Radio Shack
22-gauge stranded wire	1'	Radio Shack

Exhibit B: Schematic Diagram

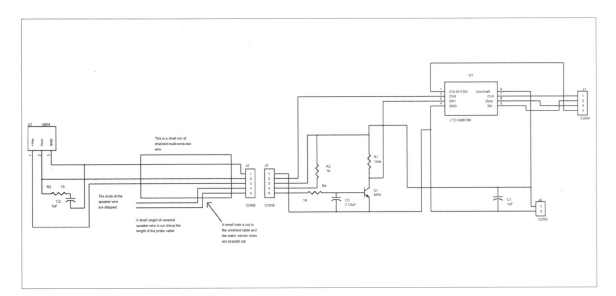

Exhibit C: SitePlayer Code

Listing 1: coffee.spd

```
;
; These are initial variables that you can place in your system
;
;$Devicename sets the name or description of the device
$Devicename "Coffee Machine Web server"

;$DHCP on sets SitePlayer to find its IP address from a DHCP server
$DHCP on

;$DownloadPassword sets password for downloading web pages and firmware
$DownloadPassword ""

;$SitePassword sets password for browsing web pages
$SitePassword ""

;$InitialIP sets SitePlayer's IP address to use if no DHCP server is available
$InitialIP "192.168.1.250"

;$PostIRQ on sets SitePlayer to generate a low level IRQ on pin 11
$PostIRQ off

;$Sitefile sets the binary image filename that will be created
$Sitefile "E:\Hacking Book\coffee_machine_hack\coffee\coffee.spb"
```

Exhibit C

Listing 1: coffee.spd *(continued)*

```
;$Sitepath sets the root path of the web pages for this project
$Sitepath "E:\Hacking Book\coffee_machine_hack\coffee"

;$Include sets the name of a file to include during make process
$Include "E:\Hacking Book\coffee_machine_hack\coffee\pcadef.inc"
$Include "E:\Hacking Book\coffee_machine_hack\coffee\udpsend_def.inc"
```

Listing 2: Index.htm

```
<html>
<body bgcolor="#99FFFF">
<h1 align="center">Coffee Machine Web Server</h1>
<hr>
<hr>
<a href="water.spi?IO0=0&SPIaddr=%00&IO3=0&SPIBus=%1E%00&IO3=1">check water</a>
<a href="refresh_index.spi?IO0=0&SPIaddr=%00&IO3=0&SPTRus=%1A%00&IO3=1">check temperature</a>
; this is the command that triggers the SPI data transaction to and from the A/D converter
<!--a href="index.spi?IO4=0&IO4=1">
<!--the value of memory location hex 03 is ^temper<br>
<!--value of 01 is ^water<br>
    <br>
temperature is ^water*2
<br>
<!--water is ^temper#C0h--!>


    <!--- input type="text" name="SPIbus" maxlength="80" size="80" ---!><br>
<!--press the link above to ectivate the transaction<br>
<hr>
<hr>
</body>
</html>
```

Listing 3: SitePlayer index.spi

```
HTTP/1.0 302 Found
Location: /index.ht
```

Listing 4: refresh_index.htm

```
<html>
<head>
 <meta http-equiv="refresh"
content="0;url=index.spi?IO0=0&SPIaddr=%00&IO3=0&SPIBus=%1A%00&IO3=1">
    <title>test</title>
</head>
<body bgcolor="#99FFFF">

<h1 align="center">Coffee Machine Web Server</h1>
<hr>
<hr>
<a href="water.spi?IO0=0&SPIaddr=%00&IO3=0&SPIBus=%1F%00&IO3=1">check water</a>
<a href="refresh_index.spi?IO0=0&SPIaddr=%00&IO3=0&SPIBus=%1A%00&IO3=1">check temperature</a>
```

Exhibit C

Listing 4: refresh_index.htm *(continued)*

```
^temper<br>
^water<br>
    <br>
<br>
<br>
<hr>
<hr>
</body>
</html>
```

Listing 5: refresh_index.spi

```
HTTP/1.0 302 Found
Location: /refresh_index.htm
```

Listing 6: water.htm

```
<html>
<body bgcolor="#99FFFF">
<h1 align="center">Coffee Machine Web Server</h1>
<hr>

<hr>
<a href="water.spi?IO0=0&SPIaddr=%00&IO3=0&SPIBus=%1E%00&IO3=1">check water</a>
<a href="refresh_index.spi?IO0=0&SPIaddr=%00&IO3=0&SPIBus=%1A%00&IO3=1">check temperature</a>
<!--a href="index.spi?IO4=0&IO4=1">
    <br>

<br>
water is ^water
    <!--- input type="text" name="SPIbus" maxlength="80" size="80" ---!><br>
<!--press the link above to ectivate the transaction<br>
<hr>
<hr>
</body>
</html>
```

Listing 7: water.spi

```
HTTP/1.0 302 Found
Location: /water.htm
```

Listing 8: pcadef.inc

```
;
; Definitions for SitePlayer standalone direct port I/O
; to use these items they can be viewed by doing a ^objectname in your HTML file
; or they can be input by making an object of the same name in a form
;
; Some objects cannot be viewed
;
; If you do not need all the objects, you should NOT include this complete file
; even if your program does not use a particular object by name.  If you include
```

Exhibit C

Listing 6: water.htm *(continued)*

```
; this file in its entirety, someone could send a URL request with the name of
; an object and make changes to your SitePlayer.
;
; So only define the objects you specifically intend to use
;

      org 0ff00h
p1            ds 1                  ;Port 1 all 8 bits

      org 0ff01h
cmod          ds 1                  ;PCA Counter Mode

      org 0ff02h
ccon          ds 1                  ;PCA Counter control

      org 0ff03h
ch            ds 1                  ;PCA Counter High

      org 0ff04h
cl            ds 1                  ;PCA Counter Low

      org 0ff05h
ccapm0        ds 1                  ;Module 0 Mode

      org 0ff06h
ccapm1        ds 1                  ;Module 1 Mode

      org 0ff07h
ccapm2        ds 1                  ;Module 2 Mode

      org 0ff08h
ccapm3        ds 1                  ;Module 3 Mode

      org 0ff09h
ccap0h        ds 1                  ;Module 0 Capture High

      org 0ff0ah
ccap1h        ds 1                  ;Module 1 Capture High

      org 0ff0bh
ccap2h        ds 1                  ;Module 2 Capture High

      org 0ff0ch
ccap3h        ds 1                  ;Module 3 Capture High

      org 0ff0dh
ccap0l        ds 1                  ;Module 0 Capture Low

      org 0ff0eh
ccap1l        ds 1                  ;Module 1 Capture Low

      org 0ff0fh
ccap2l        ds 1                  ;Module 2 Capture Low
```

Exhibit C

Listing 8: pcadef.inc *(continued)*

```
       org 0ff10h
ccap3l        ds 1                          ;Module 3 Capture Low

       org 0ff11h
io0           ds 1                            ;Port 1 Bit number 0

       org 0ff12h
io1           ds 1                            ;Port 1 Bit number 1

       org 0ff13h
io2           ds 1                            ;Port 1 Bit number 2

       org 0ff14h
io3           ds 1                            ;Port 1 Bit number 3

       org 0ff15h
io4           ds 1                            ;Port 1 Bit number 4

       org 0ff16h
io5           ds 1                            ;Port 1 Bit number 5

       org 0ff17h
io6           ds 1                            ;Port 1 Bit number 6

       org 0ff18h
io7           ds 1                            ;Port 1 Bit number 7

       org 0FF19h
COM    ds 128                       ;serial port output (only takes up really one byte)

       org 0FF1Ah
Baud          dw 0                         ;baud rate counter register (WORD)

       org 0FF1Ch
SPIbus        ds 128               ;SPI bus commands (only takes up really one byte)

       org 0FF1Dh
SPIaddr       db 0                          ;destination of SPI incoming data

       org 0FF1Eh
UDPsend       db 0                          ;flag to send out a UDP message

       org 0FF1Fh
HalfSec       db 0                          ;half second (0.50135) down counter stops when 0

       org 0FF20h
UDPrcvr       db 0                          ;enable UDP receives or not

       org 01h
water db 0                     ; place to get at incoming SPI data
  .    org 03h
temper        db 0
```

Exhibit C

Listing 9: UDPsend_def.inc

```
;
; These are definitions of objects to be used with the UDPsend
; Serial command or the UDPsend object location
;
; To send a UDP message to a specific computer on your local network:
;  set the UDPMAC address to the computer's ethernet adapter MAC address
;  set the UDPIP address to the computer's IP address
;
; To broadcast to many computers simultaneously:
;   set the UDPMAC addresses to all 0ffh's
;   set the UDPIP address the local network broadcast address
;   which is typically xxx.xxx.xxx.255
;
; To broadcast to all computers on all logical local networks:



;   set the UDPMAC addresses to all 0ffh's
;   set the UDPIP address to 255.255.255.255
;
; To send to a remote PC through a gateway:
;   set the MAC address to the gateway's MAC address
;   and the UDPIP address to the address of the remote machine
;

        org 2D0h
UDPMAC              dhex 0ffh
UDPMAC2             dhex 0ffh
UDPMAC3             dhex 0ffh
UDPMAC4             dhex 0ffh
UDPMAC5             dhex 0ffh
UDPMAC6             dhex 0ffh

;IP address in the format UDPIP.UDPIP2.UDPIP3.UDPIP4
UDPIP               db 0ffh
UDPIP2              db 0ffh
UDPIP3              db 0ffh
UDPIP4              db 0ffh

UDPPORT             dw 2552
UDPADDR             dw 0
UDPCOUNT            dw 1
```

Appendixes

III

In the appendixes that follow, you will find some additional information that may be useful when you design and hack your own projects.

In this part

Schematic Capture Software

As you design your own hacks, you may need to draw a schematic diagram of the circuits involved.

Schematic diagrams can be drawn by hand (a time-consuming process) or by using a computer-aided design (CAD) tool. There are numerous schematic capture software packages available for both the professional and the hobbyist. If you have a few dollars to spend, I recommend the OrCad package available from Cadence Design (*http://www.orcad.com*). It is one of the most popular and well-supported packages available. As of this writing, the company offers a free CD with a "light" version that allows schematic capture of up to 60 parts. If you want to try out low-cost or free tools, check out the following web sites:

http://members.aol.com/atpclogic/index.html
http://www.advancedmsinc.com/
http://www.pulsonix.com/

Several drawing packages, such as Visio, include some schematic symbols, which can be used to generate simple schematic diagrams. You can also create your own schematic symbols inside a drawing software package.

Communication   B

In Chapter 10, How to Build an Internet Toaster, I use several wires to send and receive serial data so that the toaster could communicate with the controlling PC. As you hack your own projects, your circuit may need to communicate with other items. Wired and wireless methods are available. Let's take a look at the options.

Wired

One of the least expensive ways to allow two CPUs to communicate is by connecting a set of wires between them. If the CPUs are a few inches apart, they can have wires connected directly. If they are farther apart, a direct connection will not work well due to noise picked up by the longer wires. To alleviate this problem, I'll cover several standards for medium range (1 to 100 feet) and for long range (more than 100 feet).

RS-232

The RS-232 standard is one of the oldest and most enduring bit-serial data interfaces. It was originally used to allow video and teletype terminals to communicate with a mainframe computer and modems. It can effectively allow two machines to communicate up to distances of 100 feet at speeds from 300 bits per second to 115,000 bits per second. This standard is still in use today to connect a personal computer to modems, printers, and other peripherals.

Many CPU and microcontrollers include hardware for an RS-232 connection. These engines are called Universal Asynchronous Receiver Transmitters (UARTs). UARTs output data in a bit-serial fashion over a single wire for each direction. Data bytes are denoted with a start bit and end with a stop bit. You can see what an RS-232 transmitted data byte looks like in Figure B-1.

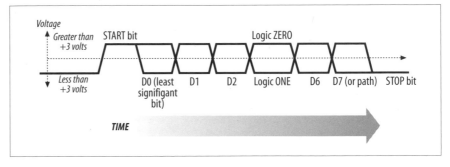

Figure B-1: RS-232

The standard is composed of a physical interface specification, a protocol specification, and an electrical interface specification.

Modems

If you need to connect two systems over very long distances and they are close to a wired telephone line, a modem can be used. If space permits, you can connect a standalone RS-232 modem to both (Figure B-1).

If your project has space and power constraints, you may be able to use small embedded modems. Cermetek (*http://www.cermetek.com/*) offers the CH2124, a 2400 bits-per-second modem that draws very little power and can be placed inside most projects.

USB

Universal Serial Bus, referred to as USB, is one of the newest low- to medium-speed standard interfaces available for the personal computer. Designed to replace the RS-232 serial interface, USB allows two or more machines to communicate over distances of a few tens of feet. Version 1.0 specifies a data rate of 12 million bits per second, and Version 2.0 specifies a data rate of 400 million bits per second. The USB standard specifies the physical interface, the connectors and type of cable, and the protocol interface. The USB interface is significantly more complicated than the older RS-232 interface. It is much harder to quickly add a USB port to a project. Fortunately, there are people who have already done some of this hard work.

If you want to start playing with USB for the control and communication aspects of your projects, I recommend that you look at the products from Active Wire Inc. (*http://www.activewireinc.com/*). Active Wire offers a number of moderately priced experimenter's kits with extensive software support for all of the major operating systems and programming languages.

FireWire

FireWire is also known by its official name, IEEE 1394. This standard, invented by Apple Computer, has become one of the most popular high-speed interfaces for peripherals. You can send and receive data at over 400 million bits per second at distances of a few tens of feet. Many personal computers, digital camcorders, and laptops have this interface built in.

Ethernet

Ethernet is used to connect most personal computers to local area networks. It can communicate at data rates from 10 million bits per second to almost 10 billion bits per second. The standard requires a large amount of software overhead, but can be used in small, embedded projects. A company called NetMedia (*http://www.siteplayer.com*) offers a small programmable web server that includes a 10-megabit Ethernet interface.

Telephones

Besides using telephone lines to connect a modem, you may want to connect a project to a telephone line for other purposes. If you do so, a few standards will help you to properly connect.

DTMF

DTMF stands for Dual Tone Multi Frequency. It is the standard method for communicating telephone dialing digits over the publicly switched telephone network. Chips that send and receive DTMF signals are common and easy to use. You can connect a DTMF receiver to a telephone interface (called a DAA, described below) plugged into a telephone line, and you can use the keys on the calling telephone as remote control devices connected to the DTMF receiver.

DAA

The DAA or Direct Access Arrangement is the circuitry required to connect to a standard telephone line. It usually provides a Ring Detect signal to indicate when the phone line is ringing, and an On/Off hook control to connect and disconnect the circuit from the phone system. You can build your own DAA or purchase a premade and pretested one from several vendors. Cermetek (*http://www.cermetek.com/*) manufactures and sells a number of different DAAs. If you want to build your own, TDK Semiconductor has a number of reference designs (*http://www.tsc.tdk.com/*).

Wireless

If your project cannot accommodate a wired connection, then wireless is the way to go. Bear in mind that it is often more complicated to make a wireless link work well and that the cost is often higher than a wired connection.

Radio control

A company called Pericom (*http://www.pti-ic.com*) offers radio-control chip sets used in toy- and hobby-level remote-controlled vehicles. The company's web site offers detailed data sheets and application notes that include a design for a standalone radio-control link (both transmitter and receiver).

Radio data communications

A number of other companies offer prebuilt radio data interface circuit boards. These boards will set up a one- or two-way data link, depending on which model you choose. Additional circuitry and sometimes software is required for some of these products to reliably transmit and receive data. Outside radio noise typically introduces errors and distortion into signals, which manifests itself in errors in data transmitted and received. These errors must be detected and corrected if the radio link is to be reliably used. The following is a list of vendors of ready-to-use radio interface boards.

> *http://www.linxtechnologies.com/*
> *http://www.radiotronix.com/*
> *http://www.abacom-tech.com/*
> *http://www.lemosint.com*
> *http://www.laipac.com*
> *http://www.maxstream.net*

If you are interested in learning more about error handling in a radio channel, take a look at the web sites for Radiotronix (*http://www.radiotronix. com/*) and Linx Technologies (*http://www.linxtechnologies.com/*). You'll find some well-written white papers describing useful techniques.

More-involved radio interface standards include 802.11a or 802.11b and HomeRF. These are full networking interfaces that require extensive software support. (If you want to learn more about 802.11 technologies, check out O'Reilly's *802.11 Wireless Networks: The Definitive Guide.*)

Infrared

Infrared light is invisible to the human eye. In the electromagnetic spectrum, it is at a wavelength shorter than red light.

Infrared (or IR) LEDs are used to communicate commands and data over short distances without wires to IR receivers. IR communication can be an inexpensive way to send wireless data, but it has a fairly short operating range of one to three feet for high-speed data and ten to twenty feet for a few command bits. It is highly directional and cannot pass through objects like a radio signal can.

In Chapter 13, How to Make RC Cars Play Laser Tag, I use a complete IR receiver module as a sensor. This same module can be used to receive remote-control data as well as higher-speed serial data from a microcontroller or a PC.

Easy-to-Use Microcontroller Boards

C

If your project requires a controller, there are a number of ready-to-use products on the market that allow you to use a high-level language to program. These products typically require a connection to a power supply and a programming cable connected to a PC.

Table C-1 shows a number of these ready-to-use controller boards. These kits allow you to get small to medium amounts of code working very quickly. I have used the BasicX and BasicStamp controllers for projects in this book due to their ease of use.

Table C-1. Easy-to-use microcontrollers

Product	Vendor	Programming language	Memory
BasicStamp	Parallax Inc. (*http://www.parallaxinc.com*)	Basic	Up to 16K FLASH, 128 bytes RAM
BasicX	NetMedia (*http://www.basicx.com*)	Basic	32K FLASH, 400 bytes RAM
BasicAtom	BasicMicro Inc. (*http://www.basicmicro.com*)	Basic	2K FLASH, 300 bytes RAM
JavaStamp	Systronics Inc. (*http://www.jstamp.com*)	Java	512KB FLASH, 512KB RAM

Power Sources

D

Many hacks require a portable power source. Batteries are easy to replace and an inexpensive source of electrical power. Solar cells provide electricity when exposed to light, and generators are also available. Let's take a look at the pros and cons of each.

Batteries

Batteries are probably the easiest portable power source to work with. Battery capacity is typically measured in amp-hours or milliamp-hours. This number is the product of the amount of current (in amps or milliamps) times the number of hours it can operate. For example, if a battery is rated at 1,000 milliamp-hours of capacity, it can deliver 1 milliamp for 1,000 hours or 100 milliamps for 10 hours.

Disposable

Batteries generally come in two types, rechargeable and nonrechargeable (or disposable). Both types are available in many different shapes, sizes, voltages, current capacities, and performance characteristics. Let's first look at the ones you toss once their power is depleted.

Zinc carbon cells

One of the earliest types of nonrechargeable batteries was the "dry" cell, or zinc carbon battery. Previous batteries were composed of solid electrodes (metal rods) immersed in a liquid solution. The dry cell did not require a liquid solution, hence the name. The invention of the zinc carbon cell is attributed to Georges Leclanche, a Frenchman. This type of battery is available in a variety of sizes and is useful for circuits that draw low-to-medium amounts of power. Table D-1 lists commonly available zinc carbon batteries and their characteristics. The capacity of this type of battery decreases when more than a few tens of milliamps are drawn. Ray-o-Vac (*http://www.rayovac.com/*) and a number of other companies still make this type of battery. Check the manufacturer's web site for details.

Table D-1. Common zinc carbon battery types

Cell type	Voltage	Capacity	Size
AAA	1.5	300–600 mAh	44 mm × 10 mm (diameter)
AA	1.5	600–1000 mAh	50 mm × 14 mm (diameter)
C	1.5	2200–2700 mAh	49 mm × 25 mm (diameter)
D	1.5	4500–6800 mAh	60 mm × 33 mm (diameter)
9V	9V	350–450 mAh	47.5 mm × 25.5 mm × 16.5 mm

Alkaline

Alkaline cells have begun to overtake zinc carbon cells in popularity, mainly due to their ability to hold more electrical power. These cells can also supply a more instantaneous current than zinc carbon cells. Alkaline cells are available in many sizes and capacities. Several companies are marketing improved types of alkaline cells that allow a larger instantaneous current draw, more capacity than their competition, and limited rechargeability. Table D-2 lists the basic characteristics of popular alkaline batteries.

Table D-2. Common alkaline battery types

Cell type	Voltage	Capacity	Size
AAA	1.5	800–1100 mAh	44mm × 10mm (diameter)
AA	1.5	1600–2500 mAh	50mm × 14mm (diameter)
C	1.5	5500–7200mAh	49mm × 25mm (diameter)
D	1.5	10,000–15,000 mAh	60mm × 33mm (diameter)
9V	1.5	550–650 mAh	47.5mm × 25.5mm x 16.5mm

Lithium (nonrechargeable)

Disposable lithium-type batteries have been a popular cell for cameras due to their long shelf life and high capacity. The charge in these batteries can last for many years without degrading. They also store more power unit weight and unit volume than other nonrechargeable or rechargeable batteries. Table D-3 lists a few of the commonly available disposable lithium cells available. This list is not exhaustive, and you should search the web sites of manufacturers such as Duracell, Sanyo, and Energizer.

Table D-3. Common lithium battery types

Cell type	Voltage	Capacity	Size
AA	1.5	2900 mAh	44mm × 10mm (diameter)
CRV3	3	3000 mAh	52mm × 28mm × 14mm
EL2CR5	6	1500 mAh	45mm × 34mm × 17mm
CR2032	3	225 mAh	3.2mm × 20mm (diameter)
CR2450	3	575 mAh	5mm × 24.5mm (diameter)

Zinc air

This type of battery consumes air as one of the chemicals in its electricity-producing reaction. Most zinc air batteries are small and designed for hearing aids, although a company called Instant Power (*http://www.instant-power.com/*) offers larger and higher power zinc air cells. Currently, this type of cell is not rechargeable.

Other nonrechargeable batteries

Several other types of nonrechargeable cells are available, including manganese dioxide and silver oxide. These cells typically do not hold a lot of energy and are expensive. Take a look at the Energizer web site for details on some of these other battery types.

Rechargeable

If you prefer to power your project from a battery that can be recharged, take a look at some of the rechargeable batteries listed here. If you are interested in circuits for recharging the different cells, most of the manufacturers will have a reference design. You can also look at chip companies that build integrated circuits designed for recharging batteries, such as Maxim Integrated (*http://www.maxim-ic.com/*).

NiCad

Nickel cadmium, or NiCad, batteries are a mature rechargeable technology. They were among the first popular rechargeable batteries used in consumer electronics. Early NiCad cells exhibited a "memory" effect where they would not accept a full charge if they were not discharged completely before recharging. NiCad cells offer reasonable capacity at a price lower than many other rechargeable cells. These cells are not used as often in consumer applications due to the presence of small amounts of cadmium, a heavy metal pollutant released when the cell is disposed of in landfills. If you use one of these cells, be sure to dispose of it through a recycling program when it is no longer used. The capacities of some common NiCad cells are shown in Table D-4.

Table D-4. NiCad cells

Cell Type	Voltage	Capacity	Size
AAA	1.25	300–320 mAh	44mm × 10mm (diameter)
AA	1.25	600–1060 mAh	50mm × 14mm (diameter)
C	12.5	2500–2750mAh	49mm × 25mm (diameter)
D	1.25	4300–4930 mAh	60mm × 33mm (diameter)
9V	8.4	120–165 mAh	47.5mm × 25.5mm × 16.5mm

NiMH

Nickel metal hydride, or NiMH, cells are a newer and higher-capacity rechargeable battery technology than NiCad. They can hold close to twice the energy of a NiCad cell, carry no memory effect, and contain no heavy metals. Standard NiMH cells are shown in Table D-5.

Table D-5. NiMH cells

Cell type	Voltage	Capacity	Size
AAA	1.25	650–700 mAh	44mm × 10mm (diameter)
AA	1.25	1600–1700 mAh	50mm × 14mm (diameter)
C	1.25	3500–3900mAh	49mm × 25mm (diameter)
D	1.25	4500–10,000 mAh	60mm × 33mm (diameter)
9V	8.4	150–165 mAh	47.5mm × 25.5mm × 16.5mm

Sealed lead acid

One of the oldest rechargeable battery types is lead acid. Edison and Ford powered their experimental electric cars with this type of battery. Lead acid cells tend to carry less capacity than either NiCad or NiMH cells but can cost less. For very large power capacity, sealed lead acid batteries offer the best cost. A lead acid cell from a single automobile or a motorcycle costs much less than using a comparable number of NiCad or NiMH cells. Table D-6 shows some of the smaller lead acid cells that can be used for small hacks.

Table D-6. Sealed lead acid cells

Cell type	Voltage	Capacity	Size
LCR6V3.4P	6	3400 mAh	5.28” × 1.34” × 2.36”
LCR12V2.2P	12	2200 mAh	6.97” × 1.34” × 2.36”
LC-R064R2P(a)	6	4200 mAh	2.76” × 1.89” × 4.02”

A number of companies make sealed lead acid cells. Panasonic has a line of well-designed and documented cells that you can find online from electronics components vendors such as DigiKey.

Lithium ion

Lithium ion cells are one of the newest rechargeable battery technologies. They are very lightweight and carry more energy that other rechargeable cells of an equivalent size. Table D-7 shows a number of standard Li-Ion cells.

Table D-7. Li-Ion cells

Cell type	Voltage	Capacity	Size
1865	3.6	1600–1700 mAh	65mm × 18mm (diameter)
1767	3.6	1300–1320 mAh	67mm × 17mm (diameter)
Prismatic	3.6	800–1400 mAh	34mm × 50mm × 10mm

This extra capacity and light weight come at a price. These batteries are much more expensive that NiCad and NiMH cells and require special charging circuits.

Many companies now make Li-Ion cells, including Sony, Sanyo, and Panasonic.

Solar Cells

Electrical power can be generated from light sources using a photovoltaic cell (also known as a solar cell). These are available from a variety of sources, including Radio Shack and DigiKey.

Each solar cell typically provides a low output voltage, 0.6V, and produces energy only when illuminated. In order to provide energy under both light and dark conditions, some sort of battery and charger connected to the solar cells must be used. This allows the cells to charge the batteries for use when there is no light source. It also evens out the power provided by the cells due to changing light conditions.

With careful design, small panels can typically power a low-power microprocessor by themselves.

Generators

Electrical power can be derived from mechanical work using a generator. A number of simple generators are readily available for the hacker.

Bicycle generators

You may remember as a kid having a light on the front of your bike that was powered by a small metal "bottle" that rubbed against the side of one of the tires. This bottle was a small generator. You can still obtain these generators for a relatively low price, anywhere from $10 to $30. The output of these generators is an AC waveform that must be converted to a DC voltage if you want to use it for anything other than powering a light bulb. Small bicycle generators typically provide only a few watts of power.

Wind-up generators

A number of companies offer flashlights and radios powered by a small generator turned by a wind-up spring mechanism. A company called Freeplay (*http://www.freeplay.net/*) offers wind-up radios, flashlights, and generators.

Resources   **E**

References

If you've been hacking hardware for a while, you know the importance of finding good reference material. There are a lot of good books out there, but one of the best books I've read on basic electronics is *The Art of Electronics* by Horowitz and Hill (Cambridge University Press). It was written for a course I took at Harvard. If you're ready to dabble in electronics hacking, be sure to hunt down a copy of this book.

Another aspect of hardware hacking you'll need information about is data sheets. When I started hacking, the Web did not exist and data sheets were printed in huge volumes called "data books." I used to have several hundred pounds of these books that I would cart around when I moved. With the advent of the Web, data sheets for almost every component you will use are available at the web site of the manufacturer.

Another great source of introductory information is the magazine *Circuit Cellar* (*http://www.circuitcellar.com/*). The articles are clear and there are lots of example circuits. *Nuts and Volts* (*http://www.nutsvolts.com/*) is also a good publication for robotics and basic electronics.

Materials

Throughout this book, I have tried to specify parts suppliers that are reliable and stock a wide variety of components. The one I use most often, as you may have discovered from reading a hack or two, is DigiKey, but you can find most any part you need from the vendors listed here:

- DigiKey: *http://www.digikey.com/*
- Radio Shack: *http://www.radioshack.com/*
- Jameco: *http://www.jameco.com/*
- Halted Specialties: *http://www.halted.com/*
- Mouser Electronics: *http://www.mouser.com/*

Index

Symbols

A

B

Colophon

Our look is the result of reader comments, our own experimentation, and feedback from distribution channels. Distinctive covers complement our distinctive approach to technical topics, breathing personality and life into potentially dry subjects.

Emily Quill was the production editor and copyeditor for *Hardware Hacking Projects for Geeks*. Mary Anne Weeks Mayo was the proofreader. David Futato and Melanie Wang did the typesetting and page makeup, with assistance from Bryan Carden. Marlowe Shaeffer and Claire Cloutier provided quality control. Mary Agner and Mary Brady provided production assistance. Julie Hawks wrote the index.

Edie Freedman designed the cover of this book using Photoshop 6 and QuarkXPress 4.1. The cover image is an original photograph by Edie Freedman. Emma Colby produced the cover layout with QuarkXPress 4.1 using Adobe's Formata Condensed font.

Melanie Wang designed the interior layout using InDesign CS, based on a series design by David Futato. The text and heading fonts are Linotype Birka and Adobe Formata Condensed, and the code font is TheSans Mono Condensed from LucasFont. The illustrations and screenshots that appear in the book were produced by Robert Romano and Jessamyn Read using Macromedia Freehand MX and Adobe Photoshop 7.

Related Titles Available from O'Reilly

Hacks

Amazon Hacks

BSD Hacks

Digital Photography Hacks

eBay Hacks

Excel hacks

Google Hacks

Linux Desktop Hacks

Linux Server Hacks

Mac OS X Hacks

Mac OS X Panther Hacks

Spidering Hacks

TiVo Hacks

Windows Server Hacks

Windows XP Hacks

Wireless Hacks

O'REILLY®

Our books are available at most retail and online bookstores.

To order direct: 1-800-998-9938 • *order@oreilly.com* • *www.oreilly.com*

Online editions of most O'Reilly titles are available by subscription at *safari.oreilly.com*

Keep in touch with O'Reilly

1. Download examples from our books

To find example files for a book, go to:

www.oreilly.com/catalog

select the book, and follow the "Examples" link.

2. Register your O'Reilly books

Register your book at *register.oreilly.com*

Why register your books?
Once you've registered your O'Reilly books you can:

* Win O'Reilly books, T-shirts or discount coupons in our monthly drawing.
* Get special offers available only to registered O'Reilly customers.
* Get catalogs announcing new books (US and UK only).
* Get email notification of new editions of the O'Reilly books you own.

3. Join our email lists

Sign up to get topic-specific email announcements of new books and conferences, special offers, and O'Reilly Network technology newsletters at:

elists.oreilly.com

It's easy to customize your free elists subscription so you'll get exactly the O'Reilly news you want.

4. Get the latest news, tips, and tools

www.oreilly.com

* "Top 100 Sites on the Web"—PC Magazine
* CIO Magazine's Web Business 50 Awards

Our web site contains a library of comprehensive product information (including book excerpts and tables of contents), downloadable software, background articles, interviews with technology leaders, links to relevant sites, book cover art, and more.

5. Work for O'Reilly

Check out our web site for current employment opportunities:

jobs.oreilly.com

6. Contact us

O'Reilly & Associates
1005 Gravenstein Hwy North
Sebastopol, CA 95472 USA

TEL: 707-827-7000 or 800-998-9938
(6am to 5pm PST)

FAX: 707-829-0104

order@oreilly.com
For answers to problems regarding your order or our products. To place a book order online, visit:

www.oreilly.com/order_new

catalog@oreilly.com
To request a copy of our latest catalog.

booktech@oreilly.com
For book content technical questions or corrections.

corporate@oreilly.com
For educational, library, government, and corporate sales.

proposals@oreilly.com
To submit new book proposals to our editors and product managers.

international@oreilly.com
For information about our international distributors or translation queries. For a list of our distributors outside of North America check out:

international.oreilly.com/distributors.html

adoption@oreilly.com
For information about academic use of O'Reilly books, visit:

academic.oreilly.com

O'REILLY®

Our books are available at most retail and online bookstores.
To order direct: 1-800-998-9938 • *order@oreilly.com* • *www.oreilly.com*
Online editions of most O'Reilly titles are available by subscription at *safari.oreilly.com*